# FUNDAMENTALS OF RURAL SOCIOLOGY

# FUNDAMENTALS OF RURAL SOCIOLOGY

JAGMOHAN DIWAN

CYBER TECH PUBLICATIONS
4264/3, Ansari Road, Daryaganj, New Delhi-110002 (India)
Ph.: 011-23244078. Fax: 011-23280028
E-Mail: cyberpublicationsdelhi@yahoo.com

*Fundamentals of Rural Sociology*



First Edition 2009

Published by G.S. Rawat
**For Cyber Tech Publications**
4264/3, Ansari Road, Daryaganj, New Delhi - 110 002
E-mail : cyberpublicationsdelhi@yahoo.com
Phone : 011-23244078,
Fax : 011-23280028

**Printed at**
Asian Offset Printers

# Preface

Sociology is science which attempts the interpretive understanding of social action to arrive at a casual explanation of its course and effects. Sociology seeks to formulate types concepts and generalised uniformities of empirical processes. History, on the other hand, is interested in the causal analysis of particular events, actions or personalities. Action is human behaviour to which the acting individual attaches subjective earning. It can be overt or inward and subjective.

Urbanisation is a powerful factor in bringing about social change. It has its impact on the attitudes of men towards caste, property, health, education, modes of living, housing, recreation and also labour. To examine the nature and extent of urban influence on rural society. It has been found advantageous form the point of view of the study of social change, to know the nature, the structure and the function of village society, in general, land tenure and fragmentation, income of households, private property, cattle-wealth, housing and health in particular.

Different sources scholars and institutions for their valuable contribution on this subject. Librarians and their staff members have been kind and helpful.

Last but not the least my publishers who appreciated this book and brought this work out in a record time.

—*Editor*

# Contents

# 1

# Definitions of Sociology and Social Action

Sociology is a science which attempts the interpretive understanding of social action to arrive at a casual explanation of its course and effects. Sociology seeks to formulate type concepts and generalized uniformities of empirical processes. (History, on the other hand, is interested in the causal analysis of particular events, actions or personalities.)

Action is human behaviour to which the acting individual attaches subjective meaning. It can be overt or inward and subjective. Action is social when, by virtue of the subjective meaning attached to it by the acting individual(s), it takes account of the behavior of others and is thereby guided. Social action may be oriented to past, present, or predicted future behavior of others. Others may be concrete people or indefinite pluralities.

*Not all action is social*: if it ain't oriented to the behavior of others, it ain't social. Also, it is not merely action participated in by a bunch of people (crowd action) or action influenced by or imitative of others. Action can be causally determined by the behavior of others, while still not necessarily being meaningfully determined by the action of others. If I do what you do because it's fashionable, or traditional, or leads to social distinction, its meaningful. Obviously the lines are blurred (pp 113-114), but it's important to make a conceptional distinction.

**Modes of Orientation of Social action**

Uniformity of social action = action which is widespread, frequently repeated by the same individual or simultaneously performed by many individuals and which corresponds to a subjective meaning attributable to the same actors.

*Usage*: probability of a uniformity in the orientation of social action, when the probability is determined by its actual practice ('it is done to conform with the pattern).

*Custom*: usage when the actual performance of the action rests on long familiarity. Non- conformance is sanctioned externally.

Action can also be uniform if the actor acts in his self-interests. The uniformity rests insofar as behavior is determined by purely rational actions of actors to similar ulterior expectations.

Types of Social Action, identified by mode of orientation:

1. rational orientation to a system of discrete individual ends. individuals can choose and adjudicate between both means and ends, though these considerations may be with reference to other absolute values.

2. rational orientation to an absolute value, involving conscious belief in the absolute value entirely for its own sake and independent of prospects for external success. Can choose b/t means, but only with relation to absolute, fixed end. Absolute values are always irrational.

3. affectional orientation. If this is uncontrolled reaction to some exceptional stimulus, it is not meaningful — grey areas.

4. traditional orientation. If this is strict imitation, it is not meaningful — grey areas.

**The Methodological Foundations of Sociology**

There are 2 kinds of meaning: 1) actually existing meaning in a given concrete case of a particular actor, or average or approximate meaning attributed to a given number of actors; and 2) theoretically conceived pure types of subjective meaning attributed to hypothetical actor(s) in a given type of action (like an ideal type).

The line between meaningful action and reactive behavior w/o subjective meaning is blurry.

The basis for understanding meaning may be either rational (logical or mathematical — clear intellectual grasp of things) or emotionally empathetic or artistically appreciative (though sympathetic participation we grasp the emotional context in which the action took place).

For purposes of ideal type analysis, it's convenient to treat irrational (from the point of view of rational pursuit of a given end) action as deviation from a conceptually pure type of rational action. We compare this analytically clear type to empirical reality, and that increases our understanding of how actually action is influences by irrational factors. The more sharp and precise the ideal type (and thus the more abstract and unrealistic) the more useful it is in clarifying terminology and formulating classifications and hypotheses.

Some phenomena are devoid of subjective meaning. What is intelligible about an object is its relation to human action in its role either of means or of end, a relation which actors can be said to be aware of and to which their action has been oriented. If you can't make this relation (for example a hindering or favorable circumstance) it's not meaningful in the sense we care about.

There are 2 kinds of understanding: 1) direct observational understanding of subjective mean of a given act (eg, if i start to shout at you, you could directly observe my irrational emotional reaction by virtue of my shouting). 2) explanatory understanding: we understand motive, or, what makes an individual do a particular thing in a particular circumstance. Since we are interested in the subjective meaning of action, we must place an action in the complex of meaning in which it took place.

A motive is a complex of subjective meaning which seems to the actor and/OR the observer an adequate ground for the conduct in question.

In most cases, actual action goes on in a state of inarticulate half-consciousness or actually unconsciousness of its subjective meaning. The ideal type case of meaning is where meaning is fully conscious and explicit: this rarely happens in reality.

Adequacy on the level of meaning: a subjective interpretation of a coherent course of conduct when its component parts in their mutual relation are recognized as a 'typical' complex of meaning. Eg, according to our current norms of calculation and thinking, the correct solution to an arithmatical problem.

Casual adequacy: there's a probability it will always actually occur in the same way. Eg, statistical probability, according to verified generalization from experience, that there would be a correct or incorrect solution to the arithmatical problem. Depends on being able to determine that there's a probability a will follow.

Subjectively understandable action exists ONLY as the behavior of one or more individual human beings. States, for instance, are results of particular acts of individual persons. There is no such things as a collective personality that acts. These concepts of collective entities DO HAVE meanings in the minds of individual persons, and so actors orient their actions to them as if they existed or should exist.

Functional analysis is a good starting point for sociology. We need to know what kinds of action is functionally necessary for survival, and also for the maintenance of a cultural type and the corresponding modes of social action. We are interested, though, in the subjective meaning of actions to component individuals. The interesting question, then, is what motives determine and lead the individual members and participants in this situation to behave in such a way that the situation came into being in the first place.

## The Concept of Social Relationship

### *Social Relationship*

The behavior of actors in so far as, in its meaningful content, the action of each takes account of the others and is oriented to the behavior of others. Mere group membership is not sufficient. The relation of the actors may be solidary, or the opposite. Eg, a 'state' ceases to exist when there is no longer a probability that certain kinds of meaningfully oriented social action will take place.

The subjective meaning need not be the same for all parties to the relationship. The relationship may be temporary or long term. Its subjective meaning may change over time.

### *The Concept of Legitimate Order*

The validity of an order is the probability that people will orient their action to it.

Types of Legitimate Order

Legitimacy of an order can be upheld in 2 ways:

1. purely disinterested motives a) purely affectual, b) rational belief in absolute validity of an order as an expression of ultimate values, c) religious attitudes, through belief

in need to follow order for salvation

2. entirely through self-interest based on ulterior motives

*Convention*: system of order where infraction meets with sanctions of disapproval and orders are considered binding.

*Law*: system of order where the above is enforced by a functionally specialized agency (e.g., the police).

A system of order with external sanctions may also be guaranteed by disinterested subjective attitudes. Eg, it can be both morally wrong and illegal to murder.

**Bases of Legitimacy**

Legitimacy may be ascribed to an order by those subject to it in the following ways:

(1) tradition, belief in legitimacy of what has always existed.

(2) affectual attitudes, legitimizing the validity of what is newly revealed or is a model to imitate

(3) rational belief in its absolute value

(4) legality. Readiness to conform with rules which are formally correct and have been imposed by accepted procedure.

Submission to an order is almost always determined by a variety of motives.

**Max Weber Class, Status, Party**

All communities are arranged in a manner that goods, tangible and intangible, symbolic and material are distributed. Such a distribution is always unequal and necessarily involves power. "Classes, status groups and parties are phenomena of the distribution of power within a community" (927).

Status groups makes up the social order, classes the economic order, and parties the legal/political order. Each order affects and is affected by the other.

**Power**

Power is the "chance of a man or a number of men to realize their own will in a social action even against the resistance of others who are participating in the action" (926).

Power may rest of a variety of bases, and can be of differing types. "Economically conditioned power is not identical with power... The emergence of economic power may be the consequence of power existing on other grounds. Man does not strive for power only to enrich himself economically. Power, including economic power, may be valued for its own sake. Very frequently the striving for power is conditioned by the social honor it entails. Not all power entails honor." Power is not the only basis of social honor, and social honor, or prestige, may be the basis of economic power.

"Power, as well as honor, may be guaranteed by the legal order, but... [the legal order] is not their primary source. The legal order is rather an additional factor that enhances the chance to hold power or honor; but it cannot always secure them".

**Class**

Class is defined in terms of market situation. A class exists when a number of people have in common a specific casual component of their life chances in the following sense: this component is represented exclusively by economic interests in the possession of goods and opportunities for income under conditions of the commodity or labor markets.

When market conditions prevail (eg, capitalism), property

and lack of property are the basic categories of all class situations. However, the concept of class-interest is ambiguous. Collective action based on class situations is determined by the transparency of the connections between the causes and the consequences of the class situation. If the contrast between the life chances of different class situations is merely seen as an acceptable absolute fact, no action will be taken to change the class situation.

A class in and of itself does not constitute a group (Gemeinschaft). ''The degree in which social action and possibly associations emerge from the mass behavior of the members of a class is linked to general cultural conditions, especially those of an intellectual sort''. ''If classes as such are not groups, class situations emerge only on the basis of social action.''

### Status Groups and Honor

Unlike classes, status groups do have a quality of groups. They are determined by the distribution of social honor. A specific style of life is shared by a status group, and the group itself is defined by those with whom one has social intercourse. Economic elements can be a sort of honor; however, similar class position does not necessitate similar status groups (see old money's contempt for the nouveau riche). People from different economic classes may be members of the same status group, if they share the same specific style of life.

The way in which social honor is distributed in the community is called the status order. Criteria for entry into a status group may take forms such as the sharing of kinship groups or certain levels of education. The most extreme of a status system with a high level of closure (that is, strong restriction of mobility between statuses) is a caste system. There, status distinctions are guaranteed no only by law and convention, but also by religious sanctions.

Relationships between Class and Status group; between Class situation, Status Situation, and Stratification.

Status groups can sometimes be equal to class, sometimes be broader, sometimes more restrictive, and sometimes bear no relation to class (duh). In most cases, status situation is the apparent dimension of stratification: ''stratification by status goes hand in hand with a monopolization of ideal and material goods or opportunities''. Class situation can take precedence over status situation, however. ''When the bases of the acquisition and distribution of goods are relatively stable, stratification by status is favored''. Technological and economic changes threaten stratification by status, and ''push class situation to the foreground.... Every slowing down of the change in economic stratification leads, in due course, to the growth or status structures and makes for a resuscitation of the important role of social honor''.

**Parties**

''Parties reside in the sphere of power'' . ''Parties are... only possible within groups that have an asssociational character, that is, some rational order and a staff of persons''. Parties aim for social power, the ability to influence the actions of others, and thus may exist in a social club, the state, or a cohort of graduate students at the University of Chicago.

Parties may represent class or status interests, or neither. They usually represent a mix.

''The structure of parties differs in a basic way according to the kind of social action which they struggle to influence.... [T]hey differ according to whether or not the community is stratified by class or status. Above all else, they vary according to the structure of domination''.

Max Weber. The Protestant Ethic and the Spirit of Capitalism

## Modern, Western Capitalism

Though knowledge and observation of great refinement have existed elsewhere, only in the West has rationalization in science, law and culture developed to such a great degree. The modern West absolutely and completely depends for its whole existence, for the political technical, and economic conditions of its life, on a specially trained organization of individuals, so that the most important functions of everyday life have come to be in the hands of technically, commercially and above all legally trained government officials. Nowhere else does this exist to such a degree as it does in the West.

The most fateful force in modern life is capitalism. The impulse to acquisition has existed always and everywhere and has in itself nothing to do with capitalism. Capitalism is the pursuit of profit, and forever renewed profit, by means of continuous, rational, capitalistic enterprise. This enterprise must be continuous, because in a capitalistic society, anyone who did not take advantage of opportunities for profit-making would be doomed to extinction.

A capitalistic economic action rests on the expectation of profit by the utilization of opportunities for exchange, on (formally) peaceful chances for profit. Where this is rationally pursued, calculations in terms of money are made, whether by modern bookkeeping or more primitive means. Everything is done in terms of balances of money income and money expenses. Whether the calculations are accurate, or whether the calculation method is traditional or by guess-work affects only the degree of the rationality of capitalistic acquisition.

Characteristics of modern Western capitalism: rational industrial organization (that is, attuned to a regular profit and not to political nor irrational speculative opportunities for profit); separation of business from the household; rational bookkeeping. Capitalistic adventurers (in search of booty, whether by war or exploitation) have existed everywhere, but only in the modern West has developed... the rational capitalistic organization of (formally) free labor.

The rationality of MWC is dependent on the calculation of technical factors, and so is dependent on the development in science of the exact and rational experiment. C'ism did not cause this development: but, the continuing development of this type science is supported by capitalistic interests in practical economic applications.

The peculiar rationalism of Western culture extends to many fields — science, mystical contemplation, military training, law and administration. Each of theses fields may be rationalized in terms of very different ultimate values and ends, and what is rational from one point of view may well be irrational from another. The development of economic rationalism is partly dependent on rational technique and law, but it also requires people to have a favorable disposition toward adopting certain types of practical rational conduct.

In this book, we will treat only *one side of thecausal chain*, the connection of the spirit of modern economic life with the rational ethics of ascetic Protestantism.

### Religious Affiliation and Social Stratification

Catholics show a stronger propensity to remain in their crafts, and become master craftsmen, while Protestants are attracted to a larger extent to the upper ranks of skilled labor and administrative positions in factories. Protestants own a disproportionate share of capital. All other things equal, Protestants have been more likely to develop economic rationalism than Catholics. Weber seeks the explanation in 'the permanent intrinsic character of their religion,' and not only in their temporary external historico-political situations.

The Reformation meant not the elimination of the church's control over everyday life, but a substitution of a new form of control for the previous one. While the Catholic church was fairly lax, Calvinism 'would be for us the most absolutely unbearable form of ecclesiastical control of the individual which could possibly exist.'

Protestantism must not be understood as joy of living or in any other sense connected with the Enlightenment. Early Protestantism (e.g., Luther, Calvin) had nothing to do with progress in an Enlightenment sense. Not all Protestant denominations had an equally strong influence on the development of members' business acumen and spirit of hard work.

**The Spirit of Capitalism**

The spirit of capitalism is "an historical individual: a complex of elements associated in historical reality which we united into a conceptual whole from the standpoint of their cultural significance".

Ben Franklin is an example of someone who espouses a philosophy of avarice which is: the ideal of an honest man of recognized credit. It includes a duty on the part of an individual toward the increase of his capital, which is assumed as an end in itself. It is not mere business astuteness, it is an ethos; infraction of its rules is not foolishness or bad business, but forgetfulness of duty.

In this ethic, economic acquisition is no longer considered a means of subsistence: it is the ultimate purpose of a man's life. This is combined with the strict avoidance of all spontaneous enjoyment of life.

*Note*: From the standpoint "of the happiness of, or utility to, a single individual, this ethic appears entirely transcendental and absolutely irrational".

People now are born into a capitalistic economy which presents itself to them as the unalterable order of things in which they must live. In so far as a person born now is involved in the system of market relationships, he must conform to capitalistic rules of action. Today's capitalism selects the subjects it needs through economic survival of the fittest. The interesting question, according to Max, is Where did thissituation come from?

It did NOT arise as the superstructure or reflection of economic situations. For example, the spirit of capitalism such as espoused by our buddy Ben Franklin was present before capitalistic order.

In order to arise, the spirit of capitalism had to struggle with its 'most important opponent,' traditionalism. For instance, workers will respond to an increase in piece rates by doing less work, collecting the usual amount of money, and going home early. Men do not "by nature" wish to earn more and more money, they simply wish to live as they are accustomed to and to earn as much as is necessary for that purpose.

Another way of attempting to increase productivity is to lower wages or piece rates, so that workers must work harder and longer to earn the same amount as before. This method has its limits. It (and capitalism) requires a surplus population which can be hired cheaply in the market. Also, too large a surplus population can encourage the development of labor intensive methods, rather than more efficient methods: low wages do not equal cheap labor. And, if you pay people too little, their efficiency and attentiveness decreases.

Thus, it would be better if labor were performed as if it were an absolute end in itself. This can only be the process of a long and arduous education (for example, being raised Pietist). Capitalism "now in the saddle" can fairly easily recruit the required workers, but this was not always the case.

Capitalism can exist with a traditionalistic character The animating spirit of the entrepreneur may be the traditional rate of profit, the traditional amount of work, the traditional manner of labor-management relations, and the essentially traditional circle of customers and manner of attracting new ones. Take the example of the putting out system.

In such a system, this leisureliness can be destroyed, without any essential change in the form of work organization (such as vertically integrated factories). The spirit of capitalism is the cause of this change. Where the spirit of capitalism appears and is able to work itself out, it produces its own capital and monetary supplies as the means to its ends, but the reverse is not true.

Protestantism was not merely a stage prior to the development of a purely rationalistic philosophy, however. Rationalism shows a development which by no means follows parallel lines in the various departments of life. Since life may be rationalized from fundamentally different basic points of view and in very different directions, we must ask the origin of the irrational element which lies at the basis of this particular concrete form of rational thought: the conception of a calling.

## Luther's Conception of The Calling

The idea of a calling — a life-task, a definite field in which to work — is peculiar to Protestants. Protestantism had a further new development, which was the valuation of the fulfillment of duty in worldly affairs as the highest form which the moral activity of an individual could assume. The only way of living acceptably to God was solely through the fulfillment of the obligations imposed upon the individual by his position in the world (his calling), NOT by trying to surpass worldly morality by monastic asceticism.

*Remember important part of Reformation*: By faith, not works, shall ye be saved. You are justified by faith, etc. So all those indulgences earned by crawling on your knees up stairways, etc. don't get you anything.

For the time being (before Calvin et al. got hold of it), the idea of the calling remained traditionalistic and its only ethical result negative: worldly duties were no longer subordinated to ascetic ones; obedience to authority and acceptance of things as they were, were preached.

**The Religious Foundations of Worldly Asceticism**

However, this idea of the calling was not sufficient for the development of the spirit of capitalism. We needed the effects of forms of ascetic Protestantism: Calvinism, Pietism, Methodism and the Baptist sects.

An important thing to keep in mind is that these folks were not motivated by acquisitive lusts, but rather by salvation of the soul.

Calvinists believed in predestination. God designated before the creation of the world who would be saved and who would get to rot in hell. All creation exists for the sake of God, and has meaning only as means to the glory and majesty of God. Human merit or guilt plays no part in the possession of grace, since that would make God's decrees subject to human influence. This doctrine 'must above all have one consequence... a feeling of unprecedented inner loneliness of the single individual'. The individual was forced to follow the path of his own destiny decreed for him from eternity without help from others or from the Church — complete elimination of salvation through the Church and the sacraments (which Lutheranism retained). This meant the elimination of magic from the world. [It also meant the doing away with a periodical discharge of the emotional sense of sin.]

Now, the elected Christian should glorify God in life by fulfilling God's commandments to the best of his ability. This requires social achievements of the Christian because God decrees that social life shall be organized according to his commandments.

Fear and lack of knowledge of whether or not one is going to rot in hell led to a need for ordinary men to find certitudo salutis (certainty of salvation). Pastoral advice to these poor, tortured dudes contained two themes: 1) an absolute duty to consider oneself chosen and to combat all doubts as temptations of the devil, since lack of self-confidence is the result of insufficient faith, hence of imperfect grace. 2) Intense worldly activity as the most suitable means to attain that self-confidence [thus we eliminate the free rider problem]. The Calvinist sought to identify true faith by its fruits: a type of Christian conduct which served to increase the glory of God. Good works do not affect salvation, but they are indispensable as a sign of election. In practice, this means God helps those who help themselves. The Calvinist creates a conviction of his own salvation.

For Catholics, good works were not a part of a rationalized system of life — they could be performed sporadically, to atone — whereas for Calvinists they are. The God of Calvinism demanded not single good works, but a life of good works combined into a unified system. The moral conduct of the average man was subjected to a consistent method for conduct as a whole. The end of this asceticism was to be able to lead an alert, intelligent life: the most urgent task the destruction of spontaneous, impulsive enjoyment. The most important means was to bring order into the conduct of its adherents. Hence we have methodically rationalized ethical conduct.

The Calvinistic doctrine of predestination was only one of several possible motives which could have supported the methodical rationalization of life. However, it had not only a unique consistency (by virtue of being based on logical deduction, rather than religious experience) and was psychologically extraordinarily powerful.

**Pietism**

This sect sought to make the invisible Church of the

elect visible on this earth. By means of intensified asceticism these folks hoped to enjoy the blissfulness of community with God in this life. Sometimes this latter tendency led to displays of emotion, which were antithetical to Calvinist restraint. Other than that, however, the practical effect of Pietistic principles was an even stricter ascetic control of conduct in the calling:

(1) Methodical development of one's own state of grace to a higher and higher degree of certainty and perfection in terms of the law was a sign of grace.

(2) a belief that God's Providence works through those in such a state of perfection.

Since some of these folks believed grace subject to repentance, by the creation of methods to induce repentance even the attainment of divine grace became in effect an object of rational human activity.

**Methodism**

Though rebirth, an emotional certainty of salvation as the immediate result of faith was an important factor, the emotional act of conversion was methodically induced. Emotion, once awakened, was directed into a rational struggle for perfection. This provided a religious basis for ascetic conduct after the doctrine of predestination had been given up by these folks.

Nothing new was added to the idea of the calling.

The Baptist Sects

The church was viewed as a community of personal believers of the reborn. Salvation was achieved by personal, individual revelation; it was offered to everyone, though not everyone took it.

The injunction was to be in the world but not of it, so

worldly enjoyments and unnecessary social intercourse with non-reborn folks was avoided. The Holy Spirit worked in daily life, and spoke directly to any individual who was willing to hear. This leads to an eventual elimination of all that remained of the doctrine of salvation through the Church and sacraments. This accomplished the religious rationalization of the world in its most extreme form.

Conscience is the revelation of God to the individual.

The rationalization of conduct within the world, but for the sake of the world beyond, was the consequence of the concept of calling of ascetic Protestantism.

**Asceticism and The Spirit of Capitalism**

In Puritan thinking, the real moral objection to possession of wealth is to relaxation in the security of possession, the enjoyment of wealth with the consequence of idleness and the temptations of the flesh, above all distraction from the pursuit of a righteous life. It is only because possession involves this danger that it is suspect at all. Not leisure and enjoyment, but only activity serves to increase the glory of God. Waste of time is thus the first and in principle the deadliest of sins. Thus, inactive contemplation at the expense of work is right out.

Labor is an approved ascetic technique, but is also considered in itself an end of life as ordained by God. Unwillingness to work is symptomatic of the lack of grace. Wealth does not exempt anyone from this.

The division of labor, which has a providential purpose in the thought of the Puritans, leads to qualitative and quantitative improvements in production, and thus serves the common good. But, in addition, specialization is encouraged by the calling, to which it provides an ethical justification; for, "outside of a calling the accomplishments of a man are only casual and irregular and he spends more time in idleness than in work." If God presents to His elect a change for profit, he must pursue it: the Christian must follow the call by taking advantage of the opportunity. The acquisition of wealth in the performance of a calling is morally permissible and enjoined.

- Asceticism turned against the spontaneous enjoyment of life. So, sport, for instance, is acceptable only if it serves a rational purpose, say, increasing physical efficiency.
- The powerful tendency toward uniformity of life, which today so immensely aids the capitalistic interest in the standardization of production, had its ideal foundation in the repudiation of all idolatry of the flesh (eg, non-ascetic, flashy or attractive clothing).

The Puritan outlook on life 'stood at the cradle of modern economic man'. This religious epoch bequeathed to its utilitarian successors "an amazingly good... conscience in the acquisition of money, so long as it took place legally" (176). In addition, the power of religious asceticism provided owners with sober, conscientious and industrious workmen. And, it provided comforting assurance that the unequal distribution of goods in the world was ordained by God.

The religious basis had died away by Ben Franklin's time. Limitation to specialized work is now a condition of any valuable work in the modern world. "The Puritan wanted to work in a calling; we are forced to do so. For when asceticism was carried out of monastic cells into everyday life, and began to dominate worldly morality, did its part in building the tremendous cosmos of the modern economic order This order is now bound to the technical and economic conditions of machine production and today determine the lives of all the individuals who are born into this mechanism, not only those directly concerned with economic acquisition, with irresistible force."

## The Religious Rejections of the World and Their Directions

Motives for the Rejections of the World: The Meaning of Their Rational Construction

Individual spheres of value presented here as ideal types have a rational consistency rarely found in reality. This essay proceeds from the most rational forms reality can assume; it attempts to find out how far certain rational conclusions, which can be established theoretically, have been drawn in reality. Perhaps, also, we can find out why those rational conclusions have not been drawn.

## Typology of Asceticism and Mysticism

Two contrasting abnegations of the world:

(1) active asceticism that is a God-willed ACTION of the devout who are God's tools. Rationally active asceticism, in mastering the world, seeks to tame what is creatural and wicked through work in a worldly vocation (inner-worldly asceticism);

(2) contemplative POSSESSION of the holy as found in mysticism. The individual is not a tool, but a vessel of the divine. Desired: other-worldly religious state; contemplative flight from the world.

Active asceticism may confine itself to controlling wickedness in the actor's own nature; in this case, it avoids any action in the orders of the world (asceticist flight from the world). In external bearing, it thereby comes close to contemplative flight. Conversely, the mystic may determine s/he need not flee from the world, and so be an inner-worldly mysticist, remaining in the orders of the world.

## Directions of the Abnegation of the World

Formulated abstractly, the rational aim of redemption religion has been to secure for the saved a holy state, and thereby a habitude that assures salvation. This takes the place of an acute and extraordinary, and thus a holy state which is transitorily achieved by means of orgies, asceticism, or contemplation. Most prophetic and redemptory religions have lived not only in an acute, but a permanent state of tension in relation to the world and its orders. The more the religions have been true religions of salvation, the greater has this tension been. The tension has been greater the more religion has been sublimated from ritualism and towards 'religious absolutism.' Indeed, the further the rationalization and sublimation of external and internal possession of — in the widest sense — things worldly has progressed, the stronger has the tension on the part of religion become. For the rationalization and conscious sublimation of man's relations to the various spheres of values, internal and external, as well as religious and secular, have then pressed towards making conscious the internal and lawful autonomy of the individual spheres; thereby letting them drift into those tensions which remain hidden to the original naive relation with the external world.

The more comprehensive and the more inward the aim of salvation has been, the more it has been taken for granted that the faithful should ultimately stand closer to the savior, the prophet, the priest, the brother in the faith than to natural relations and to the matrimonial community. Prophecy has created a new social community; thereby the relationships of the sib and of matrimony have been devalued.

Communities of villages, members of the sib, the guild or of partners in seafaring, hunting and warring expeditions have known two elemental principles: first, the dualism or in-group and out-group morality. For in-group morality the principled obligation to give brotherly support in distress has existed. All this followed the principle of "your want of today, may be my want of tomorrow" (this principle was not rationally weighed, but it played its part in sentiment).

Accordingly, haggling in exchange and loan situations, as well as permanent debt-enslavement and similar kinds of enslavement, were confined to outgroup morality and applied only to outsiders.

The religiosity of the congregation transferred the ancient economic ethic of neighborliness (I'll help you out today, since I may need you to help me out tomorrow) to the relations among brothers of the faith. What had previously been the obligations of the noble and the wealthy became the fundamental imperatives of all ethically rationalized religion (to care for orphans and widows, to give alms). The principle that constituted the communal relations among the salvation prophesies was the suffering common to all believers (whether or not the suffering actually existed or was a constant threat, whether it was internal or external). The more imperatives that issued from the ethic of reciprocity among neighbors were raised, the more rational the conception of salvation became, and the more it was sublimated into an ethic of absolute ends.

**The Economic Sphere**

The tension between brotherly religion and the world has been most obvious in the economic sphere. All the primeval magical or mystagogic ways of influencing spirits and deities have pursued special interests. The sublimated religions of salvation, however, had been increasingly tense in their relationships with rationalized economies.

A rational economy is a functional organization oriented to money-prices which originate in the interest-struggles of men in the market. Calculation is not possible without estimation in money prices and hence without market struggles. Money is the most abstract and impersonal element that exists in human life. The more the world of the capitalist economy follows its own immanent laws, the less accessible it is to any imaginable relationship with a religious ethic of brotherliness. Ultimately no genuine religion of salvation has overcome the tension between their religiosity and a rational economy.

The paradox of all rational asceticism is that rational asceticism has created the very wealth it rejected.

There have only been two consistent avenues for escaping the tension between religion and in the economic world in a principled and inward manner:

1. the Puritan ethic of the vocation. Puritanism, as a religion of virtuosos, renounced the universalism of love and rationally routinized all work in this world into serving God's will and testing ones state of grace. Puritanism accepted the routinization of the economic cosmos, which along with the whole world, it devalued as creatural and depraved. It involved a renunciation of salvation in favor of the groundless and always only particularized grace. Actually, this standpoint of unbrotherliness was no longer a genuine religion of salvation. A genuine religion of salvation can exaggerate brotherliness to the height of the mystic's acosmism of love.

2. Mysticism. The mystic's benevolence does not inquire into the man to whom and for whom it sacrifices. Mysticism is not interested in his person. Mysticism is a unique escape form this world in the form of an objectless devotion to anybody, not for man's sake, but purely for devotion's sake.

**The Political Sphere**

The consistent brotherly ethic of salvation religions has come into an equally sharp tension with the political orders of the world. Local (community, tribe, household, etc.) gods and magic were not a problem The problem arose when these barriers of locality, tribe and polity were shattered by universalistic religions. And the problem arose in full strength only when this god was a god of 'love.' The problem of tension with the political order emerged for redemption religions out of the basic demand for brotherliness. In politics as in economics, the more rational the political order became, the sharper the problems of these tensions became.

The brotherliness of a group of men bound together in war appears valueless in brotherly religions; it is seen as a mere reflection of the technically sophisticated brutality of the struggle. It's consecration appears as the glorification of fratricide.

The only two consistent solutions (first three guesses don't count...): puritanism and mysticism Puritanism believes God's commands should be imposed on the world by the means of the world — violence, so "just war" is not a problem for Puritanism (God is on their side). The mystics take a "radical political attitude" of "turning the other cheek" which makes them appear "necessarily vulgar and lacking in dignity in the eyes of every self-assured worldly ethic of heroism."

Organic social ethics (where religiously substructured) stands on the soil of brotherliness, but, in contrast to mystic and acosmic love, is dominated by a cosmic, rational demand for brotherliness. It point of departure is the experience of the inequality of religious charisma. The fact that the holy should be accessible to some and not all is unbearable to organic social ethics. It therefore attempts to synthesize this inequality of charismatic qualifications with secular stratification by status, into a cosmos of God-ordained services which are specialized in function. Certain tasks are given to every individual and every group according to their social and economic position as determined by fate. Without something like the Indian doctrine of Karma (which says there's a reason why you're bottom dog), every organic social ethic unavoidably represents an accommodation to the interests of the privileged strata of the world.

From the standpoint of inner-worldly asceticism, the

organic ethic lacks the drive for an ethical and thorough rationalization of individual life. In such matters, it has no premium for the rational and methodical patterning of personal life in the interest of the individual's own salvation. The organic pragmatism of salvation must consider the redemptory aristocracy of inner-worldly asceticism, with its rational depersonalization of life orders, as the hardest form of lovelessness and lack of brotherliness. It must also consider the redemptory pragmatism of mysticism as a sublimated and unbrotherly indulgence of the mystic' s own charisma. Both inner-worldly asceticism and mysticism ultimately condemn the social world to absolute meaninglessness (or, at least they hold that God's aims concerning the world are utterly incomprehensible).

The rationalism of religious and organic doctrines of society cannot stand up under this idea; for it seeks to comprehend the world as an at least relatively rational cosmos in spite of all its wickedness: the world must hear at least traces of the divine plan of salvation.

The organic ethic of society is an eminently conservative power hostile to revolution. Virtuoso religion is a potentially revolutionary force. Its revolutionary turn may assume two forms:

(1) (from inner-worldly asceticism, with an absolute divine law) it becomes a religious duty to realize this divine natural law. This corresponds to an obligation to crusade.

(2) (from mysticism) The commands of the world do not hold for the man who is assured in his obsession with god.

**The Aesthetic Sphere**

The development of intellectualism and the rationalism of life make art become a cosmos of more and more consciously grasped independent values which exist in their own right. Art comes to provide a salvation from the routines of everyday life, and begins to compete directly with salvation religion. [The refusal of modern man to assume responsibility for moral judgements tends to transform judgements of moral intent into judgements of taste.]

**The Erotic Sphere**

The brotherly ethic of salvation religion is in profound tension with the greatest irrational force of life: sexual love. The more sublimated sexuality is, and the more principled and relentlessly consistent the salvation ethic of brotherhood is, the sharper is the tension between sex and religion. A principled ethic of religious brotherhood perceives that inner, earthly salvation by mature love competes in the sharpest possible way with devotion to a supra-mundane God. Inner-worldly and rational asceticism (vocational asceticism) can accept only the rationally regulated marriag

**The Intellectual Sphere**

The tension between religion and intellectual knowledge comes to the fore wherever rational, empirical knowledge has consistently worked through to the disenchantment of the world. Every increase of rationalism in empirical science increasing pushes religion from the rational into the irrational realm; but only today does religion become the irrational or anti-rational supra-human power.

The less magic or merely contemplative mysticism and the more pure doctrine a religion contains, the greater is its need of rational apologetics. The more religion became book-religion and doctrine, the more literary it became and the more efficacious it became in provoking rational lay-thinking, freed of priestly control. However, there is no "unbroken" religion working as a vital force which is not compelled at some point to demand the credo non quod, sed quia absurdum (some saint said this, but i can't remember which one, it means "i believe it because it is absurd". i think it was said in reference to the trinity), the sacrifice of the intellect.

Redemptory religion defends itself against the attack of the self-sufficient intellect, by raising the claim that religious knowledge moves in a different sphere.

The need for salvation, consciously cultivated as the substance of religiosity, has resulted from the endeavor of a systematic and practical rationalization of life's realities. All religions have demanded as a specific presupposition that the course of the world be somehow meaningful, at least in so far as it touches upon the interests of men (this claim arises first as the problem of unjust suffering and just compensation for the unequal distribution of individual happiness in the world). From here, the claim has tended to progress toward an ever increasing devaluation of the world. For, the more intensely rational thought has seized upon the problem of a just and retributive compensation, the less an entirely inner-worldly solution could seem possible, and the less an other-worldly solution could appear probable or even meaningful.

The intellect, like all culture values, has created an aristocracy based on the possession of rational culture and independent of all personal ethical qualities of man. The aristocracy of intellect is hence an unbrotherly aristocracy. Worldly man has regarded the possession of culture as the highest good. In addition to the burden of ethical guilt, however, something has adhered to this cultural value which was bound to depreciate it with still greater finality, namely, senselessness (if the cultural value is to be judged in terms of its own standards).

The pure inner-worldly perfection of self by a man of "culture", the ultimate value to which "culture" has seemed to be reducible is meaningless for religious thought. This meaninglessness follows for religious thought from the obvious meaninglessness of death when viewed from the inner-worldly standpoint. The cultivated man can die weary of life, but never satiated with it; for, the perfectibility of the man of culture, in principle, progresses indefinitely, as do the cultural values.

Culture appears as man's emancipation from the organically prescribed cycle of natural life. For this reason, culture's every step forward seems condemned to lead to an every more devastating senselessness. The advancement of cultural values seems to become a senseless hustle in the service of worthless, moreover self-contradictory, and mutually antagonistic ends. The advancement of cultural values appears the more meaningless the more it is made a holy task, a "calling."

The need for salvation responds to this devaluation by becoming more other-worldly, more alienated from all structured forms of life, and by confining itself to the strict religious essence. The reaction is the stronger the more systematic the thinking about the "meaning" of the universe becomes, the more the external organization of the world is rationalized, the more the conscious experience of the world's irrational content is sublimated. These specific intellectual and mystical attempts at salvation in the face of these tensions succumb in the end to the world dominion of unbrotherliness. One the one hand, their charisma is not accessible to everyone. Hence, in intent, mystical salvation means aristocracy; it is an aristocratic religiosity of redemption.

# 2

# The Nature and Origin of Society

## Society and the Individual

Man as a social being, we are here confronted with the central problem of sociology, - namely, the sociability or, as we prefer to call it, the sociality of man. That a man may or should belong to this or that type of association is a secondary matter. The essential fact behind it is that man has always belonged to a society of one kind or another, and that without it he cannot exist at all. When we speak of society as related to the individual, we have in mind no special type of society in particular; it may be the state, the tribe, the family or any other group in which man has lived. But this question has been historically associated with that more inclusive society: the state. That is why in order to follow more clearly the authors who have written on this subject, we shall also have in mind the state or larger society when there is no danger of confusion in the issues with which we are dealing.

The question of the nature of society is largely connected with the question of its origin. It is the former, as we shall presently see, on which the latter depends as a kind of corollary. That man has not only a *capacity* for social life but also an *intrinsic need* of it, is a self-obvious fact. Emotional development, intellectual maturity, the necessity of a certain amount of material goods and comforts for the full exercise of his liberty and progress in self-perfection, are unthinkable without society. No human being is known to have normally developed in isolation. In the notorious case of Kaspar Hauser (1828), who from his childhood until his seventeenth year was brought up in the wood of Nuremberg, it was found that his mind was not developed, and in spite of subsequent education, thanks to which he made a little progress, he could never make himself a normal man. The accounts of the noble savage free from all social restraints and quenching his thirst in the streams and rivulets of the forest and appeasing his appetite with the fruits freely bestowed by nature, are idyllic tales void of all historical value.

Even the 'man in the cave', who unintentionally left in Altamira, Lascaux and similar places, a monumental record of his way of life – a hunting expedition with its corresponding division of labour–was no less social than his modern counterpart, and probably as sociable, if not more so. Even the Ifugao of Luzon and the Andaman islanders, who are reckoned among the most centrifugal of the primitives, not only live in society; they observe a complex system of customary law which keeps them together. All this and many other proofs that could be adduced tend to show conclusively that society is nothing accidentally added to or superimposed on human nature.

It is something which is consonant with it and fulfils a vital need in man's constitution. Indeed, as Aristotle said, man is social by nature. C. E. M. Joad explained this point very lucidly from the view-point of the political philosopher: Whether Neanderthal man lived in society, the political philosopher does not know, nor does he very much care; it is a question that he is prepared to leave to the anthropologist. He is content to point out that, since it is impossible to explain the coming into existence of society, unless the capacity for living in it was already present in the human beings who were members of it, and since this capacity cannot have arisen, as it were, out of nothing, we are driven to postulate the presence of this capacity from the earliest moment at which human beings are first entitled to be called Human; or rather, if the phrase be preferred, we are driven to postulate the *potentiality* for this capacity, a potentiality which must from the first have expressed itself in some kind of social organization, however rudimentary. Thus a new meaning must now be given to the definition of man as a social or political being. Not only is man a being who only attains his real nature in society; he is a being who has always lived in some form or other of society, even if his earliest society was only that of the family group.

The psychological development of the social consciousness of the child is also a confirmation of the natural sociality of the human being. In the early stages he hardly distinguishes between persons and things and is only confusedly aware of his own self. As the becomes conscious of himself, he also realizes the existence of other things similar to himself whose nature he apprehends through an inborn power of mutual recognition within the species, or a common sympathy, or any other similar reaction among human beings which was expressed of old in the famous dictum –'As a man, noting human is alien to me', *Homo sum, humani a me nihil alienum puto* (Terence).

In this process individuality and sociality develop together. A baby who is just a few weeks old, smiles when his mother smiles to him; cries when he is chidden. He plays later on with other toddlers of his age, deals with them as equals, and develops towards them the attitudes of generosity and selfishness, joy and anger, sympathy and aversion. He is not moulded by society in utter passivity nor is he the mere receptacle of the social influences-which he displays in facing new situations testifies to his individuality and even to his creativeness. His entrance for the first time in the larger world of a school, his experiences as he grows up, specially during the period of puberty are decisive landmarks in the process of individualization as well as of socialization, the net outcome of which is, what in modern terminology is called, personality or character. The natural sociality of man, which is so evident, has never- the less been repeatedly called into question in history for various reasons. Some of these are mutually opposed – the individualistic and organismic opinions which we must now analyse in the following lines.

***Individualistic Opinions :*** One of the most widespread misconception about man is the individualistic idea. About 600 B.C. in China we find Taoism holding that the individual's greatest satisfaction in life was not enjoyed by him as a member of society, but as a being isolated from everybody and being a law unto himself. L ws and social institutions were mere devices to cramp his human development. This conception greatly influenced ancient China even in the times of Confucius.

One or two centuries later the Greek sophists, especially Glaucon and Adeimantus, also taught that men by nature were selfish and unequal; that everyone's hand was against his fellows; and so they decided to make a compact in order to get rid of that state of anarchy. The result of this compact was society.

These ideas, which in reality had never died in the history of human thought, appeared again in full force in the political and social thought of Europe in the seventeenth and in the two subsequent centuries. The rationalism and atomism which prevailed in the philosophies of those times were also applied to man. Man was conceived as an abstraction separated from any other realty. His rationality and individuality were taken into account, but society, the milieu in which and by which they naturally developed, was thought of as accessory.

The classical representatives of this school of thought are Thomas Hobbes (1588-1679), John Locks (1632-1704), and J.J. Rousseau (1712-1778). The three of them taught in various ways that before the existence of civil society men lived in assort of pre-social state, called the state of nature, and in virtue of a contract among themselves, society came into existence.

According to Hobbes, man in the state of nature was in perpetual conflict with his neighbours; he was a wolf to his fellowmen; his life was 'solitary, nasty, brutish, and short'. Moving in the midst of such unenviable conditions, he decides to make a contract with his fellowmen in order to form a society and live in peace with all. Fear, therefore, is the root origin of society. As a result of this pact a government arises sovereign and absolute, containing in itself the wills of all. The sovereign's actions become the people's actions in accordance with the principle that 'he who acts through his agent, acts through himself.' Hence Hobbes's individualism ended in absolutism. In fact, his masterwork, *The Leviathan* (1651), was written to justify Cromwell's tyranny.

Locke, on the other hand, believed that man in the state of nature was enjoining an ideal liberty, free from any social restraints; but in order to ensure the exercise of his liberty he entered into a contract by which the individuals conferred power, not to the government, as Hobbes thought, but to the community. This contract is not absolute, because the natural rights of life, liberty and property, remain in the hands of the individual. In order words, not every right in society comes from the state.

J.J. Rousseau in his *Contrat Social* (1762) held that man, in the state of nature, was a noble savage: peaceful and unsophisticated; but growth in numbers of men and the quarrels arising among them compelled a man to make a contract with his fellowmen 'in virtue of which everyone, while uniting himself to all, remains as free as before.' Out of this contract a general will emerges which is really sovereign and includes by a tacit agreement the individual wills of all. Hence if any individual will is at variance with the general will it shall be compelled to submit or 'shall be forced to be free.' Thus by this peculiar device the possibility of conflict between the general and the individual will is excluded, while everybody cannot help but remain free. This intrinsic contradiction in Rousseau's theory has given rise to the most conflicting theories ranging from democratic liberalism to totalitarian idealism.

In the light of what we have already said in these pages about man's sociality, it seems hardly necessary to insist on any refutation of these theories. They only serve to stress a truth which some social scientists sometimes forget, - namely, that thought society is natural to man, his whole life is not exhausted in terms of society. His personality and freedom remain active in the turmoil of social life. In addition to this we may also remark that in the state of nature, these theories imply that man was already living in society, outside of when he could not have developed mentally nor have acquired those ideas and feelings which led to the social contract. From the historical viewpoint, on the other hand, the state of nature, as described by these authors, never existed nor could have ever possibly existed.

***Organismic Theories :*** These theories, by overemphasizing the importance of sociality, to the philosophical background and the pseudo-justification for the totalitarian regimes and theories of modern times. These organismic theories may be grouped under two types : organismic theories strictly so called; and idealistic or group-mind theories, which we shall study in the next section.

These writers compare the social or political structures to a living body endowed with organs, nerves, limbs, etc. In this body the individuals are nothing but cells subordinated in their composition and functions to the organism. This was the opinion held in the Middle Ages by Nicholas of Cues; in more recent times by Bluntschli, Spengler, Novicow, and Herbert Spencer. This last-named writer compares the social structure to an animal body whose system of nutrition has its counterpart in society, in the industrial and agricultural systems; the circulatory system with the heart, arteries and veins, corresponds to the communication and transport systems of a nation; the nervous system, to the government, and so on. Yet in Spencer's mind this parallelism is no more than a metaphor. As a reality it is a blatant disavowal of his individualistic system; for when he attempts to reconcile individuality with organicity, his argument for the latter falls to pieces.

Not a few writers used to describe society by a general comparison with an organism. Others have driven this simile to extremes and hold that in reality the individual in society behaves as the cells of the body whose activity and life are meant for the sake of the whole. If this were true, the individual would then exist for the sake of society, not society for the sake of the individual.

In reply, therefore, to all these organismic theories we may say that it is true that individuals in society are intimately connected with it, and that society itself is not an artificial device, as the individualists maintain; still the dissimilarities between society and an organism are radical.

Firstly, as Spencer himself said, society, unlike an organism, has no 'common sensorium', no central organ of perception and thought. It is not society that thinks and wills in individuals, but thought. It is not society that thinks and wills in individuals, but it is individuals who think and will in society. In the second place, the life cycle of the individual organism is ***toto coelo*** distinct from that of society. We can speak analogically of a society being born, attaining maturity, reproducing and dying; but these vital functions are only true of the organism or of the individuals as such, not of society. In the third place, there are profound differences, both structural and functional, between the relations of the cells to the organism, and those of the individuals to society. The life of the cell is exclusively for the sake of the organism, so much so that if a group of cells display a special activity out of harmony with the whole, cancer or any other dangerous diseases will follow. In society the opposite is true; the existence of persons of character or men of genius who break away from the old stereotyped ways and lend leadership to society, is a necessary condition for its healthy development and progress. In the organism, be it a plant or an animal, the cells receive the vital impulse to function and co-ordination to work from the higher organs of the body; in society it is the higher organs which receive their inspiration and direction from the individuals. In other words, in society it is the individuals who act teleologycally; in the organism it is the organism itself which acts teleologically.

Again it does not further the cause of the organismic theories to object that the individuals cannot exist without society; for neither can they exist without oxygen. Yet they are not a constituent part of the oxygen of the air. Besides this, if man cannot exist without society still less can society exist without men. We can imagine the cat without the grin, but we cannot imagine the grin without the cat. As MacIver puts it.

The only experience we know is the experience of individuals, and it is only in the light of their struggles, their interests, their aspirations, their hopes and their fears that we can assign any function and any goal to society. What we speak of the 'group interest' we mean only the interest in the group which its members or any of them feel.

**Group-mind Theories**

The second type of the so-called organismic theories, the idealist or group-mind theories, has been propounded with great detail and ingenuity by a host of philosophers and thinkers. Here we can only offer a schematic idea and criticism of some of its most representative versions.

Plato himself had called civil society a mind 'writ large' and divided it into three classes-philosopher-rulers, warriors, and workers-corresponding to the three parts in which the human mind was supposed to be divided. But except for the fact that the society conceived by Plato in Republic was distinctly totalitarian, the comparison of the body politic with the human mind did not go beyond a metaphor.

According to Hegel (1770-1831), the father of modern idealism, society as manifested in the state, is a natural organism representing a phased of the historical world process or Absolute. The state, not the individual, is the real person; its will is the manifestation of perfect rationality, that is, the synthesis of universal and individual freedom. The state is the divine idea on earth. The individual has reality only in so far as he is a member of the state. The perfect life consists in living according to the will of the Absolute.

This and similar opinions were followed in the main by the English idealists, T. H. Green, F. H. Bradley, and B. Bosanquet; in America by J. Royee and R.W. Emerson; in Germany by the so-called 'arm-chair' socialists such as Wagner, Schmoller and Schaefle.

According to Bosanquet the system of volitional dispositions of every individual his 'standing will' or true character, and implies a real will of true self. This real will, as distinct from the actual character or inclinations of the individual, is an ideal will based on 'a fully articulated idea of the best life for man', essentially social and *qualitatively identical* in all individuals. It is, therefore, one will, real or general, and embodied in the state.

Otto Gierke held that our internal experience testifies not only to the existence of the Ego, but also to the fact of our being a part of a higher whole, which whole, as such, we cannot distinguish with our consciousness. 'But there are times', he writes, 'when the spirit of the community reveals itself to us with an elemental power, in almost visible shape, filling and mastering our inward being to such an extent that we are hardly any longer conscious of our individual existence as such. Here, in Berlin, in the *Unter den Linden,* I lived through such an hour of consecration on the 15$^{th}$ of July, in the year 1870.'

This hour of 'consecration' was decided by the famous telegram sent by William I of Prussia to Bismarck, which gave rise to the Franco-Prussian war of 1870, and the publication of which filled the German people with enthusiasm. As Sir E. Barker remaks: 'It is also his emotion which serves for him (Gierke) as evidence of the existence of spiritual reality or personality, which transcends the individual.

In Durkheim's opinion the social mind also has an existence distinct (not apart) from the mind of the individuals, and is superior to them. This mind or collective consciousness is the higher form of psychic life. It tends to absorb the individual mind from which it differs not only in the richness of content but also in kind. Particular minds exist in the social mind as the atom exists in the molecule absorbed by the higher synthesis of the whole.

The idea of the group mind found a new exponent in the eminent psychologist W. McDougall, whose work *the group mind,* published first in 1920, exerted a wide influence in the English speaking world. He forcibly disowns any brand of German idealism directly derived from Hegel; but he presents his own opinions in such a way that it is not easy to distinguish them from the theories that he repudiates. Thus he writes:

> The aggregate (of individual units) which is a society, has a certain individuality, is a true whole which in great measure determines the nature and the mode of activity of its parts; it is an organic whole. The society has a mental life which is not the mere sum of the mental lives of its units existing as independent units; and a complete knowledge of the units, if and in so far as they could be known a isolated units, would not enable us to deduce the nature of the life of the whole in the way that is implied in Spencer's analogies.

As Fouillee puts it 'the essential characteristic of human society is that is an organism which realizes itself in conceiving and in willing its own existence. Any collection of men becomes a society in the only true sense of the world, when all the men conceive more or less clearly the type of organic whole which they can form by uniting themselves under the determining influence of this conception. Society is then an organism which exists because it has been thought and willed, it is an organism born of an idea.' In this sense, society has never yet been perfectly realized but it is the ideal towards which social evolution tends.

Some contemporary writers tend to identify the individual with the group so closely that logically fall into the same difficulties as the exponents of the group mind theories. Such phrases as: 'Civilization creates above all this inner force that we call the human soul'; 'Civilization creates man'; or 'the individual is a myth, except as he is a member of the group' are liable to produce such conclusions that their very authors may recoil from them.

*Criticism :* As the principles on which the group mind or the general will theories are built are similar-both refer to the existence pf a higher mental synthesis out of individual acts- we shall study the two together by stressing occasionally the aspects in which they differ from each other. For brevity's sake we shall include both under the head of group mind theories, though the term has been sometime explicitly rejected by some of these writers.

The basis of these theories seems to be a threefold identification: first, identification of the mind with its mental acts or processes (attitudes); secondly, identification of the mental processes with their objects (interests); and thirdly, identification of the objects or interests with the ideal object (general will, group mind, Idea, Absolute, etc.). Of these, the second identification (the mental processes with their objects) seems to be the most characteristic of these theories.

The first identification, that of the mind with its mental acts, became prominent since Decartes' times; *I think therefore I exist* was the formula on which this identification was based. Starting from this presupposition, Wundt, with some German psychologists of the second half of the last century, popularized the idea of a 'psychology without a soul', as the soul, or mind had become fused, or rather confused with its own acts. Once this stage was reached, the door was flung open to the subsequent phases of the group mind theory.

In his work, *the group mind,* McDougall himself defined the mind as 'an organized system of mental or purposive forces; and in the sense so defined every highly organized human society may properly be said to possess a collective mind.' To this statement, definitely redolent of idealism, Maciver replied that 'when we speak of the mind of an individual we mean something more than this. The mind of each of us has a unity other than that of such a system. To this McDougall retorted that no other kind of unity may be assigned to constitute a mind unless a soul or substance is assumed. 'But,' he adds, 'I do not suppose that MacIver accepts or intends to refer to this conception.

But is the identification of the mind with its mental acts justified? Has the existence of a substance mind or soul been validly excluded from the field of psychology? This question has to be decided not on school assumptions but on its own merits by examining our own mental acts.

When we reflect on ourselves we become aware that beneath the system of our mental processes there is an underlying reality permanent and identical throughout time and space. I, who an now writing, am the same person who is listening to the tick of the clock ad the chirping of birds outside my window. I am still enjoying the last joke made last night by a friend, and thinking of tomorrow's trip. Under all these transient affections there is a permanent underlying reality- the I or Ego which recognize them as its own and gives them unity and consistency.

In the same way one may reflect that he is the same person who, two years ago in Calcutta, incurred such and such a debt, and is now going to his office. The past mental acts no longer exist, yet he still exists as the permanent centre and substratum of them all. This standing reality has been traditionally recognized as the individual mind, soul or self.

These and similar reflections lead us to reject or at least to take as not proven the so-called identity between the mind and its mental acts. These or similar difficulties perceived by L. T. Hobhouse must have led him to write the following lines on this question:

When Dr. McDougall goes on to identify a mental system with a mind he raises a very definite question which compels those who, like myself, have used such, terms as Social Mind to consider our terminology very carefully. For his discussion – by its very success in propounding a tangible meaning for what has been a hazy conception makes it clear that the question raised is not merely, not even primarily one of the nature of society, but of the nature of the mind or rather of its unity.

The next question to be discussed in connection with theories is the second identification-namely that of our mental acts or processes with their objects; or in the terminology used above, of our attitudes with their corresponding interests. According to this position if the members of a community desire, for instance, the common good, a fusion of their minds with the object takes place, which gives rise to the group mind or general will. But such a supposition is not possible; attitudes or mental processes cannot be common, though their objects or interests may be. I may desire the common good with the same degree of intensity and enthusiasm as my neighbour– a situation which is extremely unlikely in practice but my will is always mine, and my neighbour's will remains his, and neither of the two can be fused or identified with the common good. When we say that our minds are closely identified in the promotion of an ideal cause, we are simply using a metaphor indicating that we are jointly co-operating towards that end. Yet strictly specking, co-operation does not connote oneness but plurality. Mind may communicate with mind, but one never becomes the other. The enthusiastic members of a Shakespearean society may become enraptured at the performance of Hamlet, but they would be the first to be surprised to hear that their minds were truly fused with one another, and that, together with Shakespeare's works, they constituted a group mind.

Even when the object is an idea, universal or concrete, the group mind hypothesis encounters the same difficulties, because this idea, inasmuch as it is an interest, continues to be an object, whereas our mental processes remain attitudes.

In other words: attitudes are not interests; while the latter may be common, the former cannot be.

The appeal made to an integrated system of mental forces as constituting a mind, has already been examined in connection with McDougall's opinion. The co-ordination or integration which belongs to the mental acts of various individuals is never the co-ordination and unity which attaches to the acts of a single individual; we can only use such concepts as group mind, group spirit, or social mind in a metaphorical, never in a real sense.

As regards the third identification,-namely, that of the object or interest with the ideal object,-little can be said to add to what has already been explained. It may be of some interest to note that this question has been especially debated in conjunction with the general will. This general will is supposed to be included idea of the best life for man'. Being perfect and harmonious, the imperfect individual wills ought to submit to it.

But here again there is a lurking confusion between act and object, attitude and interest. One thing is my will and another is what I will. On the other hand, what I in fact will is different from what I ought to will. If obviously cannot be the object of my will; if it is perceived, it is the object of a particular will, not of a general will if what I ought to will is really not willed, then there is a distinction between the so-called 'general will' and my own. But whether I will it or not, my individual or personal will remains as individual and personal as ever. The general will is a contradiction in terms – if it is a will, it is not general; if it is general, it is not a will.

Obviously then there are objects and aspirations common to certain groups of men which are loosely called the 'national soul' or the 'national mind'. There are also individual and collective ideals after which civil society has been constituted;

but it is not easy to see what is gained by identifying and fusing those ideals objects with the individual mind.

The fact that these theories became official in totalitarian societies for the suppression of individual liberties renders them very suspicious. But apart from practical considerations, to obliterate the human mind and will by merging them into a sort of hypostatized general mind or will, idea, or Absolute, is to undermine the whole fabric of the social sciences and of society itself by removing their most precious support – the autonomy and worth of the human person.

## The Nature of Social Unity

Now that we have arrived at the end of eh discussion the reader may pose the following question: 'If there is such a thing as social unity or union, in what does it consist? Some contemporary sociologists seem to evade this question by saying that the individual and society are two aspects of the same thing and so there is no possible conflict between them. But it is obvious that conflicts between them do exist; the individual is not society, but only a tiny part of it. Hence this answer is not satisfactory. Between the part and the whole between man and society, there is a type of unity which we may consider. This, to be sure, is not an artificial or physical unity as that existing between the stones of a building or the parts of a clock. This solution is already discarded by our own rejection of individualism. Now is it an organic or synthetic unity as that of the cells of the body or the atoms of a molecule which are merged in the whole. Not even is it a mere functional unity in which every member is quantitatively affected by a change produced in any of the other functional parts.

The union which we find in society has certain characteristics, it is true, of both the functional and the organic, but it is neither the one nor the other. It is sui generic; if is simply social, that is, without the company of his fellowmen, the individual cannot live at all nor develop his own personality. But even when living and communicating with them he still has a life of his own, an autonomy and character which cannot be fused or confused with the lives of other men. Social values are in the last resort personal values. Even those qualities or powers which belong to society a such are realized only in its members, present or future; for the life of society has no meaning except as an expression of the lives of the individuals.

Dr. Timasheff describing the nature of society and the kind of union which belongs to it, writes;

Materially speaking there are only individuals in a state of interaction, but this interaction creates a new unit, a social group, society is, therefore, a relation among individuals; its members. This relation is of course necessary: being in society is an essential property of every individual. This concept is so far removed from the so-called organismic theory of society ... On the other hand by describing social groups as concrete systems, the existence of society as such or the fact that it is something more than the sum of individuals, is by no means denied : society is the sum of interacting individuals, and this interaction is what differentiates society from the mere aggregation of individuals.

## The Mainsprings of Social Life

*The Question and the Answers* **:** Having studied the nature of society and its relation to the individual, we must opinions of psychologists and social scientists – such is the question about the ultimate drives of social life or the mainsprings of man's behaviour in society. This question is frequently studied by psychologists in conjunction with the wider one about the dynamics or ultimate forces of human behaviour in all its comprehensiveness. In this respect the inquiry into the ultimate sources of social life is a particular case of a more general problem with which it is closely connected.

The immediate motives which may prompt a person to join a particular group or society-self-interested or otherwise-are excluded from our query which is only concerned with the ultimate motives or tendencies which man has as a social being for living in society. Nor do we mean to say that these motives or drives are conscious. Usually they are not, though occasionally they may become conscious. This question should also be distinguished from a similar one about the ends or ideals of social life; but with these we are not here concerned.

Of the opinions hitherto advanced about the ultimate motives of social life, only a summary can be given here of those considered to be more important.

Lester F. Ward divided what he called social forces into essential and non-essential. Essential social forces are those upon which the existence of society and of man himself depends; non-essential social forces are those 'not indispensable to the life of either the individual or the species.' Essential social forces are the preservative and the reproductive, whereas the aesthetic, moral, and intellectual are not essential.

According to W. G. Sumner and A.G. Keller the basic motives of society are hunger, love or sex passion, vanity, and fear. F. H. Giddings, already mentioned in a previous chapter, reduced the springs of social behaviour to a fundamental principle called consciousness of kind. This is, in his opinion, a primary sociological postulate inspired in the notion of sympathy which was propounded by Adam Smith. It means 'a state of consciousness in which any being, whether high or low in the scale of life, recognizes another conscious being as of like kind with itself. The four fundamental wishes proposed by W. I. Thomas as the roots of social life we already know : response, recognition, security, and new experience.

Vilfredo Pareto placed the basis of human behaviour

on six fundamental residues or 'manifestations of sentiments and instincts'; instinct for combinations, group persistences, need of expressing sentiments by external acts, residues connected with sociality, integrity of the individual and his appurtenances, and sex residue.

Some decades ago Freud's system, which seemed to explain most human activity by the sex impulse, became very popular. Now it has lost most of its scientific appeal as a unique or universal explanation. Nietzsche's conception of Will zur Macht (The Will to power), and Bergson's idea of élan vital were also proposed and accepted by many as the fundamental drives making for society.

An opinion widely held in our own days is that which locates the ultimate motives of social behaviour in a special instinct of gregariousness or sociality. This theory was propounded by W. McDougall with the thoroughness and subtlety which characterize his writings. In the later editions of his works, setting aside the concept of instinct, he uses instead the term propensity by which he understands the driving force behind the goal-seeking innate behaviour tendencies.' These inborn tendencies are not only the basis of our mental life, but also explain all our activities from the simplest to the most complex, as they are in reality the 'hormic energy' or propelling force activity behind them.the most current criticism leveled at McDougall's theory stresses the difficulty of distinguishing between innate and acquired tendencies or drives. Even if these propensities exist, they do not throw much light on the interpretion of human behaviour. To say, for instance, that wars occur because there is in man an innate propensity to self assertion or pugnacity, is not very illuminating unless the existence, nature, and conditions of this propensity are explained. The same applies to gregariousness or any other kind of 'instinct' or propensity.

On the other hand, it must be acknowledged as it is practically accepted by common agreement among psychologists – that human behaviour is largely determined by inborn factors. They only object to acquired habits, dispositions and environmental influences.

We cannot enter here into a detailed examination of these various theories; that would take us beyond the scope of this book. The summary of them made in these pages will suffice. Yet without denying the elements of truth which they contain, we think that most of then are either incomplete or otherwise inconclusive. Neither fear nor the wish for new experience, nor the will to power may be held to be the ultimate springs of social behaviour. At most they are secondary or derivative.

But there is a more fundamental consideration which compels us to take exception to these theories. Many of them, including that of McDougall, tend to envisage this question atomistically, as if sociality were a part or a compartment of human life. This attitude seems to proceed from a tendency to indentify sociality with sociability. The former appertains naturally to man as a social being, whereas sociability- the quality by which a person is disposed to companionship, conversation, and similar activities may well be due to a psychological disposition, inborn or acquired, in the same way a affine ear for music corresponds to a physiological disposition of the acoustic nerve.

This cannot be said about sociality. For sociality is not a part or quality, but a condition or aspect of man. Paradoxically enough, man can live without being sociable, but not without being social. Sociality colours and pervades his whole life and activities though it does not exhaust them. Man is all social, but he is something more than that. *Totus socialis sed non totaliter.* This is why the quasi-oraganic character of the 'consciousness of kind' propounded by Giddings, and the 'social forces' of Lester Ward which explain the fact of sociality seem to us more acceptable than the other theories. Yet the excessive generality of the former and the narrowness of the latter which refuse to include the aesthetic, moral and intellectual tendencies of man among the essential forces of society, weaken their validity.

*The Classical Solution* : An explanation which seems to avoid the pitfalls of the others in accounting for the most intimate motives of man's social behaviour, is the time-honoured Aristotelian-scholastic solution with which not a few of the modern theories agree as A. H. Maslow's "Human Needs" theory proposed in his work Motivation and personality 1954. according to this solution the fundamental drives or inclinations of man are reduced to three : the self-preservation inclination, the procreative, and the intellectual. This last is subdivided or propensities, to which perhaps others could be added. These inclinations are not disconnected from each other; there is between them a reciprocal and organic action whose extreme complexity constitutes one of the most difficult, if not insoluble, problems of psychology.

The self-preservation tendency, which in some way or other is common to every being, is the inclination that man has to exist, not in general or in the abstract, but as a human being. It includes some secondary inclinations which are either actualizations of it or tendencies arising under certain conditions to facilitate or improve the exercise of self – preservation. Such are food hunger, excretion-hunger, rest-hunger, etc., of which Tolman and other psychologists speak

"The procreative tendency is not a mere biological inclination; it is more complex in the sense that it gathers round itself such concomitant tendencies as sex, parental love, wish for protection, etc. All of them combined give rise to the institution of the family which is probably give rise to the institution of the family which is probably the most complicated social group.

The third inclination is the intellectual. Its ultimate object is truth or reality in all its aspects. If this reality is a norm according to which man's actions are finally good or evil, we have morality. If this reality is the supreme Being or some supernatural beings, we have religion. If its objects is beauty, as perceived or expressed, we have art. And if its object is one's neighbours in so far as they are connected with one by social relationship, we have society.

For neither can the self-preservation and procreative tendencies of man operate irrespective of thought and intelligence, nor can any one of them normally develop independent of society. The unity and type of interaction existing between them is such that we cannot separate them or give prominence to one to the exclusion of the rest. Thus an over-insistence on the self-preservation tendency, coloured at times with fear, vitiated the political writings of Hobbes, Spinoza, and Rousseau as well as those of the Marxist writers. In the same way special stress on sex radically weakened the claims of the Freudian psychoanalysts to be the legitimate interpreters of human or social behaviour.

The problem, therefore, does not seem to be well stated by our merely inquiring into the ultimate motives or mainsprings of social behaviour. The ultimate source of sociality is not one or a few particular needs or tendencies of man, but man himself, with all his natural and fundamental inclinations, which require society as a sine qua non for his life as a human being. Man, as Aristotle so plainly proclaimed, is by nature social.

If we go further and ask what kind of reality does sociality belong to, we may answer with Aristotle himself, and in agreement with the ideas expressed in these pages, that society being essentially a mental phenomenon, it belongs to the sphere of intelligence in contrast with gregariousness which is an animal or sensitive phenomenon proper to irrational beings. It is possible that sociality in man implies also a gregarious instinct or tendency as a background; but taking into consideration the objections proposed against the doctrine of instincts in man, this possibility does not seen to have been proved as a matter of fact.

**The Origin of Society**

Having studied the nature of society and of sociality we must now briefly make some observations about the origin of society.

It goes without saying that this question is parallel to the one about the origin of man. Sociality is inborn in him; hence as soon as he saw the light of day with others like him, society became a fact. Society was not superadded unto him by virtue of a pact or special provision; it emerged gradually and followed its own line of development.

The question about the origin of society must not be misunderstood, as sometimes happens, with the more concrete problem about the determining factors or occasions which have given rise to various types of societies or states. About these, no general rule can be offered, for history shows that the ways by which new societies came into being are of the most diversified nature; such are wars, pacts, migrations, discoveries, family growth, efficient leadership, religious movements and the like.

Such current suppositions, as the social contract theory or the force theory, may be interpreted, not as providing a general explanation of the origin of society, but as indicating the way in which certain societies began to exist. The same applies to the divine right theory or the patriarchal or matriarchal theories about the origins of society.

On the other hand, the explanation given by certain versions of the evolutionary theory regarding the origin of society, seem to offer a generally valid explanation in accordance with the principles and facts proposed in these pages. According to the former, society was not made, but emerged spontaneously in the process of social evolution without having any pre-social stage to precede it. This theory is principally concerned with the evolution of the state or the sequence of stages through which the modern differentiated state came into existence. It is widely held among evolutionary writers that kinship and the family were the first social bonds uniting man with man; after this the village community and tribe developed, until it was possible through various events, to arrive at such advanced forms of social organization as the city and the nation state.

The classical natural law theory-which is sometimes confused with the social contract theory-does not admit of any mythical state of nature in which man was not living in society. It is more concerned with the natural sociality of man, and less with the stages through which it developed, though its conclusions are quite compatible with most of the contemporary forms of social evolution. It concurs with the Aristotelian view of man and society, and emphasizes the worth of human personality as the central point and raison de etre of society.

# 3

# Impact of Industry on Social Change

The present century, especially in the last decade, is such, that together with science and technology, it must be reckoned as one of the most powerful agencies for social change in recent times, and will undoubtedly continue to be so for many years to come, even beyond the present century. Here we must briefly survey its influence on modern Indian society and study some of the repercussions that it may have for the future. Modern industry came to India in the last century after the Industrial Revolution of Europe, and was allied with a modern system of education sponsored by an alien power.

Whatever the merits or demerits of the case may be, the fact is that since then profound changes have been spontaneously initiated, first slowly, and later on more acceleratedly, particularly concerning the social stratification of the country. The caste system, which had reigned hitherto undisturbed, began to meet with serious competition by the rising class system, particularly by what has been called the Indian "New Class".

## Class as Effect of Industrialization

Over and against the caste system based on birth and

endogamy and having the Brahmin at its apex, the class system began by placing on top the professional wealthy man with his material power and prestige acquired mostly by individual effort as contrasted with the accident of birth. In this system the main factors determining class prestige are the following : occupation, education, and wealth, to which birth may be added.

This means that, other factors being equal, the more a given factor increases, the same level of education, wealth, and birth, the higher his occupation is the higher his prestige will be. The same apply to birth in spite of our professions of equality. This would be more so in India where the caste system with its insistence on birth still keeps its hold. Thus of two equally place managers, the Brahmin or Kshatriya will be more respected than the Vaisya or Sudra in the cases in which this last one may be able to attain this position.

But whatever the extent may be to which the class system has influenced Indian society, the fact is that its principles and values are operative and are accepted and assimilated not only by individuals but also by social groups. The existing tendency towards conforming with these values, which are supposed to be western, is what many sociologists after Dr. M. N. Srinivas call westernization in opposition to sanskritization which is the tendency to conform with the traditional values of the Brahmin caste system. This drift exists mostly among lower castes and tribals many of whom still remain untouched by industrialization.

## Characteristics of Class

The main characteristic traits of class in opposition to caste are the following : Individualism; insistence on economic and professional values; rationalism, and urbanism.

The modern class structure relies on the intrinsic worth of the individual to the exclusion of any privileges which would arise from birth or family connections. It is true that these still have their force due mostly to the help that they provide to the members of the group either through direct influence or by enhancing their personal worth through education or other environmental advantages. But what finally counts is the individual who, while sharing the mode of life of his own class with all its restrictions, remains nevertheless free to rise in the social scale through his own personal effort and worth. The transition "from office boy to president of the United states" and other such "promotions" are difficult, but compared with the absence of individual mobility within the caste, it is a reality. As a contemporary writer observed: "In a caste system an individual displays the attributes of his caste because he is a member of it. In a class system, ar individual is a member of his class because he displays its attributes".

This individualism is ultimately based on the economic and professional or functional values cherished by society and realized by individuals. The more appropriate is the "mix" of occupation and money which the individual succeeds in achieving, the higher his status will be, especially if it is combined with "birth" whose worth is sometimes enhanced by carefully contrived "genealogical connections".

All this goes together with rationalism or the tendency to rely more on reason than on myth, on eality rather than on fancy. What the stars foretell or what the configuration of the planets is, has little appeal to the modern man as he realizes that work, study, and personal endeavour together with social influence will principally determine his future in life. Modern man may be a believer and religious man but is careful to distinguish between the spiritual and the material order.

A consequence of this rationalism is the growing disregard for the taboos and prohibitions inherent in the caste system.

A person who has assimilated the new values does not care to observe the commensal or food taboos, the drinking and smoking taboos, and even less, untouchability. At home he may observe some taboos, more as a concession to the pressure of tradition than as a matter of conviction. Undoubtedly the neglect of these taboos even in agricultural and other sectors is largely the result of industry and the new tendencies in education. Whateven may be thought about the caste system itself, caste taboos are certainly on their way out.

That the class system, with its inherent values brought in by industry, is on the increase interfering and frequently clashing with the traditional system creating thereby tensions and maladjustments does not need demonstration. So the very man who in his village is respected as a Brahmin, may be employed in a factory under a man of an inferior caste whereby his prestige may suffer and his people at home, especially the young, may not regard him as highly as before. Much could be said about those cases in which traditional and modern values collide affecting not only groups but also individuals and inducing in them a kind of cultural schizophrenia. Thus workers in a factory may believe that the bosses run the business by divine disposition and at the same time may accuse them of being tyrannical and dishonest. They may on Dassera day be praying with them at the machines, and next week go on strike damaging the same machines and shouting slogans against the bosses. These events may not be frequent, but they do happen.

### The "New Class"

Together with the diffusion of industrial values affecting in different degrees the whole social structure, there is a special sector where these values are most genuinely assimilated, which for want of a better name has been called the Indian "New Class". This is composed of various economic categories very dissimilar among themselves among which the wealthy classes and the middle classes are most conspicuous. Industrialists, managers, technicians, businessmen, teachers, head clerks, office workers etc. with their complement of students and management trainees variously make up this class which is really open to those who can qualify for it.

Moreover it is by the younger generations that the values of this class are more readily assimilated not only because modern industry is a comparatively recent phenomenon, but also because a kind of second Industrial Revolution or expansion occurred in India immediately after independence under the leadership and inspiration of Pandit Jawaharlal Nehru followed by a flowering of industrial education in technical schools and colleges as well as in management and business administration institutions. The impact of these changes on the young members of the new class is not merely that their habits and customs are modern, but also that in their mentality and way of thinking they have little in common with their ancestors so that the so-called "generation gap" is a reality with them. It is of this group that A. Beteille writes in the following vein:

For the rising executive fluency in the art of English conversation and familiarity with Western party manners are likely to be greater assets for mobility than a knowledge of the rituals of the twice born.

For them it is more important to belong to a smart set than to have been born into the highest caste. Domestic furniture, interior decoration and tastes in theatre, films and music show a pronounced western orientation.

**Industry and the Position of women**

Another general effect of industry, especially through its alliance with education is to be seen in the position of women and their role in the family and society. Not only are their rights of property protected by law, but the educational system itself has also thrown open its doors to them where they are often doing better than their male counterparts and even taking some departments by storm. Even when these lines were first written (1961) the press reported that the majority of students applying to the Arts section in the Colleges were girls. To this it may be added that not only they have free access to lucrative occupations but also that some white-collar jobs as typists, stenographers and secretaries are largely monopolized by them.

This is indeed a far cry from their traditional position some-what overdrawn in the following lines:

They (women) were expected to grow up as obedient daughters and die as subservient wives; they had almost no social rights and were confined to the four walls of the house. It is suggested, in the name of such a sage as Tulsidas, that "drums, uncivilized people, untouchables, animals and women deserve beating." But today, constitutionally our womenfolk are the best placed in the world as far as equality of opportunity goes.

At any rate they are normally accepted in public and political life, and now for the first time in the history of the country the post of prime Minister of India is held by a lady. Again, while admission in factories has largely contributed to the freedom of working class women, the introduction in the home of electrical appliances and other domestic inventions, which only an industrial society could provide, has considerably relieved them from the drudgery previously associated with housekeeping. Now any mother can attend to the family and look after her children without undue worry. Morever, due mostly to the practice of birth control and other contraceptive measure the number of children are constantly decreasing while the mobility of the family made possible by the economic improvement of the higher class and the facilities afforded by the new means of conveyance is constantly increasing. Whether these and similar changes will work in the long run for the happiness of society and the family itself is an ethical question into which we cannot enter.

Another effect of the rapid progress of industry and technology affecting mostly the family is the rebelliousness or protesting attitude of teen agers especially in affluent societies. As they are free from economic pressures and owing to the new subjects and skills introduced in the modern educational curricula, they find themselves more informed than their elders, the "generation gap" widens, communication and mutual understanding become difficult, and friction and disobedience are more likely to occur.

There are other causes to account for this rebelliousness, especially in developing nations where political and economic reasons play a considerable part in accordance with the special conditions of each country which must be studied in each particular case. At any rate, these events are related to and favour the drift from the traditional joint family to the individual family where the members are more free from institutional restrictions as mentioned in chapter 4 of the present work.

**Urbanization and "Modernization"**

Urbanization is another of the consequences of industrialization. As will be seen in the next chapter, this does not mean that the city as such is the effect of industry. Most of the cities of the past were political or administrative centers and not a few were important nets of communication. What is meant is that in modern times industry is the greatest propelling force in the creation and growth of cities particularly since the industrial Revolution. Such cities as Manchester and Liverpool in England and Pittsburgh and Detroit in the U. S. A. are clear examples of this. On the other hand Calcutta,

Bombay. Madras and Kanpur owe their rapid growth to industry, while Jameshedpur and Kotah among others, may be considered as purely industrial cities or townships. What this means for individuals and society in terms of behavioural adjustment. This adjustment become more difficult when the villager is not pulled but pushed to the city driven by poverty and need. Much has been discussed by sociologists about the causal relationship between industrialization and urbanization, but whatever one's opinion may be there is no doubt about the impact of the former on the latter. Industrialization is likely to affect in a very significant way, not only the rate of growth of particular urban areas but also the type of growth in urbanization as well as the relative level of economic development involved in urbanization.

Another important effect or by-product of industrialization is the acquisition by the persons involved of a definite type of life-interests and orientation which may be designated by the term modernization. In order to study this process among the workers of a number of development nations including India, A. Inkeles proposed to them some questions and choices which were meant to convey their modernity. These referred to openness to new experiences, self-assertion including freedom from fatalism, high aspirations, ability to plan, interest in current politics etc., and other such attitudes commonly associated with a modern outlook as opposed to a traditional one.

His findings were that not only the factory workers considerably led in modernization to agriculturists, but also – and most unexpectedly – that the factory competed with the school itself as an agent of modernity. If is true that the school had a lead over the factory of 3 : 2, but it must be considered that the school is meant to be directly an agency of modernization, while the factory's object is to produce material goods. Thus modernization here comes as a marginal product at zero marginal cost. On the other hand it is a matter of common knowledge that school children of industrial centers score higher in I. Q. tests than their counterparts in agricultural villages.

## Industry's Impact on Religion

The influence of religion on the economic system has been the object of much discussion among sociologists since Max Weber first published his famous work on the subject. There we must touch on the reciprocal question concerning the influence of industry on religion about which there is already a vast literature. The general impression conveyed by most writers, particularly non-specialists, is that the forces making for industrialization work to the detriment of religion- a conclusion which is supposed to have been proved by the recent history of the western nations. But matters are not as clear as that, particularly because religion is an internal attitude which is not easily amenable to observation and measure. It is true that at the rise of modern industry and even later religious practices externally declined, and attendance in churches and temples considerably decreased.

But this could aptly be interpreted as the result of the transition from an agricultural to an industrial society, where owing to the demands made by the new occupations on the workers' time, constant attendance at religious services become more difficult. This is more so if it is considered that this transition meant a change from an established to an adaptive society as Elton Mayo remarked with the consequent relaxation of social bonds and disorganization of previously well integrated communities whereby religious practices not necessarily religious convictions were bound to suffer. Sure enough, church attendance declined in England, France, Germany, and in most parts of the European continent. But such was not the case in Ireland, Poland, or even the U. S. A. insofar as Catholics were concerned. This seems to indicate the difficulty of proving the decay of religious feeling whatever may be about the external practices as well as of distinguishing between the influeace of industry itself and other concomitant factors. What seems to be out of doubt is that the rationalistic outlook fostered by industry militates against the irrational and magical aspects by which religion may be affected. But concerning religion as such, nothing irrational seems to appear in it, though at times it may confront man with supra-rational phenomena.

Whatever may be said about this, some authors, as L.T. Hobhouse, writing at the end of the last century believed that religion rather than decreasing, had increased, as the missionary revival of that century seemed to show, which seems to corroborate the impression that the negative influence of industry on essential religion is still a matter to be proved. As regards India there is hardly any sociologist who holds the negative impact of industrialization on religion, in a research conducted in 1957 by Dr. P. H. Prabhu, about "some Effects of Urbanization on Industrial workers and maladjustments, but in spite of that he found that among his respondents all of them Hindu males – 68.86% used to observe religious rites in their village while in the city the ratio increased to 71.27% and added.

The attitude of a very large majority of our respondents, as many a 70% towards religious duties is positively favourable. 6.79% of them, on the other hand, expressed positive disbelief in God and, in about 5.58%, frustration has shaken their faith in God, even though they have not become disbelievers, 1.86% have tried to rationalize their non-observance of religious duties by saying that they do not attach too much importance to mere prayers. This analysis belies the general belief that urban influences destroy faith in God.? This was also confirmed by miss Kunji Patel who found that of the 348 workers, whom she interviewed, practically all visited the temple with more or less frequency, though only 32 of them or 6.3%, had no time for it.

The conclusions essentially square with the findings of our past student Mrs. Rashmi, G. Mehta (nee Ved) in a sample of 325 women workers spread over 26 factories in Bombay belonging to various religious denominations. The women were divided into workers in traditional industries and those in modern industries, and it was found that those who ordinarily attended the temple or the church were 90% in traditional industries and 94% in modern industries. As regards regular prayer the score was 98.66% in traditional industries and 98.66% among modern industry workers. Similar percentages applied to other religious practices. It is true as Miss Patel wrote that "young and educated workers are not much interested this joining religious associations, pujas, bhajans etc. and that these attitude is more so in more educated people specially student, among whom it is not difficult to find atheists." But it is not proved that attitude is due to industry. The most that may be deduced, as mentioned above, is that industry as an agency or factor of social change tends to envisage religion in a more rationalistic and positive way in accordance with the values that it fosters.

# 4

# Social Policy and the Sociology of Education

Pragmatic, and focused on details of school and classroom organization. There was much discussion of administrative problems and of methods for managing conflicts between schools and families, special interest groups and problem students.[1] However, the close cooperation between sociologists and educators did not last. The development of sociology was heavily influenced by the model of the German University, where the goal of scholarship was to contribute to the general body of theory and research upon which the development of sociology a distinct academic discipline was based. It was assumed that the highest levels of scholarship were manifested in research that was empirical, methodologically sophisticated, value free, and tied to general theory. The ideal of value-free analysis was thought to demand the insulation of academia from practical, pragmatic, and political concerns. When judged according to these ideals, Educational Sociology appeared sadly wanting. Sociologists increasingly regarded the subject as an applied field, theoretically fragmented and devoid of adequate research methods.[2]

Educators also became disillusioned with Educational Sociology. The grand claims of perfecting society were not to be realized, and sociologists could offer few definitive solutions to educational problems. To many educators, sociologists appeared increasingly elitist, obsessed with highly technical research methods on the one hand, and grandiose and inapplicable theories on the other.

In time, Educational Sociology fell into disrepute. Educators and sociologists both turned inward toward their own diciplines, each attempting to develop their own unique body of theory and research.

Educational Sociology became a historical phenomenon. Its passing was marked officially in 1963 when the *Journal of Educational Sociology* became the *Journal of the Society of Education* and when the American Sociological Association's section on Educational Sociology became its section on the Sociology of Education.

Today, the Sociology of Education closely approximates the scientific ideals of sociology as a whole, but it also profits significantly from the input of professional educators. A 1970 survey of the members of the Sociology of Education section of the American Sociological Association indicated that a substantial portion of the membership is closely connected with education. (3) These members hold teaching certificates, administrative posts, and teaching positions within departments of education at colleges and universities. Those with educational connections tend to emphasize the practical application of sociology to the daily operation of the schools. Among their primary concerns are equality of educational opportunity, school desegregation, curriculum content, intergroup relations in the school, and teaching as a career There is some divergence in the research priorities of these members and those of other academic sociologists, but these differences should not be exaggerated. During the last two decades, a rapproachment has developed that has brought educators and sociologists closer together. This is evidenced by the increased number of sociologists employed within education departments and by organizational changes, such as that at the University of Chicago, which incorporated the Department of Education into the Social Services Division. (4) Furthermore, inter- disciplinary cooperation was evident in recent federal commission reports on excellence in elementary, secondary, and higher education.[5] It has become obvious to many that sociological theory and research are relevant in the search for the solution to educational problems, and that experience with the operation of educational institutions can contribute to the development of social research and theory building. We hope this book will help further this favorable trend.

## Theory in the Sociology of Education

Abstract concepts are helpful to students of educational institutions in the same way that a flashlight is helpful in the dark. Each illuminates certain aspects of reality and helps make sense of what is otherwise hidden and chaotic. We cannot deal with everything in our surroundings at once. Concepts help by focusing attention on certain phenomena while distracting us from others. By imposing a simplified order on the complexities of social life, they offer us a clearer intellectual path. At the same time, though, they keep some aspects of reality in the shadows and distort our perceptions of others.

At present, two contrasting conceptual paradigms are widely used by scholars in the Sociology of Education. The adherents of each proclaim the virtues of their own particular approach, and both have made important contributions. These paradigms are most commonly referred to as consensus theory and conflict theory. Historically, the consensus approach has been dominant, not only in the sociological study of education but also in virtually all other areas of sociology. Recently, however, there has been an outpouring of work using the conflict perspective, with a renewed appreciation of its usefulness.

Despite the fact that many sociologists actually use elements of both theoretical perspectives in their work, and although there are areas of overlap between them, it is possible to distinguish the key elements of these two schools of sociological thought. The consensus and conflict theorists offer alternative interpretations of the forces that bind societies together and the role of educational institutions in society. First, we will sketch the basics of consensus theory and illustrate its application to the analysis of schools and classrooms. Then we will follow a similar procedure with conflict theory. Our introductory discussion of theory in the Sociology of Education will conclude with certain cautions about the uses and limitations of grand theory and a few words about the importance of empirical research as an anchor for theoretical speculation.

**Consensus Theorists**

Consensus theorists generally agree that societies are in some ways like biological organisms. Both are composed of many distinct, but interdependent parts, and each part makes some contribution to the survival of the whole. Both tend to maintain a state of relative equilibrium. When something disturbs one part of the system, or threatens to destroy it, all of the other parts react to bring the system back to an even keel. Our own bodies destroy threatening bactera, keep body temperature within tolerable range, and maintain proper levels of oxygen in the blood. In an analogous fashion, societies adapt to the physical environment, maintain adequate levels of production, distribute essential goods and services, keep violence under control, and so on.

But the analogy must not be overdrawn. Social institutions are not biological organs and individuals are not biological cells. Human behavior is purposive and goal directed. We can all think, and our thinking, our perceptions of the world around us, our attitudes, and our values all affect our behaviour.

Consensus theorists point out that societies cannot survive unless their members share at least some common sets of perceptions, attitudes, and values. As their name implies, consensus theorists often stress the beliefs and interests that we share in common and give less attention to those beliefs and interests on which we differ. Let us look more formally at the key elements implicit here.[6]

*Structure and Function.* Consensus theorists, like many other social theorists, see societies as being made up of "parts". These "parts" make up the social structure of each society. There is some disagreement as to whether these "parts" are best thought of as social institutions, patterns of social behavior, social roles, or some other type of unit. In the remainder of this text, we will sometimes be talking about the institutional structure of society, especially when we look at the interrelationships between the school and such other institutions as the family or the economy. We will sometimes be talking about patterns of social behavior, such as in our discussions of school-community relations, and we will sometimes be talking about social roles, as when we talk about what constitutes being a "teacher" or a "student."

Consensus theorists are distinct from other social theorists in their emphasis on the contributions that each "part" of society makes to the survival of the whole. This contribution is its "function," and consensus theorists are concerned with showing how the recurrent survival needs of societies are met by their institutions, norms, and social roles. Consensus theorists are often criticized for exaggerating the positive contributions that various parts of society make to the functioning of the whole and for ignoring the destructive effects of other elements.

*Integration.* Consensus theorists also stress that the various parts of society, however they are defined, are integrated with each other. A change that occurs in one part of society will affect all the others. But these parts are not just interdependent they are coordinated and complementary. They seldom stand in opposition or conflict with one another. Each part supports the workings of the others as well as the society as a whole. Even consensus theorists recognize that integration is never complete, however. Some parts may overlap or fail to mesh completely. In general, though, consensus theorists emphasize the ways in which the various elements of the social structure work together to maintain the overall social system.

*Stability.* No society is completely static, and consensus theorists recognize that at least some social challge is inevitable. For example, events may occur outside a particular society that impinge upon it and force it to change in response. Nevertheless, consensus theorists stress the forces that keep societies relatively stable rather than those that press for radical and abrupt change. Consensus theorists point to the persistence of such basic institutions as the family and to similarities in the values and behavior of various generations as evidence of how slowly societies actually change.

*Consensus.* Agreement on important perceptions, sentiments, values, and beliefs is another theme of consensus theory. Of course, societies vary in terms of the nature and extent of consensus; it is easier to achieve consensus in small folk societies than in large modern industrial states. Consensus theorists point out, however, that in any society, modern or folk, large or small, there is a shared set of abstract and complex assumptions about the world without which social life would be impossible. This consensus is achieved through socialization, and, in modern societies, the function of socialization is primarily performed by the family and the schools. Consensus theorists have been criticized for overemphasizing similarities among people and ignoring the diversity of interests, values, and beliefs that exist in complex pluralistic societies.

**Durkheim's Sociology of Education**

Like numerous social thinkers both before and after his own lifetime, Émile Durkheim was interested in the fundamental question of how societies are held together. This concern with the basis of social order is a central theme running through many of his works.

Durkheim's approach to the problem of social order emphasizes two basic ideas. First, Durkheim believed that complex societies are held together by the mutual interdependence of their members. Individuals do not and cannot meet all their needs by themselves. Instead, individuals specialize. There is an intricate division of labor such that each individual produces some portion of the goods or services required by the other members of society and exchanges them for the goods and services one needs but does not produce. In an advanced technological society such as our own, such exchanges are effected through a system involving labor, wages, markets, industrial enterprises, and so on. The complexity of our division of labor makes us all mutually interdependent, and, according to Durkheim, contributes to social stability. [7]

At the same time, however, Durkheim recognized that mutual economic interdependence was not enough. There must be some agreement among us about what we are doing and what we should do. Furthermore, we must all agree to participate and to subordinate our own personal interests to those of the larger society whenever this becomes necessary.

According to Durkheim, we are all born into society as asocial beings. Obviously, we do not know society's language, skills, or customs, and we must learn these to survive - both as individuals and as a group. But our learning must also include something else. We must develop a sense of commitment to society, and internalization of its most central values and ideas. We must change from being egoists, responding greedily to our own endless self-centered desires, into moral citizens, responding in terms of our duty to the state and our loyalty to something greater than ourselves.[8]

Durkheim did not doubt that there were central ideas and values in all societies: "respect for reason, for science, for ideas and sentiments which are at the base of democratic morality" [9] were some of the examples he gave for his own society. This is not to say that Durkheim totally ignored diver- sity, but he did not emphasize it. He recognized that the very division of labor in society requires some degree of differentiation of values and ideas. Different occupations require different aptitudes, practices, and modes of viewing the world.[10] But Durkheim stressed that there must be an underly- ing consensus regarding the central values and beliefs of society, or it could not survive.

If a consensus of values and beliefs is necessary, though, how is it to be achieved? How do we transform each new generation of asocial infants into responsible adults? The answer for Durkheim was through moral education.[11] For Durkheim, moral education consisted of socialization experiences that result in the internalization of society's central values and beliefs. Such internalization, when totally successful, is a powerful form of social control, because individuals then believe that their own society's norms represent the only right or moral way to behave. From then on, they will be self-policing. Even thinking about violating their internalized beliefs and values will arouse feelings of guilt and shame that will deter the potential violation.

But how is society to accomplish such socialization? According to Durkheim, each society must accomplish it in ways that are appropriate to the values and beliefs it needs to instill. In some societies, the family (especially the extended family) might play an important role. Durkheim argued that in the decades immediately preceding his writing, the Catholic Church performed this vital function in his own society, France. With increasing industrialization, urbanization, and secularization, however, the values and beliefs taught by the church and the manner in which it taught them no longer represented the central values and beliefs of French society and could no longer be the basis of its moral order. Some other mechanism for moral education had to be found, one more attuned to the needs of a modern state; for Durkheim, that mechanism was the schools. The schools could transform us. They could help us overcome our initial egoism and teach us discipline and self-control. They could encourage us to adopt the fundamental principles of our society as our own.

One can see that from Durkheim's perspective the task of the school is critical to society's survival. In line with this view, Durkheim believed that educational institutions must be closely guarded. The state, whose interest in survival the educational institutions serve, must outline the basic principles to be taught there. It must carefully supervise the schools to assure that these principles are taught. It must "see to it that nowhere are children left ignorant of them, that everywhere they should be spoken of with the respect which is due them."[12]

Within the schools the specific tasks of moral education must be accomplished by the teacher. According to Durkheim, the teacher is the representative of the state. "Just as the priest is the interpreter of his god, the teacher is the interpreter of the great moral ideas of his time and his country."[13] Teachers must not subvert society by teaching their own personal values and beliefs, for to do so would reduce the nation to ". . . an incoherent multitude of little fragments in conflict with one another."[14] Teachers must be firmly committed to those beliefs and values central to society, for it is through the teacher's commitment to these central principles and the personal example set by the teacher that the child experiences and incorporates the moral order:

> Let him be attached to these ideas, let him feel all their grandeur, and the authority which is in them . . . cannot fail to be communicated to his person and to everything that emanates from him. Into an authority which flows from such an impersonal source there could enter no pride, no vanity, no pedantry. It is made up entirely of the respect which he has for his functions and . . . for his office. It is this respect which, through word and gesture, passes from him to the child.[15]

According to Durkheim, then, the primary function of education is to socialize new generations to overcome their egoism and to become productive members of society. Education contributes to the maintenance of the social system and the conservation of the national character. All children in a society must be exposed to it and therefore, to a point, education must be the same for all children in a society. Yet Durkheim also recognized that diversity is necessary. Because different occupational subgroups require different values and beliefs, children destined for these different groups need to have their own unique educational experiences. Nevertheless, some common educational core must remain; consequently, education is more uniform for young children, when the common principles are being taught, than for older ones.

It is easy to see the ideas of consensus theory in Durkheim's work on education. He emphasized the integration of society, the interdependence of its parts, the functions that are necessary for its survival, and the ways in which these functions are filled by different institutions. He stressed consensus of values and beliefs and their contribution to societal stability. At the same time, Durkheim spent little or no time dealing with possible conflicts between different groups. Who decides which values and beliefs should be taught? Are the interests of the "state" ever in conflict with the interests of the students? Through what mechanisms do we decide which children are destined for different occupations and therefore deserving of different types of education? Are teachers really the agents of the "state," or do they represent their students' families or the students themselves? These and many other important questions are not readily answered within Durkheim's theoretical framework.

**Talcott Parsons on the Classroom**

Talcott Parsons was one of the most eminent theorists of the consensus school. Most of his work analyzed large social systems such as societies, but in his essay "The School Class as a Social System"[16] he applied the consensus mode of analysis to the classroom. The fact that his theories are applicable to social systems so large and so small highlights the very high level of abstraction of his basic concepts. Once again, the themes of structure-function, stability, integration, and consensus are illustrated.

The discussion begins with definitions of two major functions of the school class - socialization and selection. The socialization function is, of course, the one that Durkheim discussed. Parson's definition of it is quite similar to Durkheim's:

> The socialization function may be summed up as the development in individuals of the commitments and capacities which are essential prerequisites of their future role performance.[17]

In our discussion of Durkheim, we also referred to the future roles that students play in society. At that time, we mentioned the problem of deciding which students were destined for which particular societal roles. Parsons argued that in contemporary technological societies these decisions are made in the schools. It is the function of the educational system to "select" students for different occupational slots as well as to appropriately soclalize those selected. The most important selection is between those who will go to college and those who will not. Although the allocation of students into separate academic and vocational programs may not formally occur until high school or even college, the process begins in a subtler form during the elementary school years. For example, some children are given higher grades, placed in "faster" reading groups, and encouraged to think about professional occupations. Those who are selected for college attendance wlll enter the more prestifious occupations and will rise to higher socioeconomic levels in society.

According to Parsons, the basis upon which schools allocate students into college-going and noncollege-going categories is achievement. Schools reward children with high grades and encouragement on the basis of what they are willing and able to accomplish. In the early school grades, this accomplishment is measured in both moral and intellectual terms. Children must show that they can behave properly, be cooperative, obey the teacher, be punctual, and so on. In the higher grades, the accomplishment is increasingly measured in intellectual terms. It is then not sufficient to try hard; one must also succeed in mastering the material.

Parsons' belief that schools reward children on the basis of achievement was central to his larger view of the integration of educational and economic systems in modern societies. Parsons argued that in modern societies people must be allocated to occupational slots according to their ability to perform adequately in those slots. Expertise is essential, as is making maximal use of whatever talent exists in the population. In less complex societies allocation to occupational and other positions could be (and usually is) based on criteria other than achievement. For example, such ascribed characteristics as a child's family background, race, ethnicity, or sex might determine what his or her adult role would be. Industrialization, however, requires allocation on the basis of achievement Parsons believed that there is general agreement throughout our society that allocation should be on the basis of achievement. Because of this agreement or consensus, teachers, administrators, parents, and the public at large understand what is being done in the schools and are basically supportive of them. One of the first socialization tasks of the school is to teach children that they will be evaluated on the basis of achievement so that students, too, can share in this basic consensus. Only then can we assure that the classroom itself will be stable and well integrated.

When children first arrive at school, they have not necessarily learned that achieved rather than ascribed characteristics are the proper bases for most societal rewards. In their own families, each child is valued as an individual and loved regardless of how well he or she compares to other children. Although the teacher is somewhat of a mother surrogate in the early school years, she or he is more objective about the child. The teacher remains affectively neutral, or uninvolved emotionally; treats all children alike according to uniform or universalistic criteria; and interacts with them only in terms of their respective roles as teacher and student. Gradually, the children internalize the values represented by this behavior.

Within the school class, some children will more completely fulfill the teacher's moral and intellectual requirements than others, and these will be rewarded accordingly. The unequal distribution of rewards in the classroom is potentially disruptive, but because the children quickly internalize the belief that achievement merits reward, the only remaining problem is to assure them all that the context within which that achievement is being measured is fair. In other words, they must believe that they all have an equal chance of doing well and that only differences in ability and motivation explain differences in their achievement. Certain mechanisms help ensure that this is the case. For example, children are generally age-segregated so that none is advantaged or disadvantaged by being substantially older or younger than the others. Children tend also to be sent to neighborhood schools, which results in some degree of homogeneity of such other ascribed characteristics as socioeconomic status, race, and ethnicity. Also, within the classroom, students are given common tasks and systematically evaluated by one lone, and therefore indisputable, authority: the teacher. Finally, friendship groups that grow up among students and various nonacademic activities that are valued by a student's peers provide alternative sources of reward. Those who do not do well academically can receive approval and support through participation in sports, extracurricular activities, or social events.

In summary, Parsons stressed the functional interdependence of educational and other societal institutions. He believed that two of the basic functions of education are socialization and selection. Through these two processes, the schools provide society with individuals well qualified for the roles they will fulfill. Allocation to these roles is on the basis of achievement and merit. Schools also both promote value consensus and depend upon it for their smooth operation.

As we shall see, Parsons' theory does not account for the considerable amount of controversy that surrounds educational goals and methods in contemporary society. He does not adequately deal with the abundant accumulation of empirical data that suggest that ascriptive and not simply achieved characteristics have a major impact on just how the educational system will allocate any particular individual. His analysis of the internal consensus of the classroom does not adequately account for the factionalization, hostility, and even occasional violence we see there.

**Conflict Theorists**

Whereas consensus theorists focus on functional integration, core values, and social stability, conflict theorists focus on the coercive nature of society and the pervasiveness of social change. To the conflict theorist, power struggle is the main dynamic of social life. On the one hand, societies are held together by powerful social groups that coerce cooperation from the less powerful; on the other hand, societies are perpetually changing and in danger of disintegration because power struggles can result in new elite groups replacing the old.

Conflict theorists view social systems as divided into dominant and subordinate groups. The relationship between these groups is exploitative, with the dominant group taking all or most of society's valuables for itself. The dominant group also imposes its own values and world view on its subordinates. The subordinates are, however, a constant threat to the stability of the system, and the dominant group must be always on guard. As part of its effort to retain control, the dominant group might create social myths which legitimize its own position, co-opt potentially threatening members of the subordinate groups, "buy off" the opposition, or use physical force. In any case, the system cannot last forever. Violence may eventually erupt and the system might be destroyed. In time, however, a new social order will emerge.

The key concepts here are conflict, change, and coercion.[18]

*Conflict.* Consensus theorists emphasize integration and the complementary character of various parts of the social structure, but conflict theorists emphasize that social institutions and groups usually work at cross-purposes to each other. The goals and programs of one group are often at odds with the goals and programs of another. Certainly, the interests of those in power are sharply incompatible with the interests of those who are subordinate. Conflict, then, is pervasive, as each group struggles for dominance. Sometimes this conflict is relatively muted, but it is often open and violent.

*Change.* The continuous power struggles between groups result in a state of constant flux. Periods of relative calm and stability clearly occur, but they are interspersed by periods of rapid change and upheaval. Placid periods may be times when the opposing forces are gathering strength for the next battle, the calm before the storm. When the storm breaks, riot,. rebellion, and revolution may result.

*Coercion.* Whenever, in the course of this panorama of struggle and change, any one particular group consolidates sufficient power, it will create a period of temporary stability and social order by coercing the less

powerful into cooperation. This coercion will not be based solely on the use of force, however. Instead, the dominant group will propagandize and indoctrinate the oppressed in an effort to convince them that their oppres- sion is legitimate. For example, a myth of the divine right of kings might be promulgated to legitimize an oppressive monarchy. Subjects who believe in this myth will be less likely to rebel against their royal oppressor because they believe his or her reign is the will of God. The powerful may also use theil resources in a positive way as rewards for desired behavior. This can still be considered coercive as the phrase, "I'll make him an offer he can't refuse," implies.

Nevertheless, force - either positive or egative - and propaganda are never completely successful. There is always remaining resistance to oppression, and this resistance, combined with other inevitable changes in society, ultimately lead to social upheaval and disintegration. In time, however, a new cohesive order rises to replace the old.

Samuel Bowles: A Conflict Perspective on Contemporary American Education

The writings of Samuel Bowles [19] provide a clear example of the application of the conflict model to contemporary educational institutions, especially those in the United States. The themes of conflict, change, and coercion appear throughout.

The heart of Bowles' argument is that the rise of public education in the United States occurred along with, and as a consequence of, advancing capitalism. Capitalism, he argues, requires a skilled and disciplined labor force, one which cannot be adequately socialized by the traditional institutions of family and church.

In precapitalist economies, skills are generally passed from parents to children under informal conditions in the home, the field, or the shop. Capitalism increases the rate of technological change, however, and the skills required from one generation of workers may be radically different from those required from the next. Furthermore, capitalism requires liter- acy, mathematical and other technical knowledge that may not be pos- sessed by the parental generation and may not be easily taught in an informal manner.

Capitalism also weakens the family and the church and makes each less effective as an agency of socialization. It increases the geographical mobility of wol kers' families, and thus weakens ties to the extended family. It sends children and parents out of the home and into different parts of the labor market, and thus weakens the nuclear family. It promotes secular beliefs in rational planning and decision making, and thus weakens the church. Social order is threatened as these institutions change and lose influence. Yet the old institutions are not suitable to the needs of the emerglng capitalist elites.

At the same time, capitalism creates conditions that are potentially self-destructive. Workers are "thrown together in oppressive factories and the isolation which ... helped to maintain quiescence in earlier. widely dispersed peasant populations . . . [breaks] down." [20] Inequalities of wealth

become more apparent and are less easily justified by doctrines such as that of the divine origins of social rank.

In the United States, an additional threat was posed by the massive waves of immigrants that arrived in the late nineteenth and early twentieth centurles. These immigrants, with their diversity of languages, values, dress, and behavior seemed to threaten the orderliness and discipline of the workplace. It was feared that they would become criminals, political agitators, or burdens to the economy. A crisis seemed at hand.

The solution to all of these problems was offered by a system of mass education. Compulsory public schooling could accomplish several important goals, all in service to the capitalist class. First, mass education could supply workers with the cognitive, intellectual, and technical skills required by the capltalist economy. Secondly, it could supply workers who had already learned the values and behavior conducive to productive labor. Children could be taught punctuality, discipline, deference to authority; and acceptance of responsibility for their work. The social relations of the school (the relationship between teacher and students, for example) could replicate the social relations of the workplace and ease the transition from the family to the world of work.

Third, the schools could teach loyalty to the state and obedience to the law. This loyalty could be achieved by convincing children that the system was benevolent and just.

The schools, then, could provide the capitalist economy with a ready, willing, and able supply of workers, while at the same time assimilating foreign and potentially disruptive groups within the population. Bowles argues that it was for these reasons that a system of mass education was finally established in the United States.

Bowles takes his analysis one step further, however. He argues that our system of mass education not only supplies skilled and committed workers, but it also actually legitimizes existing inequalities in the social division of labor by suggesting that these inequalities are based on merit rather than on coercion. For example, the educational system appears to be open to all and to reward people on the basis of ability and willingness to work. Children are taught that they all have an equal chance of proving their worth, of receiving prestigious educational credentials, and of going on to positions of affluence and power in the larger society. However, Bowles argues that this is a myth. In fact, the educational system rewards children differentially on the basis of their class origins. Children from elite families become the elite of the next generation. Children of the poor remain poor. Consequently, the social division of labor is reproduced in each generation. Furthermore, because the system gives the appearance of openness and promotes this ideological myth, children believe that those in the dominant class are there because they deserve to be and that those who are poor are poor because they are lazy or uneducable. This effectively blinds most people to the oppressive nature of the system.

Bowles' analysis, then, points to the conflicting interests of various societal groups and the ways in which those in power can use such social institutions as the schools to justify and maintain an essentially coercive and exploitative system. Bowles' analysis does less well in explaining evidence that schools do permit upward mobility or in accounting for efforts to reform schools in the interests of greater social equality. When he does deal with these issues, however, Bowles argues that they are merely subtle mechanisms to maintain the system and not meaningful avenues to equality. Finally, Bowles' approach may blur important differences between social systems: They are all oppressive. Yet we know that educational institutions vary from society to society and, in each particular case, the balance of their contribution to societal inequality versus equality falls at a different point along a continuum. The bold outlines and stark contrasts Bowles draws between the oppressed and the oppressors may blind us to significant comparative variations.

**Willard Waller on Conflict in the Classroom**

Willard Waller's The Sociology of Teaching[21] was first published in 1932 and has become a classic in the field. There are many reasons for its continuing acclaim, one of which is its description of the school as a social system in which stability is constantly endangered by both internal and external forces. The themes of conflict, change, and coercion are evident throughout.

Waller describes the school as

> ... a despotism in a state of perilous equilibrium .... a despotism threatened from within and exposed to regulation and interference from without. It is a despotism capable of being overturned in a moment, exposed to the instant loss of its stability and its prestige. It is a despotism demanded by the community of parents... . It is a despotism resting upon children. . . .[22]

Clearly, Waller sees the school as a coercive institution. At the top are the teachers, given their authority by the community outside the school. At the bottom are the children, relatively (but not totally) helpless under their yoke. Here, the interests of the teachers are in unavoidable and universal conflict with the interests of the children. The teacher is the taskmaster, attempting to make the students learn the formal curriculum. The students are subordinate to them, but are much less interested in schoolbooks than in their classmates and informal activities. The teacher, then, must coerce the students into obedience and learning:

> The teacher-pupil relationship is a form of institutionalized dominance and subordination. The teacher and puptl confront each other in the school with an original conflict of desires, and however much that conflict may be reduced in amount, or however much it may be hidden, it still remains. The teacher represents the adult group, ever the enemy of the spontaneous life of children. The teacher represents the formal curriculum, and his interest is in imposing that curriculum upon the children.... The teacher represents the established social order in the school, and his interest is maintaining that order....[23]

Note that Waller sees the age difference between students and teachers as one source of their perpetual conflict. Waller stresses that children have a culture of their own, one that develops primarily in the playgroup

> and is passed on from one generation to the next. Children, he points out, see the world differently from adults, they value different things, and prefer different types of activities. Adults, however, have power over children and try to force them to accept adult values and perspectives.

The teacher, then, is faced with a difficult and continuous struggle to maintain discipline and promote learning. Waller describes the major mechanisms of social control available to teachers, in descending order of efficacy, as: commands, punishments, management, shows of temper, and emotional appeals. Grades and examinations are, of course, important mechanisms of coercion. However, none of these methods is completely effective. Some "set the students and teachers at one another's throats."[24] Others result in long enduring feuds between certain students and their teachers. At ally time classroom orcler can collapse, with the teacher losing all control. Inevitably, however, if the teacher is to remain a teacher, he or she must reestablish order and maintain it. The teacher must win!

Waller points out that the coerciveness of this system is resented by both students and teachers, but none can escape it. However, students will subvert the teacher's rules, minimize the importance of academic success, and divert their enthusiasm and energy to other pursuits. In particular, students will turn to extracurricular activities and informal social relationships for alternative sources of reward and satisfaction.

In summary, Waller sees coercion rather than value consensus as the basis of classroom order. He believes that the interests of teachers and students conflict and that they engage in perpetual power struggles. At any time, classroom order can collapse, but it will be reestablished. Children, at least, have no hope of winning.

**Cautions Regarding the Use of Grand Theories**

The aim of this brief review of conflict and consensus theories as applied to education has been to illustrate the crucical importance of organizing conceptual frameworks in sociological work. Of course, no set of concepts is sufficient in itself to illuminate and organize all the complexities of social life. Sociology simply has not come that far yet. As it stands, the best one can do is to carry a large conceptual tool kit. Then it will be possible to pick out those concepts that are particularly useful for the task at hand.

Theory by itself has some clear limitations, though.

First, there is the problem that each explanation taken by itself seems persuasive. Durkheim and Parsons, Bowles and Waller may all sound convincing. There is no way in which theory, devoid of research, can tell us which alternative is best. Nor can it answer more specific questions about social life, such as "What percentage of students in this class have internalized values similar to the teacher's and what percentage have not?" Secondly, such grand abstract theories as we have been discussing can easily shade over into simple ideological rhetoric. Such rhetoric is characterized by rigid beliefs, over- simplification, the absence of self-skepticism, and a resistance to questioning. The conflict framework can deteriorate into an intellectual legitimization of revolutionary change, and the consensus theory can become a reactionary defense of the status quo.

As ideology, both conflict and consensus theory become sterile and monotonous. Adherents of each perspective talk past each other, neither hearing the other. Yet, dialogues between sociologists using diverse theoretical models constructively and with a willingness to test their ideas empirically can be useful indeed. We hope to illuminate some of the potentials of such a dialogue in the chapters that follow, although the contrasts between confiict and consensus theories are more relevant to some of the issues we will be discussing than to others.

Through the remainder of this book, however, we will emphasize the importance of empirical research as a check on theoretical speculation and as a contribution to theory building. The process of hypothesis testing is chastening. The usual case is that the data are complex, subject to different interpretations, and unrefiective of clear-cut differences. There is a tentativeness, a desire for further evidence, and a recognition of complexities that grow out of a commitment to research.

This is not to say that sociologists should not have ideological positions or that their research much in some way be totally "value-free." Values enter research in any of a myriad of ways, from the choice of topics to be studied, through the formulation of hypotheses, the methodology adopted, to the final interpretation of the data. But a clear description of the research procedure and the publication of results permit each of us to assess the validity and reliability of the findings. The credibility of the research will rest, to a great extent, on our confidence that the values of the researcher have not led to more of a distortion of reality than an illumination of it.

## Research in the Sociology of Education

In recent years, there has been increased commitment to empirical research among sociologists interested in education. Conrad's review of the research literature in Educational Sociology during the decade of 1940 to 1950 showed that many writers used anecdotal stories and moral exhortations to buttress their arguments rather than rigorous and systematic research: " . . . only a fraction (of the studies) used standard tests, interviews, or observation, and almost no study was reported which used experimental techniques."[25]

The last three decades have brought a dramatic rise in research standards, however. Few pieces are not published that do not have at least some kind of empirical reference or documentation. Carefully reported field observations, large-scale surveys of national samples, and experimental designs are common. Statistical techniques for the analysis of complex and subtle relationships among numerous interacting variables have also been developed and permeate the literature.

Nevertheless, there is still room for improvement, particularly in tying the growing body of empirical findings back into theoretical paradigms so that general principles of social life can be established. A glut of discrete findings, with no organizing framework, can be as useless as the untested speculations of the "armchair" theorist.

**Social Policy and the Sociology of Education**

In some recent periods, sociologists have had increased opportunities to participate in the formation and implementation of national policies in education, law enforcement, welfare, the mass media, and so on. They have been invited to serve on commissions established by both government agencies and private foundations. They have served as fact finders and have formulated policy alternatives on the bases of their research and sociological expertise. Especially during the decade of the 1960s and its War on Poverty, federal funds were provided to sociologists to support experimental and demonstration projects through which new social programs were established. Federal financing has also been available for work on social indicators or the development of measures of social change. Additionally, sociologists have been called upon to evaluate continuing social programs, to assess their effectiveness and make recommendations for their continuation, modification, or termination.

In response to these opportunities, many sociologists have oriented their research more directly toward issues of policy concern. Policy-oriented research tends to concentrate on several particular themes.[26] One central theme of policy research is *goal clarification*, or sensitization to what our objectives and priorities actually are. Cross-cultural and historical analyses are particularly useful here because they highlight the wide range of goals that might be chosen and the variety of structures that might be used to accomplish them. A second major theme of policy research is its emphasis on large-scale *social trends* and on predicting how such trends might alter our institutions and our needs. Developing social indicators is an important example of this kind of policy research. Third, there is an orientation toward *institution building* in policy research. Policy-oriented researchers are often more interested in evaluating and reconstructing societal institutions than in contributing to the elaboration of abstract theoretical models. There is an *activist* or *moral* component to the researcher's work, a desire to improve social life. At times, there is even an optimism about social reform that is reminiscent of the faith of the Progressivists we mentioned earlier.

The deemphasis on grand theory, which is characteristic of policy research, is compatible with the needs of policymakers. Those responsible for policy development and implementation must be interested in research that deals with variables over which they have some control, rather than more abstract and intractable ones. Discussing the relative importance of value consensus or coercion for the maintenance of social order may be exciting to the sociologist, but it is of little use to the politician or the administrator. Policymakers work within a framework of what is possible for them to do, and their concerns are therefore more mundane than those of the professional social theorist. On the other hand, the unique contribution of the social scientist can be to enlighten the policymaker so that everyday problems can be seen in a larger context, as examples of more general phenomena and as products of a complex of social factors.

Research with a policy orientation has certain clear advantages and pitfalls. Chief among the advantages are the opportunity to exert some influence on national policy, and the excitement that comes from dealing

with important and controversial issues. It is an opportunity, also, to be active rather than merely contemplative and to test one's ideas in real life. But there are also several problems inherent in policy research. First, there are the difficulties of producing high-quality research under the perennial constraints of too little time, money, and freedom. Government funding is unpredictable to say the least, and regulation of what questions the researcher may ask or who can be watched is often a problem. Secondly, there is the pressure to come up with politically acceptable results. A Republican administration may not want to hear that increased spending on social services is necessary. A Democratic administration might not want to be told to strengthen big business in the interest of a stronger economy. A third and related difficulty is that policy research is only one of many inputs into policy decisions. Particularly when the results of the research are incompatible with the interests of those who commissioned the research, sociologists may find themselves ignored or at least relatively neglected when final decisions are actually formulated. Finally, policy researchers cannot even be certain that their research will be made generally available. Many research reports have been "buried" in the file and have not surfaced again. Results relevant to many individuals, and especially to those who were the subjects of a study, may be kept from them by decision makers.

For these and other reasons, there is a certain ambivalence toward policy research among professional sociologists. We would, however, prefer to see it encouraged. Particularly in the field of education, sociology has a great deal to contribute to policy decisions. We hope this text will illuminate at least some of these potential contributions.

## The Socialogy of Education : For Whom?

Many students who take this course are skeptical as to its practical usefulness and interest. Some of the reasons for this skepticism are traceable to the historical differences in the development of the fields of education and sociology we spoke of earlier. We hope that by now all of you have had your imaginations stirred and that you already believe the Sociology of Education has something to offer the sociologist, the educator, the liberal arts student, and the future citizen.

For the sociologist, the Sociology of Education offers a basic understanding of some of the processes through which culture is transmitted from one generation to the next, how social order is maintained, and how societies change. For the educator, the Sociology of Education offers a "set of concepts that will allow him (or her) to take account in . . . decision-making of organizational, cultural, and interpersonal factors . . ."[27] For the liberal arts student who does not intelld to become either an educator or a sociologist, the Sociology of Education contributes to the development of a "sociologist imagination." As an amateur sociologist one can employ the analytical skills acquired here for fun, for the simple pleasure of translating what may appear to be individual troubles and experiences into social problems and group phenomena, or for utilization in planning social

action programs. For the future citizen and potential parent, the Sociology of Education offers some understanding of the relationship between edu- cational policy and the economic, political, and social life of the nation.

We have all been students; many of us have been or will be teachers or school administrators. All of us are citizens, and many are already voters. Our lives and our futures are inextricably entwined with education. We should do our best to understand it.

## REFERENCES

1 Judson T. Landis, "The Sociology Curriculum and Teacher Training," *American Sociological Review*, 12 (February, 1947), pp. 113-16.

2 For a more detailed discussion of the divergence between the disciplines of education and sociology see Donald A. Hansen,

"The Uncomfortable Relation of Sociology and Education," in *On Education: Sociological Perspectives*, eds. Donald A. Hansen and Joel E. Gerstl (New York: John Wiley and Sons, Inc., 1967), pp. 3-35.

3 Gene F. Sommers and Richard L. Hough, *Educational Sociologists Survey of the American Sociological Association Section on the Sociology of Education* (n.p.: Center of Applied Sociology, 1970), p. 25

4 We are indebted to our late friend and mentor, David Street, for these insights.

5 National Commission on Excellence in Education, *A Nation at Risk* (Washington, D.C.: U.S. Department of Education, 1983); Study Group on the Condition of Excellence in American Higher Education, *Involvement in Learning: Realizing the Potential of American Higher Education* (National Institute of Education: Washington, D.C., 1984).

6 This discussion relies heavily upon that of Ralf Dahrendorf, *Class and Class Conflict in Industrial Society* (Stanford, Calif.: Stanford University Press, 1959), p. 161ff.

7 Emile Durkheim, *The Division of Labor in Society*, trans. George Simpson (Glencoe, Ill.: The Free Press, 1960).

8 Emile Durkheim, *Education and Sociology*, trans. Sherwood D. Fox (Glencoe, Ill.: The Free Press, 1956), p. 72.

9 ***Ibid.***, p. 81.

10 *Ibid.*, p. 68.

11 Emile Durkheim, *Moral Education*, trans. Everett K. Wilson and Herman Schaurer (New York: The Free Press, 1961).

12 Durkheim, *Education and Sociology*, p. 81.

13 *Ibid.*, p. 89.

14 *Ibid.*, p. 79.

15 *Ibid.*, p. 89.

16 Talcott Parsons, "The School System," *Harvard Educational Review*, 29 (Fall 1959).

17 *Ibid.*, p. 297.

18 The following discussion draws heavily from Dahrendorf, *Class and Class Conflict in Industrial Society*, p. 162ff.

19 Samuel Bowles, "Unequal Education and the Reproduction of the Social Division of Labor," in *Schooling in a Corporate Society*, ed. Martin Carnoy (New York: David McKay, Inc., 1972), pp. 36-64. See Samuel Bowles and Herbert Gintis, *Schooling in Capitalist America: Educational Reform and the Contradictions of Economic Life* (New York: Basic Books, 1976) for a more thorough discussion.

20 Bowles, "Unequal Education," p. 41.

21 Willard Waller, *The Sociology of Teaching* (New York: Russell and Russell, 1961). We should note that most sociologists probably would not identify Waller as a conflict theorist. Still, the themes of the conflict perspective appear quite clearly in his analysis of classroom dynamics, as shall presently be illustrated

# 5

# Primary Concepts of Sociology

India is predominantly rural, and, to know Indian society in all its aspects is useful for planners, administrators and also educationists.

Rural society in India has a typical economic, political and religious structure. The unique characteristics of this community are under-going structural and functional transformation as a result of various going structural and functional transformation as a result of various forces. This transformation has been quickened after the achievement of Independence, which has played a decisive role. Through several methods, reconstruction of Indian rural society has been attempted and they have changed the life and activities of the people of rural society to a considerable extent. An investigation into the village life, in general, covering such aspects as health, housing, education, ceremonial and customary practices, land tenure, family, caste organizations, leadership and panchayats, and the changes that have been brought about in the structure and function of the village organizations is helpful for proper planning of rural society. It is presumed that of single village could give a complete picture of Indian rural life, because of the diversity of life found in rural India.

Urbanisation is a powerful factor in bringing about social change. It has its impact on the attitudes of men towards caste, property, health, education, modes of living, housing, recreation and also labour. To examine the nature and extent of urban influence on rural society. It has been found advantageous form the point of view of the study of social change, to know the nature, the structure and the function of village society, ingenral, land tenure and fragmentation, income of households, private property, cattle-wealth, housing and health in particular.

It is interesting to know rural political life and rural leadership. For a long time caste panchayats used to perform judicial and executive functions. They are taken over now by village panchayats. In recent years, elections have revolutionized the political life of the rural people and have brought about a silent revolution in rural India. Moreover, the political alliances of rural people with various political parties, and the internal structure of village political groups and leadership of rural society are landmarks in present day rural social life.

**Definition of Society**

It is necessary to define any subject before it can be scientifically studied. Sociology makes a scientific study of society. Hence before embarking upon a study of sociology it is necessary to determine the nature of society. In common parlance, the word 'society is sued in myriad of meaning, for example, a group of women is called a 'women's society'. The word is also used for some specific institutions like Brahm society, Arya Society etc. But the popular meaning of the word does not serve the purpose of the scientific study. Sociologists should define society so that it can be distinguished from human groups and institutions.

Different sociologists have defined society differently. Some of the major definitions are the following:

"Society is a system of usages and procedures, of authority and mutual aid, of many groupings and divisions, of controls of human behaviour and of liberties." According to this definition, society is a dynamic and complex system. In it are included different activities, professions, economic, political and other activities relations with one another, rights and duties, etc. of individuals and their behavour in the various aspects of human life. It is also inclusive of such divisions among men as group, community, associations and classes, etc. In this way, society, according to this definition, is a complex web of mutual relationships and interactions.

*Giddings*—"Society is the union itself, the organisation, the sum of formal relations in which associating individuals are bound together." This definition of society places the emphasis upon its organisational aspect. Society is not merely a conglomeration or collection of scattered, individual human beings. Its members are bound to each other. Between them exist some formal relations which are based upon, and pertain to, family, race, class and other institutions. Society is an organized group of individuals.

Before starting a detailed discussion into the nature of society, it is essential to know clearly whether our study has reference to some specific society or to society in general. At this stage, it is essential to know the difference between 'society' and 'a society'. The difference is: (a) Society is general, 'a society' is specific. (b) Society is abstract, 'a society' is concrete, (c) Society cannot be limited within any space or time. But 'a society' is demarcated by geographical limits. In this way, the societies of people who live in India, Russia, China and other countries are differentiated form each other whereas the name 'human society' or merley 'society' would apply to all peoples of all countries in the world.

Society is not merley a collection of individual beings. Reuter has written, "'A society', as distinct from society is any organisation by means of which people carry on a life." Similar to this definition by reuter we have Ginsberg's opinion, viz. that 'a society's is a group of individuals related by same relations or forms of behaviour. Society consists, not of individuals, but in their mutual interactions and mutual interrelations. It is a complex structures formed by these mutual relation it is a system, a pattern. Individuals or people do not merit the name 'society' but 'a society' is sometimes used to denote people.

**Nature of Society**

The nature of the society, it is necessary to keep in mind the mentioned differences between society and 'a society'. In this way society is abstract because it is constituted of the social relations, customs and laws, besides other elements. In the words of Odum, "In another aspect society may be visualized as the behaviour of human beings and the consequent problems of relationships and adjustments that arise." According to Reuter, "Society s an abstract term that connotes the complex of inter-relations that exist between and among the members of the group." In this way, society exists wherever there are good or bad, proper or improper relationships, between human begins. These social relationships are not evident, they do not have any concrete form, hence society is abstract. In this context the definition given by Maclver and page is quite appropriate. But particular or specific society is concrete.

Some sociologists have viewed society as a group of people. Hankins writes, "We may for our purpose here defined society as any permanent or continuing group of men, women and children, able to carry on independently the process of racial perpetuation and maintenance on their own cultural level." Gillin, too, has accepted society in the form of a permanent group. But it has already been mentioned while the differences between society and 'a society', were being considered, that group of individuals is 'a society', not society. Wright rightly writes, "though society is a real thing, It means in essence a state or condition, a relationship, and is therefore necessarily an abstraction." Lapiere and Fransworth also agree with Wright. According to them, "it is that pattern, not the people, which we term society." In the words of Reuter, "Jut as life is not a thing but a process of living, so society is not a thing but a process of associating." Actually, groups of human beings have been adorned with such names as association or community sociology.

### Society is an Organisation of Relationships

Society is an organisation, a system or a pattern of relationships among human beings. Parsons has written. "Society may be defined as the total complex of human relationships in so far as they grow out of action in terms of means end relationship, intrinsic or symbolic." Colley puts it thus—"Society is a complex of forms of processes each of which is living and growing by interaction with the others, the whole being so unified that what takes place in one part affects all the rest."

Some sociologists, social relationships invariably possess a psychical element, which takes the form of awareness of another's presence, common objective or common interest etc. There is neither any society nor any social relationship without this realization. Society exists only where social beings behave towards one another in a manner determined by recognition of each other. Only those relationships which are so determined are social. Social relationships differ from relations between other objects only by virtue of this psychic element. There is a kind of awareness in them. They have in them an element of emotion and feeling, urges, sympathy and sentiments. In their absence, the relations between lower and beloved, husband and wife, father and son, teacher and taught, and others, cannot even be conceived. These elements can be bad as well as good but their presence is essential. Without the psychic element the relation between two people is in no way superior to the relation between two objects. Some sociologists, among the Morris Ginsberg, have doubted and questioned the indispensability of this psychic element in social relationships. According to Ginsberg, in many social relations individuals have no knowledge whatsoever. For example, changes in the relationships exists in the market influence the lives of people but the affected persons do not evince any knowledge of them. This opinion of Ginsberg does not appear correct because whatever the change, it has some influence upon the mental condition of the people, and they do become aware of it even though they may be unable to discover its causes or gauge its exact degree. When prices of commodities sold in the market fluctuate even a common labourer makes some inquiry and questions the seller, an even though he may be unable to trace the fluctuations in their cause he is still aware that some change is taking place.

In this way, briefly, society is an abstract organisation, pattern or system. In is not a group of people but a structure of their interactions and mutual relationships. These relations have a psychic element in them. Thus, society includes all actions, relations and mutual behaviour of people. In the words of Maclver, "Society we shall use in the very widest sense, to include every kind and degree of relationships entered into by men and other social creatures with one another...Society, when used without qualification, means the whole system of social relationships.

**Control of Human Behaviour and Liberties**

Society is a system of usages and procedures of authority and mutual aid, of many groupings and divisions, of control of human behaviour and liberties." Thee social relationships are not of one kind. Some of them are simple and some complex, some are permament and some temporary. These include behaviour, or custom, modes of operation, authority, assistance and other types of relations. Thus it is necessary to understand all these to understand society.

Man is a social being. His very existence and development rendered impossible in the absence of society. He has to establish relations with other members of society to fulfill his own needs. These relations lead to mutual behaviour. This behaviour becomes progressively complex and takes on the form of usage or custom. The daily life of almost all the member of society proceeds smoothly due to thee customs. By virtue of these, each new generation comes into possession of definite patterns of behaviour, and is saved from the effort of experimentation. These customs possess much importance in social life. These customs are the determinants of the actions of individual members of society, in respect of dietary habits, marriage, festivals, education, rituals, behaviour, etc. the differences which are discernible between the lives of people belonging to two different societies can be ascribed to differences in these respects, for example, a very great disparity exists between the diet, marriage customs, bahaviour, etc, of the Indian People and the Europeans. And within India itself all these are vastly different in the various castes, according to their respective customs and traditions. The puritanor rigouristic element looks these usages as primarily religious and is apt to view their infringement and disobedience with concern. Such activity is looked upon as sinful. The panchayats of these groups arrange to punish miscreants. Taking the people of American society as an example Maclver has stated that the basis of custom is not law, but general acceptance or agreement on the part of public. Principles of good behaviour are determined with reference to custom and not law. These customs are so divergent in different societies that an action looked upon as commendable and laudable in one society can even be condemned in another. And yet, each society emphasizes its own customs and organizes the life of society in accordance with them.

**Modes of action or procedures**

The second element in the organisation or system in society consists of the modes of action or procedures. Maclver has used the word procedures fro institutions. In this way procedures or institutions like marriage, inheritance, education, religious beliefs, political parties, etc. play an important part in society.

Authority is indicative of that relation which regulates or controls the related individuals or classes in such a way that one evinces a sense of authority is the inevitable inequality in society. There is greater similarity then dissimilarity in society but even then inequality is found in every society in some form or the other. In the family, race and in respect of situation, wealth and many other things, the members of society enjoy different status consequent upon which is an inequality in their social position. The inequality is invariably present in society. This inequality and authority is as much evident today in the relations between industrialists and labourers as it was in the relations between the labourers and farmers, and slaves and their owners in the ancient days. Even in communist countries there is a vast difference between the ruled and the rulers, and their relations are based upon authority. Actually, the system of authority is a necessary prerequisite of system in society. According to Maclver, a major characteristic of the modern age is a proper distribution of authority. In every society some individuals and classes are given authority on the basis of some specific conditions. The social relationships of people are determined by this. In society, even inequality is based upon mutual relationships.

People possessing diverse characteristics often assume

complementary roles. People of opposite sexes are able to achieve more intense and intimate relations than individuals of the same sex because each fulfils the deficiency of the other. In the same way, people who differ form one another in respect of income, status, wealth, education, etc. help and assist each other. Assistance has major importance in social relations. People who have the same interest and same objective combine together to form different kinds of groups and achieve their objective through mutual assistance. Human civilization and culture develop because of this assistance. It is this assistance which gives birth to the individual, nourishes and develops him.

### Groups and Divisions

Some of these groups are natural while others are constituted intentionally, keeping in view some specific objectives. Both primary groups like family and club, and secondary groups like trade unions, labour unions, etc, are extremely important for the development of social life. The organisation and system in society groups according to geographic divisions as well. In this way people are divided into country, provinces, districts, villages etc. Besides groups, the human societies are also divided into various classes according to ancestry, heritage, wealth, social status, etc. groups and classes are different parts of the organisation of the human society. Without control over human behavour, man's social life cannot progress properly. In society an individual cannot behave just as he happens to wish sine he has to bear in mind the consequences of his actions upon other people. In the adjustment; of the individual to society, the society has to exercise certain restrictions upon the individuals. This control of human behaviour is exercised through traditions, mores, folkways, taboos, laws and norms Every individual in a society has to behave in a way consistent with the traditions, mores and folkways of his own society. A person forfeits his right to respect and a good name by indulging in actions which are condemned by society, besides occasionally rendering himself liable to prosecution. Controls of this kind are essential for the organisation of society.

Human society is dynamic. Its life force lies in the change. Thus, in society the individual must be given livery in respect of many kinds of changes. In all the civilized societies of the world people have the freedom to get education, choose a desired profession, marry and beget children, think independently and to express their thoughts in an appropriate manner. Control upon an individual's behaviour is designed, not to destroy his liberties but to make an adjustment between this interests and the interests of the other members of society. In this way, "Society is a system of usages and procedures, of authority and mutual aid, of may groupings and divisions, of control of human behaviour and of liberties." In society—An Introductory Analysis, Maclver and Page have described in detail all these elements of the social system. Here it is necessary to keep in mind that the social system is not any stationary or immobile system, but a dynamic one. Thus, at one particular time indifferent social systems and at different times within the same social system the forms or nature of social usages, procedures, authority and mutual aid, groupings and the controls and liberties of human behaviour are continually changing.

**Society involves both likeness and difference**

Maclver has written that society cannot exist without both likeness and difference. Likeness and difference are undoubtedly mutually contradictory but they are both essential for society which is a dynamic and evolving or developing system. Society is a complex web of social relationships. In this web sometimes difference is more attractive than similarity since different individuals or classes are sometimes the complements of one another by virtue of thee differences. Social relationships are based upon a similarity of interests, objectives, mores, needs, etc. Men do not form a society in association with animals because their interests, mores, objectives, etc. are dissimilar and widely divergent. Human society can be comprised only of human beings because they share many characteristics and in common many features of nature, interests, anatomy mind, etc. The fundamental elements of human psychology vary within very small limits at all times and places. For example men and women of all ages and all countries have experienced and exhibited a very natural attraction for each other, and even in the future one cannot imagine this attraction losing its intensity; the edifice of human society, the family, rests upon this mutual attraction. Human society is divided into many societies. These different societies have vast differences in interests, traditions, behaviours, etc., and it is due to these differences that people of one society look upon an individual from another as a stranger. But among the people within one society one finds strong social relations which are the result of a similarly of traditions, mores, etc. In this way actually, the foundation of human society rests upon similarity. Maclver has written correctly, "In early society and among some of our primitive contemporaries, the sense of likeness is focused on kin-membership, i.e., real or supposed blood relationships. The conditions of special likeness have broadened out in modern societies. But the basic conception of likeness that primitive man identified with the kin remains in even so extensive a principle of union as nationality. And if the struggling principle of one world is to win out, it must necessarily rest upon the recognition of the fundamental likeness of the entire human race."

But similarity alone is not adequate for social organisation. The economic structure of society is based upon division of labour in which the professions and economic activities of people are different or dissimilar. The social structure of humanity is based upon the family, at the base of which is the mutual attraction between individuals of different sexes, viz., men and women. The culture of society prospers with the differences in thought, ideals, viewpoints, etc. Father-son, man-women, husband-wife, brother-sister, ruler-ruled, in brief, in all relationships in society, the rights and duties of individuals differ from, and for this reason are supplementary to, each other. Consequently, the progress of the system in society is smooth. Individuals differ from each other in respect of their interests, capacities, abilities, predictions, tendencies, etc. These differences do not imply mutual conflict; instead, by it the organisation of society is further strengthened Try to imagine a society in which all people are either weavers of all adults, or all old or young. Having realized the chaotic state of this society, the importance of difference in society will be readily apparent. It would not be a misnomer to say that in the absence of differentiation, the very existence of society maybe threatened or endeangered.

Both these elements are essential for the existence, organisation and development of society. Despite the fact that there are different races, nations and countries in the world today there is a growing consciousness of one universe', and 'universal government' is not longer an inconceivable impossibility. But this unity of the world cannot be achieved by abolishing the differences of the various cultures. One in the Many' is a profound truth of universal existence. Only by establishing unity through a syntesis of differences can a prosperous world society be created. Society is a web of human relationships. In order that these relationships may be prosperous and harmonious, both similarity and difference are essential. For example, the underlying cause of the intimacy between man and women is difference but if there were no similarity or concurrence whatsoever between them they could not jointly create a contended family. In this way both likeness and difference have their respective importance in human society.

**Characteristics of Human Society**

"Society is co-operation crossed by conflict." Generally speaking, the distinctive characteristics of human society are the following:

*Similarity*—Society is the name given to the system or organisation or the relations or activities among individuals. It is essential that these individuals should be similar to each other to some extent. Actually, in the complete absence of a common interest or common objective, it is not possible even to imagine any social relations. The needs of human beings differ from those of animals; hence human beings and animals cannot mutually form a society. Social relations cannot exist between them. The proverbial birds of a feather flock together. People of similar temperaments prefer to lie in societies or groups. According to a Sanskrit proverb, horses stay with horses, cows with cows and deer with deer. Aristotic has said that 'Man is a social animal' the meaning of which statement can be tranced to a realisation of man's similarity with his own kind, their similar needs, similar emotions or feelings, similar aims, etc. Social consciousness is the outcome of this similarity. It is this which creates the sense of unity in mankind. It is similarity which develops the feelings of love, affection, sympathy, brotherhood, etc., which one human beings has for another, giddings it calls the consciousness of kind. The increase in the sense of similarity among mankind is being accompanied by a widening of the sphere of society. In ancient times tribes originated when blood relations were reckoned as equal or similar. When the sense of similarity spread the tribal society expanded and embraced an entire nation, becoming a national society. After a further increase in this sense it led to talk of a human society.

*Differences*. But similarity is not the sole characteristic of society. Difference in social relations is also an essential element of society. Reciprocal give-and-take are based on difference. The strong relations between man and woman in human society are based no ton similarity but on contrast. There is greater attraction between tow individuals belonging to opposite sexes than there is between two persons of the same sex. According to the famous psychologists Freud, a daughter loves the father more while a son lavishes greater affection upon the mother. It is only by virtue of dissimilarity that people can fulfill each other's wants. Had all the individuals among humans been similar in respect of intellect and physique, their social relationships would have been extremely limited and their social structure would have resembled that of ants or bees among which there is one queen, a few males and the majority are servants. The reason why human society has achieved its present level of prosperity is its inherent multiplicity. In all of man's organisations, whether small or big, be it family, caste, race, association or community, the individuals are complements of each other by virtue of their dissimilarity. The activities in human society are based upon reciprocal give-and-take. This reciprocal exchange is due to a difference in interests, capacities, aptitudes, etc. the institutions of marriage and sexual relations are the outcome of biological differences. Division of labour is the foundation stone of the economic structure of society. The only reason why this is so is that every individual is not capable of performing any and every task while he can perform some particular task better than others. In the absence of dissimilarity and difference of many of the economic activities normally carried on in society would collapse. In society, rights and duties are determined on the basis of differences. It is because of the fact that the ruler and the ruled, the father and the son, teacher and taught, husband and wife are different that their respective rights and duties differ.

Intensity of likeness comparatively to difference. But

comparatively speaking likeness or similarity enjoys greater importance in society than does difference. Division of labour is based upon cooperation. The relations between man and woman, rich and poor, kind and his subjects, husband and wife, teacher and taught, father and son, etc. are based not upon difference or dissimilarity, but upon a concurrence of objectives, aims. Tendencies, etc. If the objectives of the ruler and the ruled are completely at variance, social organisation will suffer. Marriages are undoubtedly contracted by persons of opposite sexes but if there is complete disparity between their nature, they can never he happy. In society, the foundation of variety and multiplicity is based upon similarities. It is due to similarity in needs and objectives that individuals collectively formed societies. The progress in family, society, community and nations, too, can be ascribed to the same cause. This does not mean that society is based upon difference. Actually, both differentiation and co-operation are essential for the development of society. Hence, it has been rightly aid, "Society is co-operation crossed by conflict."

**Other Characteristics of Society**

In addition to the aforesaid three essential elements society has certain other characteristics elements. Among these are:

*Organisation*—Every society has its own individual and unique organisation in which there is division of labour of one kind or the other. People who are completely disorganized cannot be said to be constituting a society.

*Assistance*—Durkheim has expressly said that, due to division of work, there is greater evidence or co-operation and assistance in society than of differences and dissimilarity. The life of society depends upon mutual assistance.

*Interdependence.* Man cannot satisfy his needs if he leads a solitary life. So, he needs society, and stays in society because it is his nature. The members of society are dependent upon each other for the fulfillment of there needs.

**Essential Elements of Community**

*Defining Community Bogardus has written*: "a community is a social group with some degree of 'we feeling' and living in a given area." According to Davis, "The community is the smallest territorial group that can embrace all aspects of social lie." In this way, there are the following essential elements in a community:

*Definite locality*. The first condition of the community is a definite locality, since without it the relation between human beings cannot be established and the we feeling' cannot evolve. In the words of Semple, "Man is a product of the earth's surface."

*Groups of human beings*. Community is a group of human beings. It cannot even be imagined without a group of human beings.

*Community sentiment*. According to Sutherland, Woodards and Maxwell. "A community is a local area over which people are using the same language, conforming the same mores, feeling more or les the same sentiments, and acting upon the same attitudes." In this way, this community sentiment is extremely essential in the people belonging to a community.

*Likenesses*. According to Green, "a community is a cluster of people, living within a narrow territorial radius, who share a common way of life." In this way the community exhibits similarity and concurrence in language, customs, mores, traditions, etc., besides many other things.

*Permanency*. A community is not transitory and temporary like a crowd. For, it is essentially a permanent life in a definite place.

*Natural.* Communities are not made or created by an act of ill but are natural. An individual is born in a community. It is by virtue of community that he develops.

*Particular Name.* Every community has some particular name, which is expressive of the individuality or personality of its locality. In the words of Lumley, "It points to identity; it indicates reality, "it points to identity; it indicates reality; it points out individuality; it often describes personality—and each community is something of a personality."

In addition to the above essential elements of a community a common life and some degree of self-dependence are also necessary for it.

According to Osbon and Neumeyer, a community is "a group of people living in continuous geographic area, having centre of interest and activities, and functioning together to the chief concerns of life."

**Essential elements of an association**

An association has the following essential elements:

*Human Group.* An association is created by human beings. It is created for the attainment of the objectives of human beings. Hence human group is an essential condition of an association

*Common interest or aims.* Association is not a mere conglomeration of individuals, but of individuals who have some aim of selfish end in common. In the words of Maclver and Page an association is described "as a group organized for the pursuit of an interest or group of interests in common."

*Co-operative Spirit.* According to Bogardus, "Association is usually a working together of people to achieve some purpose."

*Organisation*. Defining association, Ginsberg writes that associations are constituted of those groups of individuals who are organized in order to complete some specific work or works, examples of which are trade unions, political parties or associations of scholars. Put that way, it is evident that organisation is an essential element of an association.

*Laws*. The organiation of association rests upon a particular set of laws. Some laws, be they written or merely verbal, are essential for an association.

### Distinction between Society and Association

| *Society* | *Association* |
|---|---|
| 1. Society is a system of social relationship. | 1. Association is a group of People |
| 2. Society is abstract. | 2. Association is concrete. |
| 3. Society is almost permanent. | 3. Association is concrete. Association is temporary. |
| 4. Society is natural. | 4. Association is established. |
| 5. There are both co-operation and conflict in society. | 5. Association is based upon co-operative alone. |
| 6. It is not essential for society to be organized. | 6. Association must be organized |
| 7. Society comprehends all conscious and unconscious relations. | 7. The basis of association consists of conscious feelings and thoughts. |
| 8. The objectives of society are not completely determined. | 8. The objectives of an association are predetermined. |
| 9. Society is inevitable. | 9. Association is a matter of violation. It is voluntary. |
| 10. Society is an end in itself. | 10. Association is merely a means. |

**Definitions of Community**

Community has been defined in more ways than one by various sociologists. Some of the main definitions follow:

*Ginsberg*—"whenever the members of any group, small or vast, live together in such as way that they share, not this or that particular interest but the basic conditions of common life, we call that group a community."

*MacIver*—"Whenever the members of any group, small or vast, live together in such a way that they share, not this or that particular interest but the basic conditions of common life, we call that group a community."

*G.D.H. Cole*—"By a community I mean a complex of social life, a complex including a number of human beings, living together under conditions of social relationships, bound together by a common, however constantly changing, stock of conventions, customs and traditions and conscious to some extent of common social objects and interests."

The following elements must be present in community:

(a) Group of people, (b) Definite locality, (c) Community sentiment, (d) Common life, (e) Spontaneous birth, (f) Particular name and (g) Psychic life.

In this way community is one such spontaneous group of people living in a definite locality, called by a particular name, in which a common life and community sentiment are evident and whose members are tied to each other by common dogmas, traditions, customs, mores and social relations. An example of such a community can be seen in Hindu community and Muslim community, besides others.

## Distinction between Neighbourhood and Community

According to Maclver neighbourhood is the simplest community. The neighbourhood comes after the family in the order of social importance and one in which there is a feeling of local unity. In this way neighbourhood is only a specific organ or part of community. There are neighbourhoods in one community. The neighbourhood has a profound influence upon the group of collective activities of an individual but the form or nature of neighbourhood has great importance, and the deepest and most intimate relations are found to exist among neighbours. They share one another's good luck and misfortune as do members of a single family. On the other hand, the neighbourhood has far less importance in the towns. In big cities like Calcutta, Bombay, etc., the neighbours do not even recognise each other. Mobility of the population, development in the means of transport and communication, materialistic outlook, individualism, and the velocity of life, are some of the causes of the indifference which neighbours in towns evince for each other.

Fairchild has written that in one are of a community, the existence of an acquaintance between people on a large scale, knowledge of each other, relations and specificity of social unity is essential, and it distinguishes community from neighbourhood groups. In this way, while the scope of community is far more extensive and comprehensive, the circle of personal acquaintances and intimates in it is also fairly large. On the other hand, the circle of neigbourhood is very small. It can be treated as a concentrated or narrow form or the smallest unit of a community.

The following table will further clarify the difference between community and neighbourhood:

| *Community* | *Neighbourhood* |
|---|---|
| 1. Community is extensive. | 1. Neighbourhood is limited. |
| 2. The circle of personal acquaintance is wide. | 2. The circle of personal Acquaintance is narrow. |
| 3. Community is a unit of society. | Neighbourhood is a unit of community. |
| 4. Prominent importance of community sentiment. | 4 Main importance of Sentiment of local unity. |
| 5. Community sentiment is caused by definite locality common life, etc. | 5. Feeling of neighbourhood depends upon continuity of residence. |
| 6. Community sentiment is stronger | 6. Sentiment of neighbourhood Is comparatively less strong. |
| 7. Community is more Organized and controlled | 7. There is no particular organisation of a neighbourhood. |

**Constituents of Community Sentiment**

Commuity sentiment is the feeling of unity among its members consequent upon this commonlife. In the absence of this sentiment, no human groupcan claimthe tittle of community, whatever the length of time for which it may have resided in one place. Community sentiment arises naturally among people who spentd a common life, live together, speak a common language, accept the same custms and traditionsor share a common goal and interest. No individualcan live unaffected by this feeling although its intensity ay not be the same in different communities,and in different members of the same community. This serves to bind the members of the community with asingle thread.

Consider the example of a rural community. All the villagers lend each other a hand in the event of need in agriculture and in other occupations. They take part in all important occasions which occur in a neighbour's home. They are present when marriages, deaths, births take place in any family. They celebrate the festivals all together and jointly face all calamities which descend upon the village. In this way a sense of brotherhood is generated among the villagers and they tend to identify another's delight and distress with their own. This same complex of emotion is called community sentiment. Due to the community sentiment, people sacrifice their own little interests in the interests of the community and being to look upon the good of the community as their own good.

Roughly speaking, community sentiment evinces the three following constituents.

*We feeling*. The most important element in community sentiment s the 'we feeling', as a result of it an individual instead of regarding himself as separate from others, believes himself to be identified with them. All the people look upon the pain or pleasure of any action of community as their own pain or pleasure. This kind of 'we feeling' can be seen among people of one sector, of one village and among those on foreign strands who hail from the same town or country. The fundamental cause of this feeling is a similarity of interests of people who live in the same place.

*Role feeling*. In the community, every individual has his own status and he should make his contribution towards the working of the community in accordance with this status. The community sentiment inevitably induces this desire for contribution because this is a part of the community sentiment. As a result of this feeling, an individual looks upon himself as a specific part of society and shoulders his responsibility accordingly.

*Sense of dependence*—the third element of community sentiments is the sense of dependence, which means that an individual believes himself to be dependent upon community and denies his existence apart from community. Due to this feeling of dependence he does not object to any designs which society has upon him and always tries to work in its favour.

As a consequence of this community sentiment, people exhibit immense interest in local life and take enthusiastic part in the solution of problems and the development of the local group. The community sentiment finds expression in the respect and observance of racial customs, dogmas and traditions.

**Changes in community sentiment in modern world**

According to Maclver, "Community sentiment is developed by the socialization process itself, by education in the largest sense, working through prescription and authority, social esteem or disfavour, until habits and conformities become the ground of loyalties and convictions." In this way the community sentiment changes in concurrence with the changes in the structure of society.

Extension of community in modern times—In ancient times the communities were very small. Due to a smaller number of the means of travel, coupled with the absence of the means of communication, the contact of people was limited to a mere hundred and was confined to a definite area. Often people did not even proceed out of the precincts of their own villages. Slowly, with the development in science, the means for transportation and communication were developed. With these facilities people started

Establishing business and friendly relations not only with their own countrymen but even with people living thousands of miles away in foreign countries. In this way the circle of community sentiment started widening.

*Inter dependence of communities.* In old days, the communities were self-dependent because, for one there was not quite so much division of labour and, for another, it was not at all easy to transport commodities from one place to another. For these reasons, the circle of the community was very limited. Today, all the communities is the world are dependent upon each other in some way or the other. As a result of this, while the circle of community feeling in being extended on the one hand, its ties are losing their strength on the other.

*Sense of universal brotherhood.* With this extension in community sentiment, and with the independence of the communities, a sense of universal brotherhood is being carried. The United Nations Organisation is the result of this sense. On the prone hand while the sentiment of nationalism has been strengthened, it has not, on the other, conflicted with the sense of universal brotherhood. Many thinkers have even conceived the idea of a World Nation.

Birth of new communities. In the modern world, the form of community sentiment has changed considerably due to the birth of new communities. In the modern towns the communities based upon occupation and industry etc, are stronger than those bound together by racial and blood ties. Different interests have merged and created new communities which pay no need even to the interests of the nation when forced into a choice between their own interests and those of the nation.

Actually, due to the effects of the industrial revolution, the present world is passing through a transition period. Thus, there cannot be any indication of definite progressin one direction, while ideas of universal brotherhood and internationalism are increasing on the one hand, it is possible to see, on the other, the presence of interests based upon colour distinction and narrow communal interests. It is definite that the sense of universal brotherhood shall triumph in this struggle because the discovery of atomic or nuclear power has made a universal organisation of human beings indispensable, since, otherwise, their very existence is threatened. A majority of the modern thinkers favour nationalism which can nurture the sense of universal brotherhood and in which other narrow interests have been sacrificed for the community sentiment of humanity.

**Distinguish between Society and Community**

| *Society* | *Community* |
|---|---|
| 1. Society is a web of social relationship | 1. Community consists of a group of individuals. |
| 2. Society is abstract | 2. Community is concrete. |
| 3. A definite geographical area is not necessary for society. | 3. A definite geographical area is essential for a community. |
| 4. There can be more than one communities in a society | 4. There cannot be more than one societies in a community |
| 5. Community sentiment or a sense of unity is not essential in a society | 5. Community sentiment is indispensable for a community. |
| 6. In society the common objectives are extensive and coordinated | 6. In a community the common objectives are comparatively less extensive and coordinated. |
| 7. In a society common interest and common objectivesare not | 7. In a community a common agreement of interests and objectives is necessary. |

necessary

Actually community is the name given to the concrete form of society existence in a definite geographical area. In the words of Manzer, "A society that inhabits a definite geographic area is know as a community."

**Meaning of Association**

An association is established with the purpose of fulfilling some common needs of people. Some of the definitions of association follow:

*Maclver.* "an organisation deliberately formed for the collective pursuit of some interest or set of interests, which the members of it share, is termed as association."

Ginsberg. "a group of social beings related to one another by the fact that they possess or have instituted in common an organisation with a view to securing a specific end or specific ends."

G.D.H. Cole. "By an association I mean any group of persons pursuing a common purpose by a course of cooperative action extending beyond a single act and for this purpose agreeing together upon certain methods of procedure, and laying down, in however rudimentary a form, rules for common action.

An association is a rationally constituted organisation of human beings, for the fulfillment of certain objectives, which has its own rule and its own modus operandi (mode of operation). On the other hand, community is a natural organisation. Its objectives are common, not specific. From among these various aims of the community, specific aims are chosen for the fulfillment of which specific associations are formed. Man is born in a community, whereas he enters into different associations in order to fulfil his various needs. Thus, association is not community but an organisation within the community.

The difference between association and community is clarified in the following table.

**Distinction between Association and community**

| *Association* | *Community* |
|---|---|
| 1. Association is voluntarily constituted. | 1. Community comes into Existence of itself. |
| 2. Membership of an association is voluntary. | 2. Membership of a Community is compulsory |
| 3. Membership of has Some definite objectives. | 3. Community fulfils all The needs of its members. |
| 4. Association is comparatively | 4. Community is comparatively more unstable. |
| 5. An intimatic community Sentiment is not found in Association | 5. Community is based upon an intimate community sentiment. |
| 6. Association has its own property, etc. | 6. Community does not have any property of its own. |

**Institutions**

Different sociologists have offered different definitions of institution, some of the major ones follow:

Maclver. "institution is a definite organisation pursuing some specific interests or pursuing general interests in a specific way."

Bogardus. "A social institution is a structure of society that is organized to meet the needs of people chiefly through well-established procedures."

Green. "An institution is the organisation of several folkways and mores (and most often but not necessarily laws) into a unit which serves a number of social functions."

Sumner. "an institution consists of a concept (idea, notion, doctrine or interest) and a structure."

Woodward and Maxwell, "In sociological parlance, an institution is a net of folk ways and mores that centre in the achievement of some human end or purpose."

**Characteristics of Institution**

It is evident from the foreigoing definitons of institution that an institution has some definite aims by virtue of which it is beneficial to society. Institution is only an organised form of racial customs, dogmas and rituals or methods. The following characteristics of institution further clarify the form of an institution.

1. Institution has some definite objectives.
2. There is a symbol of an institution which can be either material or non-materials.
3. Everyinstitution has some rules which must be compulsorily obeyed by individuals.
4. The institution has definite procedures which are formulated on te basis of customs and dogmas.
5. Institutions depend upon the collective or group activities of man.
6. Institutions are means of controlling individuals.
7. Institution is more stable than other means of social control.
8. Institutions are formed for the fulfilment of primary needs.

**Social Importance of the Institution**

In connection with the social importance of the institution. Maclver has written that it transfers cultural elements form one generation to another, introduces unity in human behaviour controls their conduct and guides man according to circumstances. Mainly, the following considerations desserve mentionwith regard to social importance of the institution:

1. In society moral ideas, knowledge and forms or modes of behaviour are transferred fromone generation to another through the medium of an institution. This helps the youner generation in its solution of the problems confronting it.
2. Institution indicates the right path to man and imposes control upon his activities.
3. The society by means of the institutions compels people, collectively, towork in conformity with social culture.

# 6

# Civil Society and Citizen Centred Society

A non-profit making, voluntary, service-oriented/development oriented organisation, either for the benefit of members (a grassroots organisation) or of other members of the population (an agency). It is an organisation of private individuals who believe in certain basic social principles and who structure their activities to bring about development to communities that they are servicing.

Social development organisation assisting in empowerment of people. An organisation or group of people working independent of any external control with specific objectives and aims to fulfil tasks that are oriented to bring about desirable change in a given community or area or situation. An independent, democratic, non-setarian peoples organisation working for the empowerment of economic and/or socially marginalised groups. An organisation not affiliated to political parties, generally engaged in working for aid, development and welfare of the community. Organisation committed to the root causes of the problems trying to better the quality of life especially for the poor, the oppressed, the marginalised in urban and rural areas.

Organisations established by and for the community without or with little intervention from the government; they are not only a charity organisation, but work on socio-economic-cultural activities. An organisation that is flexible and democratic in its organisation and attempts to serve the people without profit for itself.

*Civil Society and Citizen Centred Society*: Today an almost universal concensus that *civil society is a vital component of a good society*, and that the stronger and more developed it is, the better governed and more stable the wider political community is likely to be. This belief underlies the widely held view that Western societies are vibrant, free and democratic because they have, and the erstwhile communist societies came to grief because that did not have, a civil society, and that if the developing world is to avoid the fate of the latter, it should foster civil society.

Large and well-meaning Western foundations devote huge resources to helping the developing world do just this, and Western governments and international institutions make it a precondition of their aid. The fact that the consensus has acquired the status of an intellectual orthodoxy is a good enough reason to subject it to a critical scrutiny. The further fact that it has profound consequences for the lives of large parts of humankind, and that similar recent orthodoxies such as the Structural Adjustment Programme of the International Monetary Fund (IMF) have turned out to be deeply problematic, reinforces the need for scrutiny. Here an outline the historical discourse on civil society its central features, its explanatory and normative strengths and weaknesses, and is attempted its proper place in a well-ordered political community.

## Meaning of Civil Society

Hobbes was one of the first to articulate it with great clarity, followed by such other writers as Locks, Grotius,

Puffendorf and Montesquieu. For them human beings were by nature free and equal and endowed with the capacities for rationality and self-determination. They could not flourish in the unregulated state of nature and needed a well-ordered society that ensured them maximum freedom to pursue their self-chosen purposes. Such a society had a public or civil authority entitled to take and enforce collectively binding decisions. The authority was derived from the consent of its members, did no more than protect the basic rights of its members, and governed according to general laws. Its subjects were free to lead such lives, pursue such purpose, and enter into such relations as they thought proper within the limits set by the laws.

Hobbes, Locke and others called this '*civil society*.' Civil society referred to a group of individuals held together, and forming a single society, by virtue of subscribing to a consensually based public authority and sharing in common the practice of civility. Civil society was a human artefact, created, sustained and capable of being changed by human begins. It was not an organic expression of human sociability as Cicero and Aquinas argued, nor a teleological requirement of human nature as Aristotle maintained. It was a rational and artificial institution, growing, no doubt, out of the natural desire to live but in no way dictated or sustained by it. It called for its own distinct institutions and practices, as well as virtues and motives that it sought to cultivate in its members by educational and other means.

Civil society was not separate from the state nor one of its institutions; rather it was a way, and for Hobbes, Locke and others the only proper way, of constituting the state. Writers of the Scottish Enlightenment, who were particularly influential in popularizing the concept of civil society, shared their predecessors' view of it. Although they added minor novel touches, they did not radically depart from it. In their view human beings were inherently social, and the concept of the state of nature made neither logical nor historical sense. They contrasted civil society with 'savage', 'primitive,' 'rude' or 'militaristic' society, and equated it with civilized society (Ferguson 1767). Civilized society was distinguished by increased wants, division of labour, growth of the arts and sciences, self-restraint, moderation, rationality, liberty, gentle and refined manners, and respect for the law, all of which were believed to be enabled by and closely tied up with the development of commerce. A civilized society was above all a commercial society, and was constituted as a civil society based on a civil authority governing by means of laws and maintaining the basic rights of its citizens.

Only a civil society was believed to create the framework necessary for the development of a civilised and commercial society. Non-European societies had remained backward because they lacked such a civil society, and had no hope of turning the corner without developing one with or without European help. Hegel marked an important stage in the discourse on civil society. He too shared the earlier view of civil society, and his originality consisted in giving it a new orientation and probing its philosophical foundations. For him, as for his predecessors, civil society or *burgerliche Gesellschaft* referred to a legally constituted association of free and equal individuals pursuing their self-chosen goals. It was characterised by subjective freedom, personal autonomy, individual rights, mutual respect and recognition, satisfaction of needs, a system of exchange, rational legal norms, abstract morality, and a minimum structure of public authority. Unlike his predecessors, Hegel argued that civil society was inherently unstable. It threw up acute contrasts of wealth and poverty, created a rootless and discontented 'rabble', and was ridden with tensions and conflicts that it could not itself regulate. It also lacked collective self-consciousness, capacity for collective self-reflection, and a sense of moral direction. For these and related reasons, civil society was incomplete, pointed beyond itself, and required the institution of the state. While nurturing civil society, the state also regulated it, gave its atomized members a sense of community, and provided a higher and fully rational level of social existence. For Hegal, the state could never be constituted as civil society as the earlier writers had maintained. It included civil society as its necessary moment, but transcended it and provided it with a rationally and moral necessary wider framework (Taylor 1975). While most earlier writers had equated civil and political society and used the two terms inter-changeable, Hegel drew a fairly sharp distinction between them. For Hegel, civil society occupied a space between the family and the state. The former was based on love, unselfish concern for its members, overlapping selves, and so on, and represented an organic unity of reason and nature. Civil society was the realm of differentiation, in which free, independent, and otherwise unrelated individuals pursued their self-interest in a spirit of mutual respect and within the limits of the laws.

The state embodied individuals' dialectical unity, and represented objective rationality, rationally regulated sentiments of love and disinterested concern for the whole, pursuit of collective well-being, and a non-instrumental view of public authority. Karl Marx represented another stage in the developing discourse on civil society. He too shared the earlier view of it, but differed from his predecessors in his analysis of the nature and dynamics of civil society and its relation to the state. As he put it, 'material conditions of life are summed up by Hegel after the fashion of the English and the French of the eighteenth century under the name "civil society"'. For Marx civil society referred to the 'whole communal and industrial life of a given stage', 'all the material relations of production possible within a definite stage of the development of productive forces' [Marx and Engels 1973: 362-3). Although Marx sometimes suggested the civil society existed in all historical epochs, his considered view was that it was unique to the modern bourgeois society, especially in respect to the autonomy and the freedom from moral and communal constraints that it had currently acquired.

For Marx as for the earlier writers, civil society was characterized by individualism, rights, pursuit of self-interest, satisfaction of needs, liberty and equality. Following Hegel but far more so than him, Marx saw civil society as the realm of conflict, indeed a state of war between organized classes. Being inherently unstable, it needed the state to sustain the prevailing economic order. Unlike Hegel, Marx argued that the liberty, equality and so on that lay at the heart of civil society were deeply distorted and rendered vacuous by the class structure of the capitalist society. Workers had no choice but to alienate their labour, and were not really free. Lacking the necessary opportunity and resources, their rights too remained largely formal and empty. This was just as true of equality and individual choice. Unlike Hegel, Marx argued that the state did not and could not transcend civil society. Being the product of and inextricably tied to the class conflict inherent in civil society, it lacked the capacity to act autonomously.

The universality that it claimed to represent was nothing but the particular interest of the dominant class masquerading as that of the society as a whole. For Marx civil society was not a moment of the state as it was for Hegel, but its basis. Once the classes were abolished and the civil society was radically reconstituted, the state forfeited its rationale. People would reclaim the power they had hitherto alienated to the socially transcendental state, and govern their collective affairs democratically. Civil society would be replaced by a planned economy based on the principle of 'from each according to his ability and to each according to his need.' Marx called such a society 'communist'. It represented the dialectical unity of civil society and the state. It was not collectivist, as it became in the hands of the Soviet Communist regime, for example, and was more like a socialist version of Locke's civil' society. Individuals were its basic units, but they were socially conscious and motivated, not egotistical and self-interested. They enjoyed maximum freedom, but sued it to expand their human powers and enrich their being rather than to accumulate wealth or increase consumption. While the concept of civil society dominated Marx's early writings, it virtually disappeared from the later ones, where Marx preferred to talk of 'material relations', 'relations of production', the 'economic' 'structure of society' and so on in contexts where he would earlier have used the term 'civil society.' Within the Marxist tradition, the term 'civil society' played a limited role until Gramsci reintroduced it and made it one of the central categories of his thought.

Since he drew heavily not only on Marx but also on Hegel, Croce and other Italian idealists, his usage was both inconsistent and richly suggestive. For Gramsci, 'it is not the economic structure which directly determines the political action, but the interpretation of it', or what Marx had called ideology. He therefore shifted the focus of attention from the material relations of society to the 'cultural and spiritual' agencies that shaped the consciousness of its members, and called them civil society. In this broad sense, civil society was not peculiar to the bourgeois society, and existed in the middle ages, where the 'church was civil society' (Gramsci 1971: 170).

Civil society referred not to the economy but to the realm of free associational activity, and included the family, universities, the press, trade unions, cultural institutions, working men's clubs and publishing houses. Unlike the state or the political society, which exercised 'direct domination', or coercion over society, the dominant class used the institutions of civil society to mobilize popular consent in favour of the prevailing economic order and to establish 'cultural and spiritual supremacy' or 'hegemony'. Working classes and their organic intellectuals needed to contest this by carrying on the class struggle not only at the economic level but also in the civil society. Gramsci's vision of the classless communist society was very similar to Marx's. People would reclaim the power they had hitherto abdicated to the state, and all social institutions including the family, the schools, the universities and the state would be run democratically. 'Coercive elements of the state would wither away by degrees', and individuals, now liberated from all unnecessary constraints and inequalities, would enjoy maximum freedom (Gramsci 1971: 263). Such free, equal and socially conscious individuals would spontaneously carry out the laws they had given themselves, and the external discipline of the law would be replaced by the internal pressure of morality. Since people would readily appreciate the legitimacy of the prevailing economic and political order, their consent to it would be genuine and spontaneous, and would not need to be manufactured, Gramsci called such a society an 'ethical state' or 'civil society' (1971: 263). Unlike the capitalist society in which the institutions of civil society were manipulated to generate consent for a hegemonic social order, the communist society represented the 'reabsorption of political society into civil society', and symbolised the full flowering of the latter with free and equal individuals autonomously forming their views. In recent years the term 'civil society' has experienced a revival and found favour among people of different ideological persuasions. The current usage draws heavily not only on the European discourse but also on the American, especially the Tocquevillan, account of the vital role of voluntary associations in American life. For Tocqueville, American democracy was dominated by the idea of equality, which had its great virtues but also the tendency to isolate and atomize individuals. The only way to hold such a society together and forge bonds of solidarity was to create an extensive network of voluntary associations. Drawing on this tradition of thought, Robert Putnam (2000) has in his influential writings stressed the value of a thick associational life in building up trust, social capital and solidarity. Michael Walzer (1994) blends the two and captures the current usage well when he says that "the words "civil society" name the sphere of uncoerced human association and also the set of relational networks formed for the sake of family, faith, interest and ideology that fill this space."

As an area of uncoerced associative life, civil society includes such associations as the family, trade unions, universities, the press, professional bodies, churches, non-governmental organizations (NGOs) and social movements. It excludes the state, which is seen as an inherently and exclusively coercive institution. Political parties are also excluded, largely because, although voluntary, their purpose is to capture the state and use its coercive resources to realize their objectives. In the light of our brief historical sketch, the discourse on civil society displays a remarkable consistency.

It refers to what I might call the area of associative freedom, that is to the freedom of individuals to enter into relations with others, pursue common purposes, and form intrinsically or instrumentally valuable associations. It refers not to freedom *per se,* nor to how individuals lead their personal lives, but to the active exercise of freedom in forming networks of social relations. The concern with associative freedom arises out of the belief that as free, equal, rational and self-determinating individual, human beings desire to, and should be able to, form such social relations as they please. Since coercion violates their dignity and rational nature, it is inherently undesirable, and should ideally be avoided. However, since human beings sometimes fail to act rationally, some more than others, coercion becomes necessary. However, it should be minimized, laced in the care of a legitimate public authority, and exercised according to clearly stated and rationally defensible laws. The basic idea behind civil society is to minimize all avoidable forms of coercion and to maximize the area of associative freedom. Since different societies have different histories, the idea of civil society plays a different part and acquires a different degree of urgency in their political discourse. In the erstwhile communist countries, the state was an overpowering presence in society and stifled all areas of life.

Not surprisingly, when communism collapsed, the demand for the long-suppressed associative freedom dominated popular consciousness and the concept of civil society became the central category of political discourse, especially among creative writers, trade unionists and political activists, who had suffered the most from its absence. Asian and African experiences were different. Despite its brutality, the colonial state there was not unduly oppressive, and left considerable space for associative freedom. At independence the idea of civil society did not therefore dominate their political discourse. Their primary concern was how to organize and structure their political life so that the state pursued developmental goals and remained accountable to its people.

Insofar as they thought of civil society, they looked to the state to nurture it and, where necessary, to create its preconditions. Since different societies hold different conceptions of human life, they take different views on the role of coercion in social life and what areas should or should not be subjected to it. In deeply religious societies, the economic life is regulated by moral and religious norms enforced by religious organizations and social pressure. It does not enjoy the autonomy that it does in the modern bourgeois society, and is not generally seen as part of civil society. Again, in different societies different social institutions limit associative freedom. In some it is tribes, in some others castes, in yet others religion. In each case the struggle to create a civil society involves different targets and strategies, and the resulting structure of civil society has a different character. We should not therefore make the mistake of thinking the civil society must have the same shape and form the world over, or that an institution that forms part of civil society in one country must also form part of it in another. Rather than universalize the Western history and model of civil society and expect all others to conform to it, we need to take different views of it and appreciate its diverse forms. It is odd, even self-contradictory, to take a monistic view of the very area of life that is supposed to be the home of plurality.

## Critical Assessment

Civil society has much to be said for it, and the associative freedom that forms its constitutive principle is an essential part of a well-organized society. Freedom, including associative freedom, is an emblem of human dignity and sense of self-worth. By freely associating with others in pursuit of personal and common purposes, human beings also express and cultivate their sociability, discover themselves, develop civic virtues, and grow to their full stature. Economic, professional, neighbourhood, civil and other associations arrest the atomization and feeling of helplessness inherent in modern industrialized society, generate multiple centres of power, cultivate moral and social discipline, provide formal and informal spaces in which to interact with others and rise above one's subjectivity, and foster social cohesion.

They also provide a vitally necessary counterweight to the state and limit its power. All states have a tendency to become remote and arrogant, and need to be checked by citizens' movements and NGOs. Furthermore, power accrues to the state through its functions. As citizens assign more and more functions to it out of inertia, apathy or indolence, it acquires more and more power and legitimacy. It cannot be controlled merely by means of an internal system of checks and balances, because that only regulates its *exercise* of power and does not *decrease* the amount of power and moral status it enjoys. We need to limit its range of functions by fostering the spirit of self-help among its citizens and encouraging them to undertake as many of them as possible through voluntary associations. A vibrant civil society ensures that citizens accept the responsibility for their shared life, and do not alienate their power to and help create an overbearing state. While these and other virtues of a vibrant civil society are obvious, much of the discourse on it exaggerates its importance and gets it out of perspective. The discourase has a built-in bias against non-voluntary associations. As we saw, it is based on the deeply held belief that as free and self-determining agents human beings should not be subject to the authority of associations they have not themselves created and which they cannot leave at will. Associations based on traditional allegiances, ties of blood, inherited loyalties or the 'accident' of birth—such as castes, clans, tribes, and ethnic and religious communities—are viewed with disfavour. They are to be discouraged, even dismantled, in order that their members can be fully free, and civil society can emerge in its purest and uncompromised form. Where they are not dismantled, for prudential reasons, their presence is regretted, and their members are seen as unfree, truncated and even inadequate human beings. This bias against non-voluntary associations is unjustified.

They do have their obvious drawbacks. They sometimes have rigid norms, oppressive practices and structures of authority, limited mutual contacts, and encourage frozen social identities and narrow loyalties. However, they also have their strengths. They are often historical communities with deep bonds based on shared collective memories of struggles, achievements and failures. They encourage a strong sense of social obligation, mutual commitment, and spirit of self-sacrifice. They provide a readily available network of support and represent a valuable resource for their members and an asset to the wider society. Since they are not deliberately created and cannot be dissolved or left with ease, they have tenacity, are free of volatile individual impulses, tend to strike deep roots in the lives of their members, and evoke strong attachments and loyalties. They are narrow but deep, demand much but also offer much, and make up for some loss of liberty by offering a sense of existential security and rootedness. They can certainly corrupt public life by encouraging nepotism and narrow partiality, but voluntary associations are not free from these vices either.

While ensuring that they do not become oppressive and deny exit to dissenting members, we should value the contribution they make to the good life. Not all voluntary associations are inherently good, nor all non-voluntary ones inherently bad. While voluntary associations form civil society, non-voluntary associations form community, In civil society we meet as strangers, colleagues, neighbours, fellow professionals, fellow trade unionists, and citizens; in a community as friends, kin, fellow ethnics, Jews, Catholics, tribespeople, and speakers of a common language. Civil society is based on reciprocity, distance, respect for rules, loyalty to institutions, and so on; community on intimacy, affection, warmth and mutual concern. Civil society nurtures associative life, community communal life. In civil society we share common interests and hobbies and 'bowl' together, to use an evocative image of Robert Putnam's (Putnam 2000). In a community, we celebrate common festivals, grieve together, holiday together, or spend Christmas together.

'Bowling alone' represents the decline of civil society; grieving or spending Christmas alone that of community.

In many Western societies, traditional communities have largely disappeared, and almost all social relations including the family are cast in the mould of civil society. This has brought both gains and losses. While individualism, the adventure of self-creation and civil society have flourished, communities have declined. The voluntarist spirit that drives civil society has a tendency to encourage expectations, attitudes and values that militate against the inherited loyalties and acceptance of non-contractual obligations and traditional bonds that lie at the heart of communal life. In many non-Western societies the opposite is the case. Communities of different kinds remain strong, but civil society is weak. While they need to foster civil society, there is no obvious reason why they must be expected to declare a war on communities. They can create a space of civil society by loosening up and restructuring rather than destroying these communities, as Indians are doing with castes, African societies with clans and tribes, and Muslim societies with their religious institutions. The Western model of civil society is culturally and historically specific and has its obvious limitations.

It should not be held up as universal norm and used to mould the rest of the world in the Western image, as in currently done by many enthusiasic governmental and non-governmental champions of civil society. The second limitations of the discourse on civil society has to do with its failure to give an adequate account of the nature and role of the state. This is so because it considers coercion inherently evil, identifies the state with it and civil society with its absence, and aims to maximize the role of civil society at the expense of that of the state. The distinction between the coercive state and the non-coercive civil society is too crude and sharp to do justice to either. The state certainly uses coercion, but it also does much more. It plays symbolic, inspirational, educative, facilitative and coordinating roles. It symbolizes the unity of society, fosters social cohesion, and gives society a sense of historical continuity and depth. It enshrines certain norms and values in its institutions and practices, and embodies a particular vision of the good life. It nurtures formal equality and encourages the ideas of fair trial and procedural justice in a society that might be wholly innocent of them. It can use its coercive power to challenge vested interests, remove unacceptable inequalities, fight pockets of coercion in different areas of social life, and increase the freedom and opportunities of its citizens. Just as the state is not exclusively coercive, civil society is not wholly non-coercive. It does, of course, ensure associative freedom, this being true by definition, but the freedom is not and cannot be without constraints. All associations affect public order and public interest, and the state cannot be indifferent to their structures and practices. It may rightly ban associations that incite religious, ethnic or racial hatred, and require that they should not discriminate against blacks, untouchables, gays or women, or impose unacceptable cot on their dissenting or departing members.

Civil society does not precede or exist outside or behind the back of the state. Instead it is made possible by the state, which both permits and protects associative freedom, and exists as a moment, a space, within it. Although associative freedom is most valuable, or rather precisely because it is so valuable, we must avoid the mistake of dissociating it from its wider context. As Marx highlighted, the formally equal civil, political and other rights are unequally enjoyed in an unequal society and even used to legitimize and perpetuate it. This is just as true of associative freedom. Although it is in principle equally available to all in a well-ordered society, in practice its exercise is highly uneven.

The poor and the marginalised are often too atomized and overwhelmed by a sense of powerlessness to have the confidence to set up vibrant associations. They also often lack the necessary skills and resources, and do not understand the complex mechanisms of the modern society well enough to target its weak spots. It is hardly surprising that civil society in almost all societies is dominated by the middle classes, and even the organizations of the oppressed and marginalised are often set up and led by the middle classes. The powerless find it difficult to organise and, since organisation represents power, their failure perpetuates and intensifies their powerlessness. Associative freedom, further, can be used to legitimise state inaction. Since the state is expected to ensure maximum space to civil society it is required to pursue minimum goals and to intervene as little as possible in economic and social life.

This is how Oakeshott, Hayek, Friedman and others justify a libertarian state in the name of civil society. For these and related reasons, we should not make the mistake of idealizing civil society in the abstract. We need to ask how it is constituted, who exercises and benefits from associative freedom, and how we should restructure civil society so that all citizens and groups can exercise it equally. Since the state can play a vital emancipatory role here, we should not allow it to be undermined by an uncritical ideological commitment to the maximum autonomy of civil society. Voluntary associations, social movements, and so on that comprise civil society lack historical continuity, and are often issue-based and unable to take a long-term and comprehensive view of society. They are not popularly elected and accountable, and sometimes they are authoritarian and remote from their members.

Their decision-making procedures are not always transparent, and their decisions open to public scrutiny. It is wrong to assume that just because an association is voluntary, it is democratic or speaks for all its members, or that a protest movement against the policies of the state necessarily serves public interest or even that of those in whose name it claims to speak. We should not homogenize the civil society, which encompasses a wide variety of networks, interests and associations not all of which are equally welcome. And nor should we take the naïve view that all coercion is inherently undesirable. Coercion tends to spring up subtly and stealthily in so many different areas of life and forms of social relations that the coercion of the state often becomes necessary to monitor and deal with it. The civil society and the state are based on different principles and play a complementary role. Neither can replace nor should be privileged over the other. A varied and vibrant civil society gives the state moral depth and political vitality, even as a justly constituted state creates the conditions in which all its citizens can build a rich world of networks and associations. Rather than set up an abstract opposition between the two, a well-considered political theory should establish a partnership between them on terms that are relevant to our times.

Locke's and Adam Smith's reduction of the state to civil society disables it from dealing with corporate capitalism and grave social and economic injustices. Hegel saw the importance of both the civil society and the state better than any other writer, but made the mistake of romanticizing the state, overestimating its independence, and underestimating the tensions of civil society. Marx and Gramsci avoided his mistakes, but naively thought that once the classes were abolished the state could be dissolved into a loosely coordinated structure of the voluntary associations of socialized individuals. Many contemporary writers, including Walzer, idealize civil society without fully appreciating how deeply it is implicated with the economy and the state. Cohen and Arato's (1992) work provides a stimulating account of how the discourses on civil society and democracy should be integrated. While drawing on the rich insights of the tradition of discourse on civil society from Hobbes to Walzer, we also need to correct and go beyond them.

**NGOs and Public Policy**

Participatory development aims to enable individuals, groups and communities to plan execute and manage development that improves their living conditions. They often need technical, administrative, organizational, financial and legal support in their endeavour. Some of these support services lie in the public domain and may be cumbersome or obstruct the development processes. They therefore need to change.

The need for the public to inform and influence policy changes arises mainly from grassroots experiences: PRA often raises important issues that can be resolved only through policy changes. For example, in June 1990 an order of the Government of India on Joint Forest Management was secured. This occurred only because an OGO spent three years lobbying the government to remove policy bottlenecks from its fieldwork. Senior administrators in charge of policy formulation are removed from the field realities and may not have first-hand knowledge of participatory processes. NGOs have such experience.

They need to, and can, influence policy to further participatory development. Apart from the constraints arising in the field due to inappropriate or inefficient policies, NGOs may like to engage in policy influencing for other reasons. To encourage better implementation of a government programme that has the essential components of a participatory approach. NGOs may work to promote more appropriate mechanisms and procedures within public agencies. For example, the Watershed Development Programme of Ministry of Rural Development in India has all the features of a participatory programme and NGOs can contribute to more satisfactory implementation activities.

To ensure that participatory features are integrated into policy formulation, and NGO may try to associate itself to a programme to influence policy changes.

To persuade public agencies to put issues that are important for a participatory approach onto there agenda. For example, by promoting gender awareness in development programmes.

The action required to influence public agencies is arduous and daunting. NGOs need to commit considerable time to take up the challenge. Instead, many NGOs prefer to continue their work, hoping that the equality of their project will attract the attention of public agencies, who will eventually appreciate the need for providing supportive policy changes. Public policy is embodied in a country's constitution, legislative acts, rules and administrative instructions.

These are prescribed in manuals, guidelines and orders issued at government level, or by government bodies/officers at different levels. But pragmatic policy decisions are also made at a more local level when the policy is actually implemented. Policy-change advocates should know precisely which of these need to change to facilitate development. Those who decide policy changes, are usually preoccupied in implementing existing policies and considering a plethora of proposals for changing current policies. Proposals for change emanate from a wide range of sources: influential political parties/leaders, interest groups, committee recommendations, research findings, public spirited experts and citizens writing letters to the editors of newspapers/ magasines. Policy makers are continually bombarded with proposals for change. They are not waiting for good ideas. Their basket is full, the bus is crowded.

Development agencies should select a few issues for advocacy out of the many that emerge in the course of their work. Such issues should have the potential to have a large impact on furthering the cause of development, particularly for the deprived areas, communities, groups and families. Even if convinced of the need for change, decision makers will take months to change administrative orders, years to modify legislating provisions and decades to amend a county's constitution. Development agencies should, therefore, give priority to ideas that require a change in practice, administrative orders, manuals, rules acts and a country's constitution – in that order.

## Plan of Action

After carefully selecting ideas for policy change, a development agency will need to work out a plan of action for familiarising and influencing the decision maker to accept and act upon the proposal.

- Build up a strong case for proposed change, why it is necessary, important or urgent and who will benefit and by how much.
- Explore, in detail, the present policy that requires change, who is authorised to decide on the proposal and the process that will be followed.
- Contact like-minded organisations and individuals likely to support and join in the presentation of a proposal.
- Formulate the proposal which should incorporate: information about the organisation(s) making the proposal and their motivation identify the problem in the field that is blocking the development and articulate precisely the policy that needs change.
- Request a personal meeting to explain the details of the written proposal.

- Send a copy of the proposal to the people interested in the issues or whose support may be required.

**Strategy for Drawing Attention**

Since policymakers receive many proposals, a strategy should be devised to draw attention to it. The strategy may:

Identify an officer whose acceptance of the proposal is crucial and those people whose opinions are valued by the policy maker.

Identify an officer who is important and sympathetic to the development programme promoted by the development agency. Take his/her advice on the best strategy for success.

Contact influential people and take their advice and help on how best to influence decision makers.

Request important officers to visit the NGO to better appreciate the work being undertaken and the context for the proposal. During such visits, presentations should be made by those who undertake PRA exercises to strengthen the case for policy change.

Use the media to create a favourable climate for the acceptance of ideas in the proposal.

**In the Event of Rejection**

If the key officer is not impressed by the proposal, rejects it or is likely to reject it, work out a strategy to overcome the obstacle. The agency may approach higher levels in government to direct the officer to consider the proposal sympathetically and expeditiously. The agency may have to wait until the unsympathetic officer is transferred or a more favourable situation develops.

If, and when, the response of the decision-maker is favourable, the agency should work to ensure that the formulation of the proposed policy change will meet its requirements.

Suggest the appointment of a policy drafting committee, with NGO representation on it, for preparing the draft of the proposed change.

Officer services of the NGO to work with the officer who is responsible for drafting the government order/ instruction.

If such offers are not welcome, retain informal communication with the implementing officers. Government decision-making on policy matters involves several levels in a department. In more important matters, several departments are involved, particularly, legal, finance and personnel. The agency should follow the progress of the proposal until the desired order is issued.

**Processes for Promoting Participatory Development**

The effort required to initiate policy changes is enormous. For example, the NGO that moved the Government of India to adopt more participatory approaches to forest management, used 49 different contacts, including personal meetings, letters and telephone calls.

Participatory approaches are being integrated into more programmes in India. Yet government bureaucracies have little experience of participatory development systems and processes. It is essential that governments recognise that participatory development requires modification to the acts, rules, administrative and accounting procedures and roles and responsibilities of personnel. Adoption of participation will require an environment conducive to free and frequent interaction with those outside government.

Drawing from John Thompson's (1995) article, the following lists some activities that will help promote the necessary institutional change.

Appointment of Working Group for each programme as a forum for open dialogue, critical reflection and continuous learning. The Group should consist of senior officers. NGO representatives, academics studying the programme and representatives of community based organisations.

Policy Resolution affirming Government's commitment to participatory approach in a programme.

Strong leadership with long term commitment and capacity to learn.

Specific responsibility entrusted to a senior officer to develop the new programme.

Pilot projects as 'learning laboratories'

Action plan indicating tentative broad targets, delegated authority and training needs.

Process Documentation Research to provide continuous feedback about development and emerging issues in the field. The system of monitoring and evaluation should include equal concern for quality as quantitative targets.

Fostering a culture of constitution and participation at various levels within an organisation and with stakeholders outside the organisation.

Organising National Support Group (NSG) outside Government but with active involvement of key officers of concerned Government department, donor agencies, NGOs and academics active in the programme.

There is an NSG for Joint Forest Management in India, which provides support for innovative initiatives and research. It is also a forum for exchange and dissemination of experiences and ideas. Similar NSGs for Watershed Development and Participatory Irrigation Management are under consideration.

The Indian Government policy on Joint Forest Management initiated in June 1990 has led 16 states to issue detailed government orders on the procedures to be followed for implementing the policy. About 2 million hectares of forest lands are now being managed by nearly 15000 forest protection committees. Working closely with the government of Gujarat, India, the Development Support Centre has facilitated a policy declaration for Participatory Irrigation Management.

This has triggered changes including: appointment of a Working Group, starting pilot projects, simplification of the procedures for facilitating participation by NGOs and farmers, more delegation of power to field officers and liberal incentives to farmers' organisations to take responsibility for managing government irrigation projects. The process continues. Policy influencing by NGOs is arduous, but I consider it to be essential and rewarding.

**Human Rights, States and Global Governance**

The very notion of human rights—that based on their own existence people have claims on and protection from excesses by society—runs radically across the central organising principle of the sovereign state in our world. The territory of our globe is actually and legally divided into discrete parcels of land and people administered by governments. The people living in each of these parcels, according to the organising principle of the state, come under control of the government of the land and none other. Governments relate to each other and not to the people subject to another government. When they decide to do so, governments acting in the name of states create organisations, such as the United Nations.

States fall under no authority, except their own, unless they agree to some limits. Yet this notion of sovereignty, so dear to the contemporary crop of nationalists, does not in fact describe anything except a principle. On a global basis, governments agree to promote human rights through such organisations as the United Nations. Their agreement suggests an implicit contradiction. How can individuals have rights protected by international surveillance if governments pretend to act autonomously, even when they agree among themselves, as most have done, to respect those rights? Why did they sign up in the first place. A glib answer to these questions would hold that governments respond to the wishes of their subjects.

The UN treaties of our time assert the human rights of participating in social decisions and provide for the protection of association and expression necessary to such participation. Yet the daily pictures of bloody heads under trucheons of so-called security agents bear witness to the superficiality of such a view. So does the elaborate rhetoric that government spokesmen use to explain away refusal to do anything about such denials of rights in other states. Is the whole panoply of human rights instruments that the overwhelming majority of governments have pledged to apply nothing more than a cynical fraud or a utopian illusion? It would be hardly more than that if the principle of sovereignty described actuality. It would be hardly more than an illusion if governments could always act in an untrammeled way.

The international organizations that deal with human rights issues – the Untied Nations and its human rights establishment, the UN High Commissioner for Refugees, the UN Children's Fund, the International Labour Organisation, the Council of Europe and some other regional bodies – all stand for the hope of enlisting the cooperation of Governments. To some extent they succeed, at least rhetorically and at most in terms of bringing national practice in conformity with international norms. Indeed no government now denies the general validity of international human rights norms or proudly admits violating them. Rather they usually try to refute any criticism that crops up – it does regularly – in the international organs. Such criticism depends, however, on the willingness of governments to instruct their representatives to voice opposition, It also depends on the ingenuity and integrity of international civil servants. This approach to human rights results in fragmentary treatment, uneven application of standards, difficulty for individuals to get what they are promised and plenty of evasion.

No general government exercises authority over stages of application. Yet somehow rules, and above all expectations, have been created about the permissible behaviour and duties of governments. The existence of these rules and expectations suggests that, even without a hierarchical command, human rights are promoted and protected – not perfectly, not necessarily brilliantly but more than ever before. These functions without overarching authority and without coercion may be called *governance*. Governance in relation to global issues is driven by interdependence of economies and societies and supported by increasingly easy communication among individual people and their organizations. It may be encouraged by the widespread acceptance of privatization of functions that governments monopolised. What we have come to call the civic society – that is relationships among people and organizations outside of formal governmental arrangements – is closely related to governance. Human rights is a striking example of a global issue where governance, not merely government, applies. Yet this fragmentary, fluid approach to global issues excludes formal popular participation. No world legislature exists. Nor do governments hasten to develop a means by which representatives of the people or the people themselves take part in making decisions on human rights. Is there then no popular voice?

## NGOs as Participants in Global Human Rights Governance

If a popular voice requires detachment from government, then indeed in governance concerned with global human rights, there is a popular voice. It emanates from non-governmental organisations. The character of that voice, however, is far from self-evident and demands sophisticated examination. NGOs steadily participate in the global organisation, with all its fractures and irregularities, for promoting and protecting human rights. NGOs have been omnipresent in the human rights activity that has surged since the end of the Second World War. That they have a role in the deliberations among governments in the UN framework has been especially striking.

It comprises three approaches, all part and parcel of governance. The first of these has to do with setting agendas for international cooperation and also for national polices. NGOs that deal specifically with human rights, and others whose work touches on human rights, try to bring violations of standards and shortcomings in national practice into the light of publicity. They inform their members and supporters of such instances. They submit information and recommendations to international organs, such as the UN Commission on Human Rights or the Council of Europe. Where possible, they lobby and advocate specific policies for national governments. Some NGOs dealing with human rights do not work across national boundaries; they direct attention exclusively to the governments of their countries.

They carry information from the transnational NGOs and those that work at the international level to their home polities. Such activity helps to set the agendas for international cooperation and national action. A second mode of participation brings NGOs into the process of formation of human rights policies in both the international and national realms. NGOs have become an integral part of intergovernmental deliberations on human rights and have had an equally prominent role in some national legislatures and bureaucracies.

A third mode of action relates to the administration of accepted polices. NGOs have contracted with international agencies to offer technical assistance on human rights to governments that request it. They have also rendered such assistance on their own. They have taken part in officially sponsored surveys and investigations of human rights applications, including some cases of severe violation. They have trained human rights observers and analysts who work in other organisations or in national realms.

In all of this activity, which contributes to global governance, NGOs have none of the formal authority of government. If they apply internationally sponsored and recognized rules, they do so out of conviction and out of the experience of helping to form them. They are based primarily in the civic society and accordingly their attention necessarily goes to it as well as to official agencies. NGOs are of course constrained by national laws and rules but typically operate at the edges of government authority and find their way around various constrains. In contrast to governments, they find most support–financial, moral, intellectual-without exercising authority. They usually emphasise their contrast with government.

## NGOs as the Voice of the People

It is tempting to stamp the title "The Voice of the People" on the NGOs that have affected international governance, such as it is, on human rights. They have worked with growing skill, penetration and insight in the development of the agenda, in deliberations of transnational bodies and on the execution of adopted policies. The most active have never relented in their criticism of violations of rights and have applauded advances. They have also acted positively to form new rules, such as those on the rights of children. In a world of governments, and the conviction among many governors that sovereignty has priority over global rules, NGOs have produced impressive results since 1945. These have no historical parallel. Yet precisely whom NGOs represent remains a tantalizing questions.

Furthermore, comprehensive data are embarrassingly absent, foreing an observer to rely on impressions. NGOs differ from governments by definition and in actuality. But some NGOs directly get some or most of their financial support from governments. These are perhaps relatively few in the human rights field; still, the NGOs working in refugee relief, where human rights are part of the agenda, get substantial or even most of their money from governments and their international organisations. Similarly, some disaster relief organisations, whose work has to do with persons deprived, frequently as a result of malevolent government, of the right to food, shelter and education, are largely government financed. Some, but certainly not nearly most, NGOs offer membership to anyone who wishes to join. In other cases, the NGO forms around leaders, raises funds and interests contributors who then receive information and other services. The creation of some NGOs is stimulated by governments or intergovernmental agencies.

Such an NGOs does not of course have the characteristic of a membership organisation. Furthermore, NGOs vary greatly in how their priorities, polices and programmes are put together. In some apparently rare cases, the membership participates directly in such decisions. More frequently, but by no means commonly, the membership is polled on policy issues. A far more usually arrangement leaves such decisions in the hands of a professional core staff.

Depending on local last, NGOs have boards of trustees

or similarly supervisory organs, but the degree of their involvement in decisions varies enormously. A related question has to do with the leadership of NGOs. As usual wit NGOs, the visible practices vary enormously. Some NGOs even claim not to have any leaders or other hierarchical organisation. Others obviously respond to a single figure, sometimes a charismatic sort, sometimes a skillful bureaucratic manager.

Whatever the case, few well-based generalizations are possible. The geographic extent of political engagement raises further questions about representation. Some NGOs that relate to human rights operate almost exclusively at the level of intergovernmental relations, typically around the United Nations and other international organizations. Others have national bases but extend their actions beyond the boundaries of their countries. Still others work only in the national realm. Some show a strong interest in promoting and working with grass-roots organizations, while others have no such association. NGOs sometimes form inter-organizational alliances only for particular issues, while others belong to groupings with a more general outlook, such as the International Council of Voluntary Agencies or the American group.

*Interaction.* From time to time, such groupings make pronouncements on human rights, counsel their members and represent their common views in the meeting halls of intergovernmental agencies. Yet NGOs usually make their own decisions about the scope of their operations, however much their names or programmes might lead an observer to assume patterns of behaviour. Finally, NGOs that have agendas centering on or impinging on human rights issues vary enormously in their abilities to persuade. Some of this variation derives from the degree to which the governments they contact are open to persuasion. Some of it depends on the issue itself.

Moreover, the skill of officials and the integrity and plausability of their output differ among organisations. So no matter whom they represent. NGOs as a category tend towards unpredictable results ranging from highly successful in their terms to little impact. The variety and variability of NGOs can hardly sustain the argument that they represent the people of the world as a legislature in a democracy does its constituents. Yet NGOs do serve one of the functions for which legislatures are designed. A set of voices beyond that of officialdom sounds through the NGOs in the human rights field. In some instances, the NGO voices emanate vertically through societies and administrative units from bottom to top of the official hierarchies.

In the human rights field, NGOs can concentrate on transnational policy, rather than limiting themselves by territorial and institutional boundaries. At their best, NGOs have the ability to poke holes in shoddy defenses of low human rights standards. On occasion, they can even offer some protection to individuals and groups who are threatened or disadvantaged. The rising level of professional proficiency in NGO outputs over the years produces voices that cannot be shut down with easy gestures from authority. Their skills and scope of concern mean that human rights NGOs, taken together, contribute to long-term creation and application of standards whether or not there is well-defined popular demand behind them. NGOs clearly fall short of representing all of the peoples of the world.

They do provide a voice from people who want a voice for all people. This activity is consistent with democratisation and liberalisation as well as some social movement of the civic society. Some governments and some other social organisations still make serious efforts to still the NGOs voice. They do so at the national level with secrecy, repression and hostility. At the local level, some nationalistic, religious or ethnic groups promote violations of human rights and resent NGOs that call attention to their deeds. NGOs promoting the rights of women become a particular target at this level. At the international level, opponents use among other things procedural maneuver and definitions, e.g., group rights, to deflect NGOs activity. Whatever the vagaries and opposition, the NGOs voice will endure. It has gained wide acceptance as a moral and ethical influence. New organisations are forming where they had earlier never been seen or permitted.

## REFERENCES

Cohen, J. and Arato, A. (1992) *Civil Society and Political Theory,* Cambridge MA: MIT Press.

Ehrenberg, J. (1999) *Civil Society: The Critical History of an Idea,* New York: New York University Press.

Ferguson, A. (1767) *An Essay on the History of Civil Society,* Cambridge: Cambridge University Press.

Gramsci, A. (1971) *Selections from Prison Notebooks,* edited and translated by Q. Hoare and G. Nowell Smith, London: Lawrence and Wishart.

Keene, J. (1998) *Civil Society: Old Images, New Visions,* Stanford: Stanford University Press.

Marx, K. and Engels, F. (1973) *Selected Works,* vol. 1, Moscow: Progress Publishers.

Putnam, R. (2000) *Bowling Alone: The Collapse and Revival of American Community,* New York: Simon and Schuster.

Taylor, C. (1975) Hegel, Cambridge: Cambridge University Press.

Walzer, M. (ed.) (1994) *Toward A Global Civil Society,* Providence RI: Berghahn Books.

# 7

# Civil Society and Political Change

The systematic study of concrete political phenomena, influencing and influenced by the rest of the social structure and cultures, very old. It is legitimate to regard aristotle's politics and a work of political sociology. Montesquieu, Forguson and Tocqueville were all engaged in what today wouldbe called political sociology.

Concepts of civil society in eighteenth-and nineteenth-century Europe emerged in the context of the development of the commercial sphere and the modern state. Conceived essentially, but not exclusively, as a sphere of market relations, civil society was viewed by Scottish Enlightenment thinkers and Hegel as a positive development, which nevertheless posed a problem for social order that had to be overcome by appealing to the moral sentiments of society or state guidance and arbitration. Later, Marx viewed civil society as an arena of alienation and exploitation that had to be overcome through revolution.

Tocqueville, in contrast, viewed civil society as a positive force in sustaining democracy in a condition of social equality and a weak central government. The idea of civil society has travelled far from its origins in Western philosophy, to the United States, Latin America, southern, central, and Eastern Europe, Africa, and Asia. Until the early 1980s, debates on civil society were largely confined to the history of ideas in Western political philosophy. With the third wave of democratisation, however, especially the dissolution of the USSR and the emergence of the public sphere as legitimate in the post-Soviet central and eastern European states (Poland, Czechoslovakia, Hungary), discussion of the proper relationship between the individual, society, state, and market came to the force, sparking widespread debate over the meaning of civil society and its place in politics. Civil society has entered the discourse of policymakers, scholars, journalists, NGOs, and laypersons in much of the world. Along with this global spread of civil society, certain scholars envisage the emergence of an international civil society (Keck and Sikkink 1998; Smith, Chatfield, and Pagnucco 1997).

They say that the global spread of civil society is not just talk. According to John Keane (1998: 33), it is a sign of "the end of a long century of political thinking dominated by statist ideologies" and the move of civil society, reborn on a grand scale, "to occupy the centre-ground of contemporary political thought" Yet controversy surrounds the meaning of civil society and the universality of the concept. The argument against universality is rooted in the Western origin of the idea and its perceived incompatibility with different traditions or substantially different circumstances in other parts of the world. The cultural relativist argument, which has been quite pronounced in Asia, assumes a single Western conception, which has remained unchanged. But, as we shall see, the meaning of the term has varied over time and the framing of civil society has depended on intellectual tradition and social reality. At present, there are several understandings of civil society. And the place of civil society in the structure of domination and its role in politics, including political change, are not settled issues. In the 1980s, for example, the "anti-politics" notion governed the visions of civil society leaders in central and Eastern Europe and Latin American (Arato 2000: Baket 2002). Emphasizing society itself as the arena of politics and change, the antipolitics conception did not envisage directly affecting the state, its politics, and policies. The primary purpose of the "society-first" conception was to liberate society from the totalitarian "lie" of the state and to promote "self-management" in a situation of truth. By the 1990s, however, this conception had given way to an instrumental notion in which the focus of civil societies in central and Eastern Europe shifted to their power to limit and influence their respective states, politics, and policies, or to capture stae power.

This chapter explicates two contemporary formulations of civil society and develops a framework in which to investigate the relationship between civil society and political change—especially in the direction of open, accountable, and participatory politics. Specially, I want to address four questions: What is civil society? How is it defined for this study? Is there a causal connection between civil society and democracy? And what is the role of civil society in promoting political change in a democratic direction?

## Civil Society: Contemporary Frames

The history of the idea of civil society and its formulation in the different streams of Western political thought over the past two millennia—classical liberalism, liberal-egalitarianism, critical theory, pluralism, Marxism, and democracy, for example—and in the religious traditions of the West and East, including Christianity, Islam, Buddhism, and Confucianism, have been the subject of a number of books (see e.g., Cohen and Arao 1992; Seligman 1982; Gellner 1994; Keane 1998; Ehrenberg 1999; Kaviraj and Khilnani 2001; Post and Rosenblum 2002; and Chambers and Kymlica 2002). A detailed historical account of the concept's evolution is beyond the scope of this chapter. Here I simply want to develop in broad terms and understanding of how the concept has evolved and to outline the key features of the two predominant contemporary frameworks of civil society.

Early European articulations contrasted civil (or good) society with society in a state of nature or with despotic government. There was no attempt to distinguish civil society from the community and political society at large. With the development of the commercial state in eighteenth-century Europe, civil society, conceived essentially as a market-organised sphere of production and competition, came to be viewed as a distinct, legally protected public realm, separate from family and state. Modern accounts of civil society usually trace the term to Adam Ferguson, a leading thinker of the Scottish Enlightenment. Ferguson viewed commerce and trade and more generally the development of the "commercial state" as ending the corrupt feudal system and reinforcing liberty and personal security (Varty 1997). But he was also concerned about the divisive and disintegrative effects of a market constituted civil society for social order. The specialisation and division of labour, the consequent separation of the commercial from the political arts, and the "avarice and vanity" of the commercial elite were perceived by him as undermining the communal bonds and public virtues (magnanimity, courage, love of mankind) on which democratic government tested (Ferguson [1767] 1995). The market had to be reined in, but not by the state. Asserting that political control would do more harm than good, Ferguson made the case for a self-regulating market that is free of state interference. His solution to the negative consequences of the "separation of the arts and professions" appealed to the moral sentiments of society.

Despite his articulation of the ideas of civil society,

Ferguson did not distinguish between civil society and the polity. He believed that "society cannot be detached from its form of government, nor can economic man be torn, in practice or abstraction, from the politician man" Oz-Salzberger 1995: xix). The German conception of civil society, which drew its inspiration from Ferguson and Adam Smith did, however, make a firm distinction between the civil society, the family, and the state. Asserting that civil society is a product of the modern state and that its development presupposes a state, Hegel conceptualised civil society as a sphere of market relations, regulated by civil law, intervening between the family and the state (Hegel [1821] 1991: 220; Ehrenberg 1999: 121-32; Ioannidou 1997: 49—62). The acquisitive urge of the burgher class and the ensuing competitive interplay of private interests that breeds poverty and inequality led Hegel to view civil society as prone to periodic instability and conflict, despite its tendency toward a natural equilibrium. To ensure "civility" and stability, he concluded, the state—which in his view was the only entity capable of representing the unity of society and furthering the freedom of citizens—had to order civil society. Hence state intervention to guide and govern civil society was legitimate. Since the time of Ferguson and Hegel, formulations of civil society, irrespective of their political philosophy, have shared a common root. They arose in the context of changing theories of power, legitimacy, and sovereignty, stimulated by the ascendance of centralising monarchies, their succession by nation-states, the development of self-regulating markets as a separate realm, and the emergence of movements for political freedom. "No longer understood as part of a universal commonwealth," civil society came to mean "private property, individual interests, political democracy, the rule of law, and an economic order devoted to prosperity".

Two contemporary formulations of civil society—that of the New Left and that of the neo-Tocquevillean, or liberal-democracy, model—are relevant to this study. Although they differ in diagnosis, purpose, and strategy, both the New Left and the liberal-democracy school share a positive take on civil society. The New Left conception is rooted in the Gramscian formulation of civil society, which departs significantly from that of Marx. Othodox Marxists view civil society, constituted by production, class, and their attendant social and political relations, as a structural problem to be overcome through revolution. Marx, in contrast to Hegel, viewed the state as a superficial structure in the service of the dominant capitalist class and depicted civil society as conterminous with the socioeconomic base of the state (Bratton 1994: 54-55). For Marx, therefore, civil society was a problem that had to be overcome, not by the state, which was its captive, but through a revolution that would put the proletariat in the driver's seat. With the workers' party in power, civil society would dissolve into the state, which would represent the true public good. Marx's depiction of civil society as an arena of alienation and exploitation that had to be abolished deprived it of analytic value in orthodox Marxism (Baker 2002: 5).

Committed to the same goal, and using Marxist categories, Antonio Gramsci arrived at a conception of civil society that differed significantly from that of Marx, Viewing civil society as not coterminous with the socioeconomic base of the state, he located it in the political superstructure. Differentiating state and civil society, Gramsci stressed the crucial role of the cultural and ideological support provided by civil society for the survival of European capitalism (Ehrenberg 1999: 208-11). The hegemony of capitalism, according to Gramsci, rested not only on material and coercive foundations but also one a measure of "consent, cooperation, and collaboration" that issued from cultural and ideological support. He therefore urged Western Marxists to pay serious attention to the cultural and ideological institutions that supported capitalism. Advocating a protracted war of position, rather than a simple revolution, as in peasant Russia, he depicted civil society as providing many sites to undermine existing values and inculcate new ones in the counter hegemonic struggle against capitalism. Gramsci's conception of civil society includes all social institutions that are on-production-related, nongovernmental, and non-familial, ranging from recreational groups to trade unions, churches, and political parties.

The voluntarism and political agency accorded to civil society in gramsci's account inform much contemporary thinking of the New Left on civil society (Baker 2002:7). Robert Cox (1999), for example, posits civil society as a surrogate for revolution—a key terrain of strategic action to construct "an alternate social and world order." Depicting globalization of production and neoliberal economic orthodoxy as benefiting the integrated class and encouraging "exclusionary and covert politics," he views civil society as the "crucial battleground" for citizens to regain control of public life and as a potential agent for transformation of the state. Others, like jurgen Habermas (1984; 1996), with due recognition of the pluralism that pervades modern society, view civil society a necessary to defend democracy against the threat posed by modern state bureaucracy, which seeks to encompass more and more of social life. Rather than posing a problem as in earlier Marxist accounts, civil society is now viewed as providing a solution. The self-reflexivity of society and the institutions of civil society are seen as vital to protect autonomous public opinion and the integrity of the public sphere, two pillars of democracy. Making a clear distinction among civil society, the state, and the economy, the new Left sees civil society as an important site for counter hegemonic struggle and assigns it a key role in defending society against the state and market and in formulating democratic will to influence the state.

Gramscian analysis and strategy have also been appropriated by advocates of the neo-Tocquevillean conception of civil society, the origins of which can be traced to the response to centralising monarchs and a powerful state in early-eighteenth-century France. Civil society as conceived in that context emphasized intermediate organisations and notions of community. Seeking to protect the privileged position of the French aristocratic class from royal absolutism, and admiring the balanced constitutional structure of Britain that preserved the interests of the commons, the lords, and the king, Montesquieu advanced an elitist notion of civil society (Ehrenberg 1999: 144-49). Inasmuch as the power and property of the aristocratic class was independent of "the will of the king and the passion of the crowd," he argued, it was "the only estate that could mediate between them" (145). The mediating role of such intermediary organisations, however, rested on certain norms and the existence of laws that would guarantee the integrity of civil society. Montesquieu located "intermediate bodies in the heart of republican theories of civil society." His contribution, together with the notion of community advanced by Rousseau and the defense of custom, tradition, and local power by Burke culminated in Tocqueville's emphasis on political and civil associations as key pillars of democracy in the United States.

Based on his observations of French history and American democracy—and contrasting the centralized French state with decentralised administration in the United States and the "vibrant culture of local activity' in New England—Tocqueville (bk. 1, chap. 12; bk. 2, chaps. 5-7), who does not use the term *civil society*, crafted his conception of associations and performing several key functions: meeting unmet social needs in the context of a weak central government; intermediating between personal or local interest and the national common good; preventing the tyranny of the majority (a major concern of Tocqueville's in light of despotic excesses in France); limiting state power; and preventing abuse by the state. His "civil society," operating in conditions of socioeconomic equality and political freedom, is composed of voluntary associations that cooperate for collective purposes. The interplay of the interests of these associations would guard against domination by a single interest and check the tyranny of the majority and other excesses of democracy. Tocqueville's conception of civil society is based on a limited state that would confine itself to the political sphere and guarantee the legal framework and other conditions (such as socioeconomic equality) necessary for the effective functioning of civil society. It was less state-centred and less certain of the relationship between the state and civil society. In fact, he viewed the associations in New England as compensating for the deficiencies of a weak central government. Several observers have noted that Tocqueville's assumption about American equality did not take account of the substantial economic and racial inequalities in American society. Thus he was effectively blinded to the negative effects on civil society of the inequalities that pervade capitalist societies (Foley and Edwards 1997).

The intermediation and limitation of state power functions that Tocqueville assigned to associations also inform the neo-Tocquevillean formulation of civil society. But whereas Tocqueville was equivocal about a generalised connection between associations and democracy, contemporary scholars posit a logical link between civil society and democracy. One important stream holds that participation in associations produces social capital that is vital to healthy democracy (Putnam 1993; 1996). In this views, a strong civil society is a prerequisite for effective democracy. The democratic transition literature assigns civil society an important role in the prelude to the transition, although not in the transition itself (Arato 2000). And the democracy-consolidation literature posits the institutionalization of civil society as a key conditions for the consolidation of democracy, making it the only game in town. Democracy advocates also view civil society, in a Gramscian fashion, as a site for the development of democratic culture, with the goal of democratising the remaining authoritarian regimes.

The liberal-democratic school and, to a lesser degree, the New Left conceive of civil society and its institutions in instrumental terms vis-à-vis the state (protecting the public sphere from the instructive state, influencing state policy, or altering the regime type) and not as a distinct site for governance and reform that is independent of the state. Consequently, they do not capture the 'society-first" formulation that dominated the thinking of Polish and Czech civil society leaders in the 1970s, which emphasised "self-organisation," "self-management," and "self-limitation." That conception envisaged a hybrid political system that would limit but not overthrow party-state control (Arato 2000; Baker 2002). The idea was to liberate society from the all-pervasive totalitarian ideology of the party-state, recover social autonomy, expand civil liberties and human rights, and create democratic space (in education, culture, media, and the like) outside the party-state. Although these actions would indirectly challenge the legitimacy of the party and the state, the primary purpose was not to change the party-state or to capture state power. The locus of action was society itself. This notion of civil society as a democratic end in itself was eclipsed in the early 1980s by a more instrumental view that merged with the neo-Tocquevillean notion of civil society. The "ethical society" notion that informed the central and eastern European formulation and the two predominant frameworks discussed here have all been stimulated by a system of needs and outcomes of a process of historical transformation. The ideas were developed and deployed in the context of specific social realities to produce, justify, legitimise, or resist a certain distribution of power, to appropriate certain privileges ad roles, or as a strategy for action. This is not to argue for cultural relativism, or to deny the possibility of comparative study, but to point out that the framing of civil society must relative to concrete realities.

## Defining Civil Society for the Study

In light of its multiple meanings, ad mindful of the need to problematise civil society and its connection to democracy, this study adopts a definition that posits civil society as, first, a realm in the interstices of the state, political society, the market, and the society at large for organisation by nonstate, nonmarket groups that take collective action in the pursuit of the public good; second, a distinct sphere for discourse and construction of normative ideals through interaction among non-state groups on the basis of ideas and arguments; third, an autonomous arena of self-governance by non-state actors in certain issue areas; and, fourth, an instrument for collective action to protect the autonomy of the non-state public realm, affect regime type, and influence the politics and policies of the state, political society, and the market. Although distinct, the four aspects are interrelated and affect one another. The political discourses among the self-organised, self-governing, non-state, non-profit, non-private organisations and the collective actions they take deploying civil means, for example, affect the autonomy of civil society and the prospects for governance that is independent of the state. They also influence society's relations with the state, political society, and the market, and the rules of the games in these arenas. The study does not view civil society intrinsically as a virtue, solution, or problem, but focuses on the discourses, values, and interactions of civil society organisations that are oriented directly or indirectly toward influencing the distinctiveness of the realm of civil society itself, as well as the rules of the political game, in the direction of open participatory, accountable politics, Several features of the definition—recognition of civil society as a distinct sphere;

the depiction of civil society as a space and a site of action; conferment of agency; membership and means of civil society; and the relationship of civil society to the state, political society, and the market—require elaboration.

### *Civil Society as a Distinct Sphere*

It is crucial to view civil society as an arena of governance in its own right, not just an adjunct or means to influence the state, political society, or the market. The notion of civil society as an end in itself is relevant not only to totalitarian and authoritarian states but also to liberal-democratic states. In totalitarian and authoritarian states, this formulation captures the effort of nonstate groups to carve out areas of governance outside the control of the all-embracing party-state without seeking to alter the regime type. As a strategy, the self-organisation and self-limiting approach may be less threatening and thus have a better chance of success. Contraction or expansion of the realm of civil society as an arena of self-governance is indicative of the depth and scope of political liberalisation in authoritarian states. In liberal-democratic states the state, in theory, is limited to providing order and security, establishing a system of rights, and enacting broad constitutive and regulatory rules within which nonstate institutions and the market organise much of the social and economic interaction of society. Civil society institutions are the normal means for sustaining governance over a wide range of issues. Viewed in these terms, the scope and vitality of governance in civil society are useful indicators of the emancipation of society from state domination, decentralisation, and democratisation of governance. They can also be a useful measure of democratisation and the consolidation of democracy in societies undergoing political transition.

### *Civil Society: Space, Site, and Agency*

Thus far, I have referred to civil society at various

points as a space, a site, and an actor. It is all three. Conception as *space* indicates the location of civil society in relation to other spheres and preserves the integrity of the public realm by not tying it to specific actors who may move in and out of this space, which may contract or expand in terms of sectors, issues, actors and roles. The space conception also permits the construction of civil society as a *site* for governance and strategic action. It is useful here to recall Gramsci's notion that civil society, as the cultural and ideological repository of hegemony, can be the battlefield in a war of position against capitalism. Civil society in his conception becomes the site for the construction of a counter hegemonic narrative. Neoliberals have also appropriated the notion of civil society as a site for struggle in their endeavour to subvert and eventually replace the remaining communist and authoritarian regimes. Civil society has been used, as well, to denote *agency,* although it should not be treated as a single collective actor. Like the society at large, civil society is a realm of power, inequality, struggle, and conflict among competing interests. It is populated by diverse formal and informal groups organisations, and although these may choose to cooperate on certain issues or reach accommodation of their conflicting interests, there is no necessary consensus among them. Civil society is invariably competitive and heterogeneous. Agency applied to organisations that populate the civil society space, not to civil society as a single entity. The tendency to use civil society in a shorthand fashion may mask the diversity, inequality, and struggle within the realm. Analytically, it is more useful to speak in terms of specific actors or groups of actors in civil society. This raises the question of membership in civil society: Which organisations qualify and on what basis?

### *Membership and Means*

The preceding elaboration cited certain characteristics

of units that populate the realm of civil society: self-organised, self-governing, nonstate, nonprofit, nonprivate institutions that employ nonviolent means to achieve a public interest of good through collective action. With the exception of nonviolent means, these features are not controversial, although in certain cases, it may be difficult to determine whether an organisation is indeed self-organised, self-governing, and pursuing a public good, and whether it is penetrated and exploited by the state, political society, or the market. It should be noted that the public good in the definition refers to the nonprofit and nonprivate interest of particular groups, not that of the entire community.

Two controversies—one omitted from the definition (voluntary associations with nonexclusionary membership) and the other spelled out in the definition (civil means)—attend the membership question. First: Should membership in civil society be restricted to voluntary associations of individuals? Or should it include ascriptive and other groups that limit membership on the basis of ethnicity, religion, or class? The neo-Tocquevillean conception identifies civil society with voluntary associations, in which membership is by consent and open to entry and exit by all qualified citizens without loss of status or benefits. Individuals can move freely among groups, shift involvement in them, and join more than none association. The emphasis is on the individual's autonomy to choose. Associations in this conception (organised around professional and other interests, social causes, or the pursuit of status and power) represent limited and specific purpose or interest; they do not pursue totalizing goals, which, if realised, would deprive other groups of public rights and benefits. A plural and fluid civil society that permits shifting and cross cutting identities (making possible escape from hereditary and ascriptive attachments) and operates within an agreed political and legal framework is frequently associated with the functions of intermediation and limitation of state power.

Limitation of civil society to voluntary associations, however, excludes other groups (based on religion, heredity, ethnicity, class, and other such features) that are not open to all citizens—groups in which membership is by assent, rather than consent, and exist is not a real option. Because such groups do exist in the public realm, their exclusion by definitional fiat would truncate our understanding of the composition and dynamics of civil society. Inclusion of such groups highlights the complex nature of civil society and the struggles and tensions that pervade it, reminding the observer that civil society comprises heterogeneous groups with diverse and competing goals. Civil society groups are not always supportive of democracy, as is sometimes assumed by proponents of democracy. Limiting civil society to prodemocracy voluntary associations also creates a circularity problem in exploring the connection between civil society and democracy. Furthermore, recognition of the potential for struggle in civil society accommodates the New Left conception of civil society as an arena for the construction of a counter hegemonic narrative. It also provides insights into the perception and reaction of governments, especially authoritarian ones, to demands from civil society groups. As observed by Robert Post and Nancy Roenblum, civil society is, in fact, a continuum of fluid and segmented organisations. But they assert that "segmentation within civil society must have limits" and add that the "freedom that produces pluralist associations should be prized and enforced." The society must afford autonomy to individuals and groups, but the balance should favour the individual's freedom to associate. When this right is curtailed, civil society fragments into rigid groups. In their view, the persistence of civil society "depends upon a complex equilibrium among diverse groups and associations."

We come now to the second controversial issue: What makes civil society civil? Many analysts advance two criteria:

the absence of violence and the absence of the will to dominate the entire public realm. In the abstract, civil society is a public realm guaranteed by civil laws of the state, which has a monopoly on the legitimate use of violence. In this context, society is pacified, and violence is excluded as a legitimate means for the pursuit of particularistic interests by organisations functioning in a stage-protected realm. In practice, however, many states are not internally pacified. A weak state may not be able to guarantee law, order, and security to all its citizens. Both strong and weak states may unleash state violence against certain segments of the population. In such situations, groups, especially certain ascriptive ones, may have to resort to their own private agencies to ensure the security of members. Such use of violence may be legitimate if deployed for purposes of protection. Intimidation and terrorization of other groups cannot, however, be legitimate tactics to advance a public interest. Groups that avowedly resort to violence to achieve political goals, like the various liberation movements, cannot be part of civil society. This does not imply that their goals and methods are necessarily illegitimate. But such organisations operate more in the realm of political society. There will certainly be gray areas. The military wing of an organisation may rely on violence, for example, while the social wing operates in civil society deploying nonviolent means. This issue illustrates the difficulty of applying the civil society concept to weak and contested states—supporting the claim that civil society (as a legally protected realm) is difficult to conceive of without a sufficiently strong state structure. This problem was not absent in strong states like Nazi Germany and Fascist Italy, however, where state violence against a certain segment of society was deemed legitimate by key segments of civil society. Violence is antithetical to civil society, but civil society is also the container of such violence. The control of violence is a major problem for civil society and the state.

Similarly, the will to dominate is not a clear-cut issue. In principle, a will to dominate that denies other citizens their public status and rights, especially the right to associate, is incompatible with civil society. As observed earlier, however, the exclusion of such organisations distorts analysis by obscuring important dynamics of civil society. Groups espousing totalising missions may not pose a problem if they have little hope of realising their objectives and the balance clearly favours groups pursuing limited objectives. But this may not always be the case. Overall, the analytical benefits of inclusion would appear to outweigh the benefits of exclusion. In this study, civil society comprises formal and informal voluntary and ascriptive organisations including churches, labour unions, farmers' organisations, academic and student groups, debating societies and reading groups, nonstate media, NGOs, occupational associations, business federations, and sports and leisure groups. Social movements "based on underlying social networks and resonant collective action frames," and that engage in contentious politics when the "political opportunity structure" opens up, are also part of civil society. New social movements that seek radical, policy reform in specified areas are part of civil society as well. Transnational and global organisations and movements, as well as diaspora and exiled communities, that significantly influence the composition and dynamics of civil society in a country should also be taken into account.[2] Although the composition of civil society is necessarily broad, it can be narrowed to focus on the key groups and actors that are relevant to the purpose at hand.

### *Relationship to Other Spheres*

Although conceptually distinct, civil society in practice is not fully independent of the other spheres. There is considerable overlap among them, with numerous avenues for interpenetration and mutual influence. Just as civil society organisations may influence the distribution of power, norms, and policies of institutions in the other realms, the structure of civil society and the purposes and interaction of its constituent units are shaped by many elements: the normative and material structures of the society at large; the divisions, inequality, and struggles that characterize society (although civil society need not mirror society at large); the structure, vitality, and policies of state institutions; the vibrancy of political society; and the distribution of intellectual and material resources, which in good part relate to the structure and function of the economy. The scope, representativeness, and effectives of institutions in these spheres determine the potential for expansion or contraction of the realm of civil society, its population density, the formal or informal nature of its organisations, whether they seek to engage, constrain, alter, overthrow, or retreat from the state and the market, the resources available to such organisations, and their methods of operation.

Especially critical is the relationship to the state. Civil society cannot exist in a condition of total anarchy—that is, where government is unable to maintain civil order, define personal and group rights, and enforce them (Post and Rosenblum 2002: 7) With political authority, a monopoly on legitimate violence, a stable legal framework, and representing the common good, the ideal Weberian state provides internal law and order, ensures external security, and establishes the rights and entitlements of individuals and groups. It creates the political, legal, bureaucratic, and tax framework within which civil society organisations can pursue their particularistic interests in a civil or nonviolent manner. The scope, purposes, and roles of civil society organisations are all closely connected to the type of regime. The space for civil society is greatest in a liberal-democratic system and least in totalitarian, authoritarian, and paternalistic regimes. In theory, such regimes severely restrict or even eliminate the space for civil society. They also seek to control, manipulate, and deploy civil society organisations to serve the interests of those in power. In practice, totalitarian and authoritarian governments have not always been successful in controlling and manipulating civil society organisations and have proved even less successful in eliminating them. But in contrast to democratic states, where civil society is a legally protected realm, in totalitarian and authoritarian states certain (non-state-sponsored) civil society organisations exist in fear of the state and often go underground. Control and manipulation are not absent in democratic states, however, and the space for civil society and the functions of civil society organisations may vary from one democratic state to the next.

The relationship of civil society to the state is often depicted as confrontational and zero-sum. This may be the case in certain situations. But in most cases the state and civil society are mutually dependent for survival. As noted earlier, civil society requires governance to survive and governments, at least democratic ones, draw their strength from civil society (Post and Rosenblum 2002). The relationship of civil society to the state can take many forms: co-operation and manipulation of civil society by the state, deep penetration and influence over the state by certain civil society actors, productive tension between the two in a context of overall agreement on the political and economic framework, contestation over certain fundamental issues, alienation and isolation of civil society organisations from the state, or outright rejection of the state by key segments of civil society. Although interconnected, civil society groups must be distinct from the state if they are to influence governance, and the state must have autonomy to protect the rights of all its citizens. This arrangement has been referred to as the principle of double autonomy.

Another important sphere is the continuum between

private life and the state is political society. Popularised by Alfred Stepan (1988: 3-4), the concept of political society denotes, at least in democratic states, the realm of formal competition for the acquisition and exercise of state power. Political parties, the primary actors in this realm, seek to mobilise public support and to constitute winning coalitions in the formal competition and management of state power through elections and the constitution of legislatures. Civil society is distinct from political society. While they seek to influence the rules of the game and affect policies, civil society organisations do not organise themselves on a partisan as is to aggregate interests formally compete for state office. In practice, however, the relationship between civil and political society is often blurred. Many civil society organisations—trade unions, churches, the media and certain interest groups—affiliate with certain political parties on ideological or ascriptive grounds. They may also wield state power through the political party in office. In the process, they become partners in governance, compromising the distinctiveness and autonomous quality of civil society Blurring also occurs when the actors and activities of political society are banned or co-opted in totalitarian and authoritarian regimes—dissidents may take refuge in civil society to survive, to construct counternarratives, and to develop networks that can be deployed when the 'political opportunity structure" opens up. The distinction between civil society and political society and their merging in practice are useful indicators of the existence of civil society evening the most authoritarian and totalitarian states in a defensive or underground form (Bratton 1994). Such differentiation is also useful during moments of political transition when proto-party elites exist civil society to form political parties and compete for state office. Civil society then reverts to its conventional state.

To conceptualise civil society without reference to economic society—especially the market—is to miss crucial insights into civil society and its operation. As observed in the previous section, eighteenth-century conceptions of civil society in Europe were rooted in the recognition of the market as a distinct public realm and the competition arising from growing specialisation and division of labour as a problem for social order. Subsequently, Marx linked civil society to a particular state in the development of capitalism. Today, some New Left intellectuals posit civil society as a defense against the encroachment of the state and the market and the threat of global capitalism. By assuming socio-economic equality or defining civil society as a nonprofit sector, the Tocquevillean and neoliberal formulations decouple civil society from the economic sphere such that the "material bases of civil society and the negative effects of the market on civil society are erased from view" (Howell and Pearce 2001: 76). The structural inequality of markets has consequences for political and civil societies. It makes it difficult to rid the public sphere of relations of power and inequality. Functioning in a nonstate, nonprofit sphere, civil society organisations, to protect their autonomy, should in theory have independent sources or revenue. But unlike the state, which relies on tax revenues, and the market, which accumulates wealth through capital accumulation, civil society can meet only a portion of its financial requirements from service fees, subscriptions, and donations. A substantial part comes from state contributions, private giving, and international aid (Salamon and Anheir quoted in Howell and Pearce 2001: 79-80). These contributions empower certain groups more than others, shape their agendas, affect the structural and discourse dynamics of civil society, and influence the demands placed on the state. Furthermore, the growing dominance of the mass media—newspapers, journals, and especially radio and TV stations, often owned privately or by the state—subverts the public communication that is central to the formation of democratic will. Without an independent financial base and access to media, the autonomy of civil society is undermined. The key point is this: Although civil society is conceptually distinct, in practice it is not completely autonomous. Its structure and function are heavily influenced by its material base and its relations with the state and market. Civil society's boundary, especially in relation to the state and political society, is porous, at times highly contested and subject to redefinition through struggle. Actors may inhabit more than one space, act simultaneously in multiple arenas, or move in and out of arenas.

## Civil Society in New Democracies

All civil societies are not equal. Some are more developed than others. Before discussing its role in governance and political change, we need to have a good understanding of how civil society operates in a particular country. This section sketches in broad terms the likely contours of civil society in a new democracy. Although civil society organisations may be in the forefront in ousting authoritarian or communist regimes, they are likely to be weak in the postouster phase (Whitehead 1997: 109-10). Usually, civil society organisations are dominated by a small elite, many of whom had privileged standing in the previous regime. They are likely to be few in number and not well organised. The norms associated with civil society—autonomy, deliberation, collective action, civility—will be underdeveloped. Moreover, the new government, often cobbled together from diverse groups, confronts many challenges, including drafting a new constitution and legal system. It may not be able to protect the rights of individuals and groups and establish laws to secure and regulate the public realm. Political and economic equality and rule of law, key conditions for a civil society, may exist only in aspiration. And civil society may be unevenly developed across the geographic and social terrains. Thus, while collective action by a coalition of diverse forces may bring about the ouster of an authoritarian or communist government, civil society often fragments in the aftermath of the political revolution. Some personalities and organisations move on to occupy the vacant state and political society; others simply lose their rationale and disappear from the scene. But in their place, new organisations may mushroom, mostly in the urban areas.

Thus, with few exceptions, civil society is unlikely to be well developed and institutionalised in new democracies. The weakness of civil society may be exacerbated if the incumbent political system or government lacks legitimacy, the nation-state as constructed is contested, and the government is unable to maintain law and order and lacks the capacity to address socio-economic problems. An overbearing state and the market may also limit the space for civil society and distort its organisation and agenda. The legacy of the authoritarian regime, especially its old actors in new garb, as well as criminal organisations, liberation movements, and the like, may also compete with civil society organisations for the public realm. The democracy-promoting effect of civil society organisations may be limited; some may be antidemocratic. Although this sketch may appear pessimistic, it is essential to recognise such possibilities. Civil society must be defined and analyzed in the context of a country's prevailing circumstances.

Two sets of issues are important in understanding how civil society operates in a country. First is the size and quality of the realm of civil society. Can citizens associate freely? Can such associations function in all issue areas? Or do certain restrictions apply? With what consequences? Is a system of rights, fundamental to the functioning of civil society, institutionalised? Investigation of these questions should yield a good measure of the size, quality, and institutionalisation of civil society in a particular country. Second: Is civil society plural and fluid with opportunities for multiple identities? Or is it segmented and polarised? Or do features of both coexist? Do civil society's actors partake in a system that is widely acknowledged as legitimate? Or is the system contested in a fundamental manner by certain groups? Do groups employ violence in the pursuit of their interests? In sum then, it is crucial to gauge the mix of organisations that constitute civil society, as well as their structural locations, purposes, and methods, if we are to understand their democratic (or antidemocratic) potential and their role in political change.

## Civil Society and Democracy

For different reasons, both neo-Tocqevillean and the New Left associate civil society with democracy. Civil society has also not only been deployed in the democratisation literature to explain political liberalisation and democratic transition but has been advanced as a precondition for democratic consolidation. Reviewing these linkages, this section makes the following claims: There is no necessary connection between civil society and democracy; civil society can have both democratic and antidemocratic effects; and the actual effect in practice hinges on the ideas, purpose, and the distribution of power among the organisations that make up civil society, the strategic connections between organisations and leaders in civil society with their counterparts in political society and the state, and the international context.

### *The Neo-Tocquevillean Connection*

Among the early theorists of civil society, Tocqueville made an explicit connection between civil society and democracy, Convinced that the profusion of voluntary public associations underpinned America's robust democracy (by protecting individual liberty, preventing tyranny of the majority, decentralising power and authority, and fostering active engagement of citizens in politics and governance), he posited civil society as an indispensable component of a stable democracy (Whitehead 1997: 98-99). Today, a remarkable consensus has emerged among democratic theorists around Tocqueville's proposition that "the virtues and viability of a democracy depend on the robustness of its associational life" (Warren 2001: 3).

There is, however, an important difference between the connection made by Tocqueville and that of the neo-Tocquevilleans. Tocqueville himself regarded civil society as a key site for governance and decentralisation of democratic governance. For neo-Tocquevilleans, the locus of activity is not society but the state. Their primary concerns relate to the core democratic institutions and processes at the state level. Civil society is viewed as a supporting structure to democratise the state. Associational life is thought to provide the social infrastructure for liberal democracy, supply the means to limit, resist, and curb the excesses of the state and market, present alternatives when they fail, facilitate service delivery at the local level, assist in conflict management, deepen democracy (by cultivating civic virtues, establishing democratic norms, and spreading democracy to more domains of life), offer a voice to disadvantaged groups, and promote economic development. Armed with such beliefs, scholars have tried to explain the degree of robustness of democracies in Western industrialised states, connect civil society to democratic change in the developing world, and prescribe policy for national governments, international donors, and multilateral lending agencies.

An important stream of contemporary thought has focused on the critical role of small face-to-face voluntary associations in promoting civic engagement, and the role of such engagement in producing social capital. Robert Putnam (1996) argues that the norms and networks of civic engagements have a powerful influence on the quality of public life, including the performance of representative government. Such networks foster the development of "generalised reciprocity and encourage the emergence of social trust," which in turn facilitate "coordination and communication, amplify reputations, and thus allow dilemmas of collective action to be resolved" (292). Dense civil networks broaden participants' self-conception, helping to transform the "I" into "we." These are crucial resources for collective action in the pursuit of the common good. The structural resources, habits, and attitudes inculcated through participation in voluntary associations promote healthy democracies. To explain this phenomenon, Putnam, relies on the concept of social capital, which he defines as "features of social organisations such as networks, norms and social trust that facilitate coordination and cooperation for mutual benefit" (292). Voluntary associations produce social capital; quality of life and representative government are better in a community with a high stock of social capital; a decline in voluntary associations leads to a reduction in social capital that erodes the vitality of democracy. Although it is based on the study of Italy and the United States, Putnam claims that his conclusion that civil society is the "key to making democracy work" is relevant to the new democracies as well. His impact on policymakers has been substantial.

The concept of social capital and its connection to democracy as articulated by Putnam has generated much debate within the intellectual community, producing critiques from several perspectives (see, e.g., Edwards, Foley, and Diani 2001; Bermeo 2000; Nord 2000; Howell and Pearce 2001). Several criticisms are relevant here. First is the issue of definition. Trust is both a precondition and an output of social networks (Newton 2001). The inclusion of functions and products as part of the definition of social capital creates a circularity problem and muddies empirical investigation. Second, social capital produced by small face-to-face organisations may be important for primary democracy (direct citizen participation) but not for democratic governance in a large, complex modern society. Institutions such as the media and education may be more important in creating the abstract trust that is necessary for the functioning of complex large-scale societies (Newton 2001). Third, Putnam takes a narrow view of democracy that focuses on performance, rather than on deepening and extending the democratic process (Howell and Pearce 2001: 48). Fourth, the benefits of civil society for democracy are uncertain. As Philip Nord (2000: xv) has observed: "Burgeoning civil society translate[s] into a democratisation of public life in certain instances but by no means always." Putnam does not consider the antidemocratic norms, values, and practices that inform civil society. If these are taken into account, civil society organisations may be a threat to democratic institutions (Whittington 2001). Voluntary associations may deepen conflict in society, create excessive demands on the government, and hasten the disintegration of democratic regimes (Bermn 2001). Thus, while social capital is an important tool for achieving a social goal, the consequence for democracy depends on the political ends for which social capital is used. Finally, to ascertain whether a robust civil society will produce beneficent or harmful consequences for democracy, it must be examined in the proper political and constitutional context and be related to the capacity of political institutions. A healthy democracy depends not only on a vigorous civil society but also on effective political institutions—a point made by Samuel Huntington decades ago (Berman 2001).

Thus the claim that associational life builds civic virtues (reciprocity, trust, recognition), which in turn underwrite democracy, should be qualified in two respects. First, democracy may build on civic virtues, but such virtues are not uniquely democratic. They may underwrite other forms of government (Nazism in Germany, Fascism in Italy, apartheid in South Africa) as well. Much depends on the political and constitutional context and the political ends for which the social capital is deployed. Second, the democratic process may itself erode the civic virtues that are supposed to underwrite democracy, which "is a way of dealing with conflict in the face of pressures for collective action" (Warren 2001: 150). Reciprocity and trust may be fractured by strategic political maneuverings, while democratic politics may sharpen differences of identity. Nevertheless, a background of cooperation may very well lead to empathetic connections that make deliberation more likely. Bargaining and compromise less threatening, and democracy easier. But democratic potential depends on associational types, their purposes, and political circumstances, issues that we shall take up later. Next, we explore the second take on the connection between civil society and democracy.

### *The New Left and Society-First Perspective*

The New Left shares certain aspects of the neo-Tocquevillean perspective: for example, it emphasises the recovery of civil society in order to defend society against the intrusive state and the threat from the capitalist market. Moreover, civil society is assigned a key role in democratising the state and influencing its politics and policies. Yet there are major differences. Political participation and communicative action, not the production of social capital and its connection to democracy, are the key themes of certain New Left scholars, such as Jurgen Habermas (1984), and Jean Cohen and Andrew Arato (1992). Acknowledging the pluralism in modern society, these scholars focus on the formulation of public will to influence the politics and polities of the liberal-democratic state. Other scholars, such as Robert Cox (1999), view civil society as a site for struggle and construction of a counternarrative for an alternative version of democracy that will cater to the needs of the excluded classes. It is unclear what this form might be. Neither of these perspectives, however, conceives of civil society as a democratic end itself. The society-first approach, in contrast, projects a vision of democracy with multiple sites, of which civil society is an important arena of governance. This notion suggests a more complex connection between civil society and democracy. In addition to the function of civil society in affecting democratic institutions and governance at the level of the state, it draws attention to democratic governance in other sites and the decentralisation of power, resources, and authority to local and nonstate institutions in order to promote self-governance and liberate society from domination by the political centre (Howell and Pearce 2001: 54-55). Although it developed in the context of Communist regimes in central and eastern Europe and has since lost some of its early luster, the society-first perspective alerts us to a much neglected aspect of the link between civil society and democracy.

### *The Democratisation Literature*

Although observers and participants celebrate the role of civil society in the political changes that swept central and eastern Europe and Asia, this is less the case in the democratisation literature, which focuses heavily on Latin America and elites. Little attention is paid to civil society's origins, it composition, or its democracy-producing effects. Viewed as a given, civil society is conceived of primarily in instrumental terms for bringing about change in the state, not as a distinct area of democratic governance. In fact, such an idea is considered dangerous for democratic politics, because it creates a "parallel to state power" (Stepan 1997). The basic premise of the democratisation theorists is that the locus of governance is the state, not society. In this context, civil society is viewed in one of three ways: as a positive but subordinate factor in explaining political liberalisation and democratic transition; as a negative force obstructing the development of political society and the democratic state in the postouster phase; and as a precondition for the consolidation of democracy.

"Elite dispositions, calculations, and pacts," write Guillermo O'Donnell and Philippe Schmitter (1986: 48), determine in large measure whether there is an opening and set "important parameters on the extent of possible liberalisation and democratisation." Once soft-lines prevail, they argue, opportunity opens up for general mobilization, which they call the "resurrection of civil society," This hypothesis is rooted in the belief that authoritarian and totalitarian states eliminate independent civil society organisations, that the public arena is dominated by state-controlled organisations, and that discussion in this arena conforms to codes and rules established by the state. Aside from a few highly motivated individuals, the majority of citizens, it is presumed, confine themselves to private pursuits. Once the government lowers the barriers, however, collective action mushrooms into an "explosion of civil society." The rapid changes undermine the legitimacy of the soft-liners who seek to perpetuate themselves in government and increase the cost of a coup by the hard-liners (53). The diverse layers of civil society come together in a "popular upsurge" that pushes transition even further (56). O'Donnell and schmitter argue that the popular upsurge is "always ephemeral," however, leaving behind "a persistent problem for consolidation of political democracy that can only be 'tamed' by the holding of elections." This leads to the demobilisation thesis: once the authoritarian government has been ousted, civil society loses its relevance and should make way for political society to take the lead in negotiating pacts and constituting the democratic state; civil society, which invariably fragments in the aftermath of a political revolution, must be reconstituted in the context of a new framework put in place by political society and the new democratic state (Arato 2000: 29-30, 63).

The popular top-down thesis is open to challenge for at least two reasons. First, authoritarian and totalitarian states have not been able to emasculate civil society except in a formal sense. Civil society in these regimes may operate informally under different guises or go underground. In the absence of such associations, it is difficult to account for the explosion of civil society. Indeed, the account offered by O'Donnell and Schmitter on the resurrection of civil society relies heavily on the activities and effects of such organisations. Moreover, pressure from below is necessary—as in Thailand, South Korea, and the Philippines—to create and augment differentiation among the elite and extract concessions from the government. Rather than being an all-elite affair (agency), openings for liberalisation and democratisation hinge on political an economic inequality and dissatisfaction in society at large, on the international context (structure), and on the actions of individuals and groups in dissident political society and civil society (agency). While structure cannot cause a specific occurrence, agency alone cannot succeed in the absence of propitious conditions. To be successful, moreover, synergy is required between soft-liners in government and leaders in dissident political society and civil society. This synergy often is found in the interaction of bottom-up and top-down pressures for liberalisation and democratisation. The salience of civil society for political liberalisation and democratisation increases sharply when viewed as and arena of democratic governance in its own right. Although important, concessions relating to individual civil rights do not free citizens from control and regulation by the party-state. The locus of authority and activity is still the state. Self-governance, by contrast, results in the creation of space outside the control of the party-state, shifts the locus of activity at least partially and constitutes an acknowledgement by the party-state that citizens can govern themselves and issues can be regulated without its involvement. Development of civil society as an independent realm of governance is a critical feature of political liberalisation.

Second, a sharp dichotomy in the relevance of political

society and civil society is not warranted. Juan Linz and Alfred Stepan (1996) disagree with the demobilisation thesis, arguing that it is "not only bad democratic theory but also bad democratic politics." In their view a robust civil society, capable of generating political alternatives and monitoring government, can "help start transitions, help resist reversals, help push transitions to their competition, and help consolidate and deepen democracy" (299). In a similar vein, Arato (2000) argues that negotiated transitions to democracy have the best prospects for consolidation—and civil society, he says, is a crucial prerequisite for successful transition. The power and legitimacy provided by civil society shore up the bargaining position of political leaders in negotiating and implementing pacts and drafting new constitutional and electoral frameworks.

A full democratic transition, Stepan asserts, must involve both political society and civil society. To be representative, political society has to be subject to the pressures in civil society and be periodically renewed by it. For its part, civil society cannot go it alone. "At best, [it] can destroy a non-democratic regime" (Stepan 2001:8). Civil society needs a strong political society to carry the transition through to completion. Stepan's primary point is that while a robust civil society is indispensable, it should not be unduly privileged, and care should be exercised to avoid making false contradictions between civil society and political society and the state. Larry Diamond (1999) agrees that democratic change cannot be understood without reference to civil society but warns against a "one-dimensional and dangerously misleading" conceptualisation in understanding democratisation. Linz and Stepan draw attention to the danger that civil society may pose for the development of political society by the idealisation of certain norms and practices that may be appropriate to civil society but not to political society.

There is general agreement among analysts on the need for a strong civil society in the consolidation of democracy. A "free and levely civil society" is the first of five necessary conditions cited by Linz and Stepan (1996) for a democracy to be consolidated. Schmitter (1997) lists several ways in which civil society can contribute to democratic consolidation: aggregating and stabilising expectations, inculcating civic conception of interests and norms of behaviour, supporting inclusive political processes, reducing the burdens of governance, and checking the abuse of power. Equally important, civil society may inculcate in the society at large the cultural and normative foundations of democracy. Arato (2000: 67-70), for his part, views the crucial role of civil society—in self-limitation, adherence to rule of law, providing sociological legitimacy, and limiting popular demand—as vital to the consolidation of a negotiated transition to democracy.

Novertheless, civil society is not an unmitigated blessing for democracy (Schmitter 1997). Certain types of civil society may make the formation of majorities more difficult, build biases into the policymaking process, lead to pork-barrel politics, and segment the political community to the point of stimulating secession. Thus civil societies may produce a mixture of positive and negative consequences for democracy—and there is no guarantee that the positive effects will always outweigh the negative ones.

### *Democratic Effects of Civil Society*

Civil society, like other realms, is an arena of power, inequality, struggle, conflict, and cooperation among competing identities and interests. It is populated by diverse formal and informal organisations with widely varying structures, resources, purposes, and methods. Not all civil society organisations have the purpose, potential, or consequence of advancing democracy. Some are decidedly antidemocratic or have such an effect (Whittington 2001; Warren 2001: 10-12). Business organisations, for example, can use their greater access to financial resources to undermine deliberative power and voting—two key means of democratic influence. Hate groups undermine democracy through their racism, secrecy, and frequent resort to violence. Fundamentalist religious organisations and groups advocating racial superiority can transform pluralism into parochialism, breeding intolerance in political life. Thus to ascertain the democratic potential and role of civil society, it is crucial to gauge the mix of organisations in civil society and identify those that can directly or indirectly advance or hinder democratic development. To highlight those that promote democracy while neglecting those that retard democratic development is to present a misleading picture.

Furthermore, the democratic potential of associations varies by type (voluntary versus non-voluntary), structural location (pro or anti status quo), and purpose (individual or exclusive social good versus inclusive public good), with certain associations having a greater potential than others to generate certain democratic effects. The most useful work here is that of Mark Warren (2001). Unlike those who exclude nonvoluntary organisations from civil society by definitional fiat, Warren says that both voluntary and nonvoluntary associations may have democracy-producing effects. Voluntary associations, because they are self-selecting and externalise political conflict, achieve a higher degree of solidarity, develop a distinctive voice in the public sphere, and have more capacity for subsidiarity, resistance, and representation. They may also be better at cultivating the civic virtues of trust, reciprocity, and recognition. But they are likely to be impoverished in giving voice to dissent and resolving conflict. Non-voluntary associations, by contrast, because of the high cost of exit, are compelled to provide a voice for dissenting groups and internalise and manage conflicts over purpose and methods, and they thus have greater capacity for deliberative and political skills.

Associations rooted in social relations are likely to have democratic effects akin to those of voluntary associations. From the perspective of political change, associations embedded in the political-legal sphere, and to a lesser degree the market medium, are likely to have greater democratic effects. Adversarial expectations make debate and conflict—and the development of political skills to manage them—the norm in these organisations. Both status quo organisations and those that seek change have democratic potential so long as they work in a context in which issues are forced onto the democratic terrain. They are bad for democracy if their power positions allow them to escape institutional bargaining and public accountability. Status quo associations have a greater capacity for subsidiarity, coordination, and representation, but limited capacity for resistance and transformation of the system. Non-status quo institutions (unions, feminist movements, consumer groups, new social movements) supply the issues of representation and resistance and have greater potential for change and transformation.

The democratic potential of associations is affected by their purposes as well. Some may aim to contribute directly to a certain aspect of democratic governance: extending citizenship rights and political participation to excluded groups (women, minorities, lower castes, social outcastes), broadening and democratising public policymaking, increasing government accountability in specific domains, promoting the rule of law, advocating distributional justice, and so forth. Although the primary purpose of most organisations may not be to promote democracy, they may nevertheless have democratic consequences that are more significant than those whose primary purpose is to advance democracy. Associations pursuing public material goods through collective action, for example, are likely to have a broad range of democratic effects. Associations pursuing status goods are less likely to contribute to democratic processes and may in fact nurture uncivil attitudes. Those pursuing exclusive identity goods, by enhancing solidarity and efficacy, enable agency—especially for disadvantaged groups—and contribute to diversity and pluralism in the public realm. They may also, however, make the development of shared identity, the discovery of commonality, and cooperation more difficult. If exclusive identity representation develops in response to oppression and suppression, they may "serve as the conscience of a democracy, challenging public judgement, and stretching the boundaries of public agendas" (Warren 2001: 131). Associations devoted to social goods such as political reform and securing civil liberties play an important role in "underwriting public sphere and political processes." Because of the wide variation in the democratic effect of organisations and the presence of antidemocratic forces in civil society, it is important to gauge the mix and ascertain the balance of power among them.

Even when important groups in civil society support democracy, their effects are likely to be conditioned by the response of the state, by the connection among civil society, political society, and legislatures, and by the international context. In responding to formal and informal associations and their activities, a state may legally sanction, suppress or merely tolerate them (Bermeo 2000). Legal sanctions might be advantageous up to a point, but they could also lead to co-operation and control, limiting the democratic potential of associations and in the long run undermining their credibility. Suppression might be stultifying, but it could also create martyrs and provoke uprisings that undermine the legitimacy of the incumbent government and enhance the image and power of dissident groups. De facto toleration of the activities of civil society groups, according to Nancy Bermeo (2000: 249), had the greatest democratic consequences in nineteenth-century Europe. Tolerance in the legal, semilegal, or extralegal realm allowed civil society groups to survive, to grow, and to expand democratic space.

The impact of groups advocating democracy can be substantial if they connect with political society and the legislature. An alliance between such civil society groups and political society can pose a credible challenge to authoritarian governments. An alliance with the reformist elements in a Communist state can open up political space. It may also lead to suppression of certain civil society groups and the elimination of reformist elements within the government. Such suppression is not, however, without cost. In a new democracy, alliances with political society and the legislature can enhance the influence of civil society groups in policymaking. Strategic connections in general have the power to enhance the effect of prodemocracy groups in civil society. For such alliances to occur, political society must be sufficiently differentiated; reformist elements should be present in Communist states; the social structure should be open; national, local, urban, and rural areas should be linked; and legislatures should be effective. An independent and accessible media committed to promoting democracy can significantly enhance the influence of civil society as well.

The democratic effect of civil society organisations can be amplified or hindered by the international environment. The contemporary context is certainly favourable for democratic development. Democracy has no alternatives. Ideologies like Nazism, Fascism, and Marxism-Leninism are not viable; possible alternatives such as techno-bureaucratic--authoritarianism, one-party-dominant political systems, and the developmental state economic model have been discredited. Although there are several holdouts, especially in Asia, formal commitment to democracy is widespread in the international system. Leading states are more supportive of democracy today than they were during the Cold War. (Consider the Clinton administration's democracy enlargement policy, for example.) The alliances forged by the United States with military and autocratic governments in the wake of September 11, 2001, suggest, however, that in certain cases strategic considerations still out weigh the goals of promoting democracy and protecting human rights. Nevertheless, good governance and the development of civil society continue to feature in the programmes of international lending agencies. Associations in developed countries and transnational movements devoted to human rights and the environment have significantly enhanced the political resources available to domestic actors in developing countries (Keck and Sikkink 1998). The global media and technological revolutions (radio, TV, fax, the Internet) have minimised the negative consequences flowing from the control of media by the state or antidemocratic groups. And the dissemination of information with greater ease and the ensuing demonstration effect have become much more consequential.

Although the international structure and the disposition of key actors and agencies are conducive to democratic development, there are constraints as well. In the wake of September 11, promoting democracy has been subordinated to fighting terrorism. And in countries like Burma, the Western states have limited influence. The involvement of external forces, especially foreign funding, tarnishes the credibility of indigenous associations and provides opponents with a nationalist card. Dependence on international support affects the agenda of associations and prevents them from developing indigenous roots and networks (Hudock 1999). The dominant role of international lending agencies in policymaking reduces the responsiveness of the executive to the electorate and undercuts popular trust in legislatures. Thus both opportunities and constraints characterise national and international conditions.

## Civil Society's Role in Political Change

Thus far, discussion has highlighted several points: Civil society is a space, an arena of governance, and organisations populating this space can be a force for affecting institutions and governance in political society, the state, and the market; civil society is not monolithic; there is no necessary connection between civil society and democracy; certain civil society organisation have greater democratic effect than others, while some may have an antidemocratic effect; the democratic effect and role of a country's civil society organisations depend on its specific domestic and international circumstances; successful democratic transition and consolidation require civil and political societies to have strong democratic forest; these forces are more consequential when they complement one another and act in mutually supporting ways; and the role and influence of civil society actors must be examined in conjunction with other actors in both the domestic (political society, the market, the state) and the international arenas.

### *System Legitimacy and Change*

Moreover, the specific functions and roles of civil society organisations will vary with the legitimacy of the nation-state and political system, the type of political system, and the stage of political development. If the nation-state and political system are widely acknowledged as legitimate, most civil society organisations are likely to emphasise reform, accountability, representation, and subsidiarity. In a nation-state that is contested or where a political system lacks legitimacy, it is highly probable that disengagement, resistance, construction of counternarratives, formation of clandestine organisations, and mobilisation of domestic and international support will feature prominently. In a system in the midst of transition, the role of civil society can be expected to change as well. In an entrenched communist or authoritarian system, civil society groups may seek to carve out public space in certain domains. In the prelude to the ouster of such governments, civil society groups in combination with segments of political society may play the vanguard role. In the subsequent transition phase, civil society groups may become involved in drafting a new constitution, in strengthening and monitoring political society and the state, in institutionalising civil society, and in fostering public participation in politics and policymaking. In the consolidation phase, civil society groups may seek to expand the space for civil society and correct the deficiencies of the new democracy (including greater transparency and accountability)—all with the goal of making democracy the only game in town. The effectiveness of these civil society roles hinges on prodemocracy groups acquiring and retaining a favourable balance of power in the different phases. This may at times be difficult to accomplish. Many analysts have drawn attention to the fragmentation of civil society in the aftermath of the velvet revolutions in central and eastern Europe. The point is simply this: the process of political change often is not linear, and the composition and role of civil society groups in this process are bound to alter as circumstances change.

### *Autonomy and Institutionalisation of the Public Sphere*

The role of civil society in political change must also be examined in terms of the arenas of political discourse and governance, which includes civil society itself, political society, and the state, Civil society is a distinct and crucial sphere of democratic governance. Here the concern is with decentralisation of power, authority, and resources to local levels and non-state institutions such that social, cultural, and some political interaction are regulated by associations free of state intervention. Citizens acquire the right to self-determination and governance in matters of immediate relevance. Civil society also provides the space and means for articulating and aggregating public interests, forming public opinion, developing agendas outside the state and the market, and creating the means to influence them. Unlike the state and market—whole primary organisation and transaction mediums are power and money respectively—freedom of association and unfettered public discourse that enable representation (or differences and commonalities), influence, and communicative power are the central pillars of the nonstate public sphere. The public sphere cultivates and shelters the political autonomy that in turn facilitates collective judgement and decision making to support self-governance by citizens and influence political society, the state, and the market (Warren 2001). Roles that expand (or contract) the space of the public realm in terms of the domain for societal self-governance—as well as in terms of institutions, actors, and agendas that enable collective action to influence political society and the state—constitute political change in the realm of civil society.

The second change involves the transformation of civil society from a group of social movements to a set of institutions (Arato 2000: 71-74). Institutionalisation of civil society involves a guarantee of fundamental rights that presupposes a constitution, separation of powers, and an independent judiciary; a politically accessible media that is independent of state and market; decentralisation of power, authority, and resources to local governments and nonstate institutions; acceptance of domestic and international NGOs as legitimate actors; and financially secure associations. In other words, civil society becomes a legally protected realm distinct from the state and political society. The third change relates to the development of the communicative mode of rational action. In this mode, agreements are arrived at through rational discourse and interpersonal interaction, not through power, money, or violence. Actors with divergent interests coordinate their interaction by negotiating definitions of the situation and remedies through discourse and reinterpretation of norms (Cohen and Arato 1992: 435).

Central to these three changes is the establishment of a system of individual and group rights—a fundamental feature of civil society. Cohen and Arato (1992: 441-42) cite three key sets of rights; freedom of thought, speech, and communication, which pertain to cultural production; freedom of association and assembly, which pertain to social integration; and the rights of privacy, intimacy, and inviolability of the person that secure socialisation. They also cite rights that mediate between civil society and the market (rights of property, contract, and labour) and between civil society and the state (political and welfare rights of citizens). The establishment of rights is a good measure of the progress made in the institutionalisation of civil society (from social movements to a settled civil society) and its constitution as a legally protected realm. In such a realm, communicative action becomes the norm. Although power and money are not absent, transactions in an institutionalized civil society hinge substantially on the force of ideas and arguments in definition a situation and remedies.

### *Change in Political Society and the State*

At the level of political society, the concern is with structures and rules for interest aggregation and representation, competition for state power, and the power and responsiveness of legislatures to demands from civil and political society. Civil society can assist (or hinder) the development of political parties and a party system, the institution of an electoral system, public participation in elections, monitoring of elections and legitimating outcomes, and the constitution and functioning of the legislature. In addition to developing political society and monitoring its activities, civil society organisations may build links to political parties and legislators in order to channel and realize the interests of their specific groups and bolster democratic elements in civil society.

Turning to the state, the concern is with change (reform or transformation) in the basis of political community, type of political system, and specific policies of domination and governance. Such changes may be discerned in a number of sites, including the ideational foundation of the nation-state, the structure of the state (unitary or federal state; creation of autonomous regions; presidential, semipresidential, or parliamentary systems), change within a political system (political liberalisation in an authoritarian system, for example, or change in the base of the vanguard party in a communist state), change in the political system itself (from authoritarianism or a Communist Party system to democracy, or *vice versa*), change in incumbent government, redefinition of the state's relationship with economic society, political society, and civil society, and change in state institutions and policies in specific areas of governance. In a system that is recognised as legitimate, civil society groups may play a variety of roles in shaping the course of such changes: setting norms, representing interests, promoting transparency and democratic accountability, and contributing to policymaking. In a system that is contested and widely regarded as illegitimate, in contrast, resistance, change, and transformation may inform the role of prodemocracy groups.

### *Socialisation Function*

Apart from these roles in relation to the three arenas (civil society, political society, and the state), civil society organisations perform a socialisation function that applies across the board. This function encompasses roles that relate to citizens' skills and communication of information—critical elements in the development of an individual's capacity for autonomous judgement and participation in the democratic process—as well as those that relate to the virtues of trust, reciprocity, and recognition, which can serve as a foundation for the robustness of the public sphere and democratic institutions of a community. Roles that belong to the socialisation function include those identified by Larry Diamond (1999), such as stimulating political skills and participation, education for democracy, development of cross-cutting identities, and dissemination of information to empower citizens, as well as others that relate to the creation of civic virtues.

The role of civil society in political change may be investigated in several ways. Taking into account the purpose of this study—to investigate political change in the direction of open, accountable, and participatory politics—and the importance of conceptualising civil society both as an arena or governance and as a force for bringing about change in political society and the state. Table 5.1 sets out the roles of civil society in the abstract by arena, functions, and examples. These functions and roles are illustrative, however, not exhaustive. They will vary with the type and legitimacy of political system and stage of system change. In the democratisation literature, for example, discussions of the role of civil society indicate how and why the role may alter in different stages of the process. In the following chapters, as we shall see, the contributors modify the functions and roles of civil society to make them relevant for investigation of political change in their respective countries.

## REFERENCES

Arato, Andrew, 2000, *Civil Society, Constitution, and Legitimacy*, Lanham Md.: Rowman & Littlefield.

Baker, Gideon, 2002, *Civil Society and Democratic Theory: Alternative Voices*. London: Rutledge.

Benjamin, Barer R. 1999. "Clansmen, Consumers, and Citizens: Three Takes on Civil Society," In Robert K. Fullinwider, ed.,

*Civil Society, Democracy, and Civic Renewal*. Lanham, Md.: Roman & Littlefield.

Berman, Sheri, 2001. "Civil Society and Political Institutionalisation." In Bob Edwards, Michael W. Foley, and Mario Diani, eds., *Beyond Tocqueville: Civil Society and the Social Capital Debate in Comparative Perspective*. Hanover, N.H.: University Press of New England.

Bermeo, Nancy, 2000. "Civil Society after Democracy: Some Conclusions." In Nancy Bermeo and Phillip Nord, eds., *Civil Society Before Democracy: Lessons from Nineteenth Century Europe*, Lanham, Md.: Rowman & Littlefield.

Bratton, Michael. 1994. "Civil Society and Political Transitions in Africa," In John W. Harbeson, Donald Rothchild, and Naomi Chazan, eds., *Civil Society and the State in Africa*, Boulder: Lynne Rienner.

Chambers, Simone, and Will Kymlicka, eds. 2002. *Alternative Conceptions of Civil Society*, Princeton: Princeton University Press.

Cohen, Jean L., and Andrew Arato. 1992. *Civil Society and Political Theory*. Cambridge, Mass.: MIT Press.

Cox, Robert W. 1999. "Civil Society at the Turn of the Millennium: Prospects for an Alternate World Order." *Review of International Studies* 25(1):3-29.

Edwards, Bob, and Michael W. Foley, 2001. "Civil Society and Social Capital: A Primer," In Bob Edwards, Michael W. Foley, and Mario Diani, eds., *Beyond Tocqueville: Civil Society and the Social Capital Debate in Comparative Perspective*, Hanover, N.H.: University Press of New England.

Edwards, Bob, Michael W. Foley, and Mario Diani, eds. 2001. *Beyond Tocqueville: Civil Society and the Social Capital Debate in Comparative Perspective*. Hanover, N.H. University Press of New England.

Ehrenberg, John, 1999. *Civil Society: The Critical History of an Idea*. New York: New York University Press.

Ferguson, Adam, (1767) 1995, *An Essay on the History of Civil Society*. Edited by Fania Oz Salzberger. Cambridge: Cambridge University Press.

Fine, Robert. 1997. "Civil Society: Theory Enlightenment, and Critique" In Robert Fine and Shirin Rai, eds., *Civil Society: Democratic Perspectives*. London: Frank Cass.

Foley, Michael, W., and Bob Edwards, 1997. "Escape from Politics? Social Theory and Social Capital Discourse." *American Behavioral Scientist* 40(5): 550—61.

Gellner, Ernest, 1994. *Conditions of Liberty: Civil Siciety and its Rivals*, New York; Penguin Books.

Hudock, Ann C. 1999. *NGOs and Civil Society: Democracy* by Proxy. Cambride: Polity Press.

Ioannidou, Anastasia, 1997. "The Politics of the Divison of Labour: Smith and Hegel on Civil Society." In Robert Fine and Shirin Rai, eds, *Civil Society: Democratic Perspectives*. London: Frank Cass.

Kaviraj, Sudipta, and Sunil Khilnani, eds., 2001. *Civil Society: History and Possibilities*, Cambridge: Cambridge University Press.

Nord, Phillip. 2000. "Introduction," In Nancy Bermeo and Philip Nord, eds., *Civil Society Before Democracy: Lessons from Nineteenth Century Europe*. Lanham, Md.: Rowman & Littlefield.

Stepan, Alfred, 1988. *Rethinking Military Politics: Brazil and the Southern Cone*, Princeton: Princeton University Press.

Warren, Mark E. 2001. *Democracy and Association*. Princeton: Princeton University Press.

Whitehead, Laurence. 1997. "Bowling in the Bronx: The Uncivil Interstices Between Civil and Political Society." In Robert Fine and Shirin Rai, eds., *Civil Society: Democratic Perspectives*. London: Frank Cass.

# 8

# The Cultural Paradox of the Global Village

The culture of a place that is everywhere and nowhere, that is at once global but renders the globe obsolete, that globalizes the individual yet strips our individuality? The place to which I am referring is the Internet, and these questions represent the intriguing paradox that the Internet presents to us, one that requires us to look beyond what we can easily see or hear or touch. When we first began to think about the Internet many of us typically thought of a television metaphor. It is not hard to understand why we might immediately make this connection. We view both media through a screen, and screen-oriented technologies often have common effects.

Both have a remote control of sorts—in the case of networked computers, the remote control is the mouse—and, like television, we are always clicking and searching for what else in on. And clearly there is no shortage of paid advertising, product placements and infomercials on either medium. Television is a convenient and obvious metaphor for the internet. In fact, we often use convenient and obvious metaphors for any new technologies that are based on how we use things, or on their content, in an attempt to understand their nature and characteristics. But overtime, we slowly discover that our first, and often second and third, impressions were, if not wrong, then most certainly incomplete. And this is because we tend to base our initial thinking and reactions on the things we notice.

There's a cute story about a man who, during wartime, would come to the country's border with a wheelbarrow full of dirt. The border guard looked at the man's papers and all was in order for him to cross. But the guard was certain the man was smuggling some sort of contraband in the wheelbarrow. So that guard took a shove, pocked around in the dirt, but found nothing.

The man was allowed to cross. The next week, the man once again comes to the border with a wheelbarrow full of dirt. Again, the border guard found that the papers where in order and dug through the dirt, but still found nothing. And again, the man was allowed to cross. Week after week, it was the same story: Man approaches the border with wheelbarrow full of dirt, guard finds nothing of interest and the man crosses. At the end of the war, the guard sees the man and asks him: "Look, I know you were smuggling something across the border, but I could never find a thing hidden in the dirt. What were you smuggling all those years?" The man answered: "Wheelbarrows." The border guard was unable to perceive what had been right there under his nose for years, simply because it did not match his conception. As we attempt to discover the nature and effects of any new technology or innovation or undertaking, we naturally draw on what we already know and what we obviously notice. We then create a mental model of how the new thing is supposed to work and react. We create conceptions, and then manage our affairs in an attempt to math those preconceived notions.

But we are not necessarily effective, that is, we often do not achieve the overall desired effects. Why do I say this? Simply because, what we conceive about our enterprises and institutions is not sufficient to fully understand all the effects that are actually happening in and around our enterprises and institutions. Like the border guard in the story, we are completely unable to perceive all of the dynamics of our environment because our conception limits our perception. Years of schooling and conditioning in the business world controls what we believe. And, what we believe controls what we are able to see.

What haven't you noticed lately? This is really an odd question, because, how can you notice that which you haven't yet noticed? And if. As I am proposing to you, this is a key question for awareness in our complex interconnected society, even if we answer it once, own can we consistently continue to answer it?

Unfortunately, it is almost impossible to achieve the requisite awareness of what we haven't noticed while we are immersed in a comfortable, or at least accustomed, environment. We are all subject to the ground-rules, that is, the rules and unperceived effects that govern our ground or context. It is like asking a fish to suddenly become aware of water. Mrshall McLuhan, the visionary who gage us "The Medium is the Message" and the "Global Village," observed, "One thing about which fish know exactly nothing is water, since they have no anti-environment which would enable them to perceive the element they live in." It is only when it is pulled from the water that the fish becomes acutely aware of its former environment.

The challenge in achieving the awareness to notice the formerly unnoticed—what we call achieving "integral awareness" of our total environment—is to create an appropriate "anti-environment." We tend to notice many things. In fact, we're very good at noticing what is entirely obvious, to the extent that we often become obsessively focused on it. This is dangerously easy to do because in our world of instantaneous communications, everyone is vying for the most precious and valuable commodity to be sought—our attention. Think about it: Every advertiser, every potential vendor and company desperately wants your attention, and will go to great, and sometimes outrageous, lengths to obtain it. It attention is the most valuable commodity, our most valued asset, it may be said that the most valuable personal skill to be effective these days is ignorance, literally ignore-ance—the ability to selectively and appropriately ignore that which is irrelevant or merely distracting. In this context, ignorance is not bliss—it is he practical manifestation of acute awareness and heightened perception.

The challenge is a tricky one: We must create an ant-environment: so that we can ignore what we notice and notice what we ignore. Moreover, e need to find the questions that we have not asked after we've asked everything we can think of. We need to raise the issues that have not yet occurred to us. Ad perhaps most important, we must anticipate the effects that have already happened of things that we are about to do. In other words, our objective is nothing less than to achieve the ability to predict the future by foretelling the present.

After such a build-up, I'm almost tempted to say, "to find out more, have your credit card ready and dial the toll-free number on your screen..." But I won't. Instead, I will reveal to you all at least one of the secrets behind Marshall McLuhan's uncanny ability to, indeed, predict the future by foretelling the present. The tool I'm talking about is the Laws of Media.

The Laws of Media: They are precisely four aspects for effects that apply without exception to all creations of humankind—everything we conceive or create. In McLuhan's lexicon, "medium is not merely limited to our conventional idea of mass-media: radio, television, the pres, the internet. Rather, a medium refers to anything from which a change emerges. And sine some sort of change in us or society accompanies anything we conceive or create, all of our tools and technologies, policies and plans, a cup of coffee or a coup d'etat—they are all McLuhan media. The Laws of Media apply regardless of whether the creation is tangible or intangible, abstract or concrete, and they serve to reveal the nature and effects of our innovations relative to us. Now to Marshall McLuhan, the questions were always more important, and indeed, more revealing, than the answers. Thus, the four Laws of Media are framed as four questions or probes.

The first probe is asked like this: What does the thing—the arte fact, the medium—extend, enhance, intensify, accelerate or enable? We can ask this question about any product, any service, any initiative, any policy. We can ask this enhance question about any word or phrase in our vocabulary, including, most interestingly, our buzzwords and acronyms. Email, for example, enhances and accelerates our ability to communicate in writing. Its rapidity and characteristic terseness intensifies the sender's meaning.

A second probe: When pushed or extended beyond the limits of its potential, the new thing will tend to reverse what had been its original characteristics. Into what does the new medium reverse? So, continuing with email as an example, it enhances our ability to communicate, but when extended beyond the limit of its potential—with spam, for instance, or dozens of unimportant FY1-or CC-type of corporate emails—email reverses into no communication at all due to an overflowing inbox.

The third Law of Media probe: If some aspect of a

situation or a thing is enhanced or enlarged, simultaneously, something else is displaced. What is pushed aside or obsolesced by the new thing; the new medium? Now when I say "obsolesced," I do not mean that the older form is eliminated, never to be heard from again. In fact, it is quite the opposite: One sure sign of a medium in obsolescence is its ubiquity. Does everyone remember what happened right before the dot-com bubble burst? There was a saying then: "You know the end of the market is near when you're getting stock advice from your garbage collector." So what does email obsolesce? In a corporate setting, email obsolesced the interoffice memo, and those large brown envelopes tied with a string tat had all those boxes for a chin of recipients. It also obsolesces synchronicity in communications—the ability to respond instantly as in normal conversation—and other socialized skills of responding to aural or physical cues, in other words, body language and tone of voice.

And the final Law of Media probe: What does the new medium retrieve from the past that had been formerly obsolesced? This reflects the aphorism that, "There's nothing new under the sun," and essentially asks, "How did we react as a society the last time we saw a medium with analogous effects?" The law of retrieval rings in precedence and historically-based experience. So what does email retrieve from the past that has long been obsolesced? Thinking way back through the history of communications, email may retrieve Hermes the messenger, scribe and herald of Greek mythology. Interestingly, from the perspective of the retrieval aspect of email, Hermes was also the Greek god of commerce, invention, cunning and theft. Has anyone here received a confidential business proposition from Nigeria lately?

The Laws of Media are simultaneous effects—emergent properties, really—of anything we conceive or create. What does it extend, enhance, amplify or enable? When pushed beyond the limit of its capacity into what does it reverse? What does it obsolesce? And, what does it retrieve from the past that was formerly obsolesced?

By applying Marshall McLuhan's thinking, we understand that the nature of a medium is known by its effects-these laws of Media effects – on us and on society. In particular, we know that the most potent effects are those that are unseen, non-obvious or simply ignored- the ground-effects. Consider the effect of television: TV brings the outside world in- from a soundstage, a political platform or a theatre of war directly into our homes. In doing so, television changed not only the nature of entertainment, but of politics and war as well in ways that were not at all obvious to television's pioneers.

The effect of the internet is quite different from that of television. Via networked computers, instead of bringing the world into our homes, we transport ourselves from our homes, and indeed from our bodies, out into cyberspace. So what is this internet world into which we are transported? What has been created in cyberspace? What awaits us there? And more important, what transformations are occurring right now that we have not yet noticed?

McLuhan gave us a guide when he distinguished between "visual space" and "acoustic space." While these metaphors usefully tie to two of our senses, they do not necessarily relate exclusively to that which is seen or heard. Visual space is linear and bounded. It is ordered and continuous, yet continually fragmented by our eye's (and brain's) automatic process of grouping and classification. In contrast, McLuhan described acoustic space as "a resonant sphere whose centre is everywhere and whose boundaries are nowhere," a world of "simultaneous relationships." Therefore, everywhere in acoustic space is here, and every-when in acoustic space is now. This describes the effect of the Internet perfectly, an every-present presence, the world of simultaneous relationships.

We can make an additional observation from the interesting metaphor of visual and acoustic space. Mcluhan pints out that a characteristic of "visual space" is that we can shut it out in much the same way we can shut off our vision by closing our eyes. We have eyelids, but we have no "earlieds." We cannot shut out acoustic space, or the space of relationships and connections that are all around us. This suggests that we cannot shut out the effects of the Internet on our business and society, even if we choose not to use the Internet directly. In other words, we, in our physical reality, are affected by the changes that have their impetus in cyberspace.

In cyberspace, we literally go "out of our minds," not to insanity, where we lose our sense of reality, but to an extension of reality that offers us many more dimensions of experience. As McLuhan predicted, "having extended...our central nervous system into the electromagnetic technology, ... [we] transfer our consciousness to the computer world as well." So how can we begin to understand the effects of this profound change in the way we experience, and connect with our world?

My mother witnessed the invention of television when she was a girl – from her ground, she always wondered how to get the little people out of the box. I grew up in an age in which the television was a fixture- almost, but not quite, taken for granted. I was socialized into a society where seeing events as they occurred on the other side of the world didn't merit a second thought. But to actually communicate and interact with any people from all around the world simultaneously—and perhaps even assume multiple personalities while doing so – well, my wonderment was equivalent to my mother's fascination with the miniature

George Burns, Gracie Allen and lack Benny.

My children, however, are now socialized in a world in which instantaneous connections from anywhere to anywhere at any time is ordinary. It's a world in which people quite naturally assume multiple identities, and play multiple roles, throughout the day both online and off. Techno-schizophrenia is not only considered normal, it's almost expected! At a time in our history when these sorts of phenomena are accepted as a common state of being, people will not only have different expectations from society and form each other, but they will acquire a significantly different worldview that even transcends time and space. The techno-psychological mantra, "Everywhere is here and every-when s now," becomes the perceptible underpinning of a reality that represents the McLuhan reversal—the evolution—of our perception and experience of the world.

In this world, the fact of such extreme connectivity reverses our notion of cultural connections and citizenship. When borders and time zones dissolve, we literally become citizens of the world. Our socialisation then yields a different sort of cultural awareness that we see manifested in the popularity of world music, and the rise of global political movements like the Green Party. It is manifested in the global scope of a variety of non-governmental institutions and independent media, involving everything from sports and philanthropy to business and politics. And it is manifested in the spread of English as a universal world language.

Now I realize that this notion of a universal world language may cause a few ears to perk up at this particular conference. So let's spend a few moments to explore this potentially controversial issue. The idea of a universal world language is quite consistent with our understanding of the effects of instantaneous communications technologies, and well-grounded in historical precedent. When Gutenberg created the moveable type press, we saw two key effects among many first, with the mass distribution of printed books, a person's ideas could suddenly be transported in multiple directions, for quite a substantial distance, without the person. Second, the capacity to produce printed materials suddenly exceeded the ability of authors to produce content in Latin, which was the predominant language of ideas at the time. As nature abhors a vacuum, so too does the ability to publish and disseminate ideas. Thus, we saw a significant reinforcement and acceleration—and extension intensification and enabling—of vernacular languages that extended to the borders of countries, and later to the far reaches of empires, roughly corresponding to the distances that printed materials could travel. Literacy increased in those vernacular languages. The ability to both read and write, engendered the materials that filled the void of content creation for a medium that could be produced in relatively large volumes by printing presses. The content that was once global-largely teachings of the Church-became considerably localized, reinforcing and strengthening nationalistic tendencies and sensibilities.

We now have the next acceleration of content creation and distribution with electric technologies—first television and now, the Internet. The distribution mechanisms are global in reach, and have a production capacity that exceeds that of all the printing presses worldwide by several orders of magnitude. Based on our understanding of the history of communications, we would expect two things to happen: One, the number of authors and content creators should increase, and so should the volume of content being produced. Two, we would expect to see the adoption of a common language throughout the area that corresponds to the reach of the distribution mechanism. What has happened? Where we once were passive consumers of content, this has reversed so that we have become prolific producers of content, throughout our electronic technologies. On television, we see hundreds of channels, ranging from the sublime to the ridiculous (although most nights, there still is nothing worth watching!). On the Internet, there are more web pages that McDonald's has hamburgers—billions and billions served, with everything from PhD dissertations to the details of a teenager's latest date. Second even though almost every language on the planet is represented on the plant is represented on the Internet and on specialty television, in every country there is a rapidly growing number f people who can understand, and speak, English—especially among youth.

So what does this change? An immediate and obvious fear is that globalisation would lead to the homogenization of culture. It is a fear that I hazard eloquently expressed by Prof. Suichi Kato in EU-Japan Fest conference entitled, "The Role of Culture in an Age of advancing Globalisation." Prof. Kato argued that technology converts culture into a commodity, mass producing and exporting cultural artefcts according to the rules of capitalism. The "law of the jungle" applies in which the strong will survive and overpower the week. This results in a homogenizing effect that eliminates local, indigenous cultures. According to Kato-san, in Japan, "internationalisation" today essentially means "Americanisation" through culture becoming commodity via technology and market economics. However, what Kato-san may term "cultural imperialism" is a conception influenced by several hundred years of history that was grounded in a world of linearity and mechanization.

But it makes no sense to merely extrapolate that past into the future. We must instead foretell the present. The fear expressed by Kato-san emanates from an industrial age ground and reflects the uniformity and homogenization that are artifacts of a mechanized era that began with the Gutenberg press. However, as we have just noticed, English as a universal language is not an instance of cultural imperialism, but a natural effect of instantaneous communications that ironically, the world at large need not fear. This possibly surprising conclusion is borne from noticing the even more surprising observation that the advantage currently enjoyed by native English speakers in international dealings is, in effect, entering its obsolescence.

Remember, we are now living at the time of only the first generation to really feel effects of the universality of English. We know that language culturally, and cognitively, conditions the mind. Over time, generations of non-native English speakers, who will become fluent in English, and often in one or two additional languages as well, will have the natural advantage. It is they who will readily be able to accept the new cultural forms and fusion that are the distinctive hallmark, not of globalisation, but of our response to the effects of globalisation.

So what is our response to the effects of Globalisation? It is not the anarchy of the NoLogo crowd, although some amount of anarchy may be useful to get the world's attention. Rather, our response to the effects of globalization is Globalism, a term coined by McLuhan Programme director Derrick de kerckhoe to describe the new personal ethics and responsibilities that we as global citizens must assume and adopt. McLuhan warned of the potential effects of Global Village when he told us, "The more you create village condition, the more discontinuity and division and diversity. The global village absolutely insures maximal disagreement on all points. It never occurred to me that uniformity and transquility were the properties of the global village...I dot approve of he global village. I Say we love in it." But McLuhan also reminds us that, "there is absolutely no inevitability so long as there is a willingness to contemplate what is happening." In other words, he tells us not only to predict, but also to create, the future by foretelling the present.

While globalism does not represent anarchy, it is subversive in its power to discover new processes in what we would call "the new modernity." In the first part of the 20th century, what we called modernism in literature, art, architecture and philosophy was based on reality and the symbolism that was unique to each society. It was used to express the understanding of a society's culture, history and philosophical ground. The second modernity, characteristic of the mid to late $20^{th}$ century, stripped the symbolic significance from things we created and emphasized their functionality, sometimes to the exclusion of their aesthetics. This we called postmodernism. Second modernity is characterized by juxtaposition of incongruities, and oxymoronic conjunctions of culture, traditions and uber-modern expressionism. It is world of figure against figure, creating a new ground or context that is divorced from a conventional cultural ground traditionally tied to geographic locale—in fact, it often pits the local in direct conflict with global—and thereby attempts to create its own new meaning. Most people, who were not members of the avant-garde, or the too-hip-for-the-room crowd, were repulsed, or at the very least, unimpressed. And it was often the specific intention of the creators of post-modern culture to be repulsive.

The new modernity—postmodenism, if you dare—is something different. It is experiential, as opposed to prescribed, pre-scripted and doctrinaire in its constructive chaos. Previously, physical objects in relation to local geography allowed us to determine much about identity. Now, in an age of instantaneous communications that eliminates the effects of geographical distance and time zones, identity is oriented by means of "scapes" that juxtapose multiple diverse environments form around the world. Thus the future, especially for emerging societies, is always elsewhere, constantly in flux, formed according to relational, as opposed to regional, patterns. Trans-national traffic of ideas and experiences that are now abstract, for a new order that is ironically and paradoxically unstable, irregular, incomplete and undefined relative to our historical and physical experience. This is the new norm to which we are slowly becoming socialized. It is "broken" in our conventional sense, but that is its virtue in the reformation of a global society. In this case, the state of being broken is not a destructive force but a liberating one. As McLuhan said: "breakdown is breakthrough"

In experiencing the new modernity, with all its instability and ambiguity, we each reflexively experience our world and the simultaneous relations that are forging a new global culture. Through an experience that is at once both direct and vicarious, each of us is moved to consider and take action relative to the problems we, as individuals, perceive in the world. Unintended consequences abound, and our ability to be appropriately reflexive is the key to the new organisation of our lives and the new modernity. This poses a tremendous opportunity for those who would adopt Globalism as their personal ethic; and a tremendous challenge to nation-states and corporations—and their leaders—who are still tied to conceptions of reactive internationalism that reflect in what we conventionally call globalisation, rather than a tran-nationalism that demands a reflexive response in global conscientiousness.

So how does this translate in a practical sense? We are experiencing an interesting and suitably ironic and paradoxical, instance of Globalism that has arisen courtesy of the George W. Bush administration, the war in Iraq and the world's reflexive response. Regardless of whether your personal politics are for or against the current administration, or whether you support or decry the invasion, the war in Iraq had a significance that transcends the removal of Saddam Hussein, the ongoing struggle against terrorism and the existence—or not—of weapons of Mass Desruction.

The invasion of Iraw that was undertaken over the objections of many nations made our global village conditions intensely exploicit—every person on earth who is within range of the Internet, television or even a radio, realized just how small is our world, and how interconnected we all are, in a way that was unprecedented in human history. For the first time, citizens for the world, imbued with a sense of Globalism, simultaneously protested en masse across every time zone in an attempt to influence what was, *de facto,* a global political process. And global political processes extend beyond mere demonstrations. The ongoing engagement of American soldiers imposes a severe financial burden on the country, a financial burden that could potentially be shared with other developed countries, and one that threatens to be a significant factor in next year's election. Yet by steadfastly refusing to assist the United States – at least for the time being – the world is playing a very active role in what was once exclusively American politics, but now, in a very real and reflexive way, is a matter of world concern, inadvertently, the Bush administration ignited a spark for the 21" century, an extreme intensification of the mightiest nation in history that resulted in the reversal of nationalism and nationalistic self-interest into Globalism.

What haven't you noticed lately? You have all noticed globalization and internationalism as the initial result of our ability to communicate instantly—anywhere and at anytime. You then noticed cultural diversity around the world and the need to localize media and content for indigenous markets. In short, you have noticed the world as it was. The challenge with which we are now faced is to begin to notice the world as it evolves, as it truly is. Globalism does not mean the end of indigenous culture, or the imposition of a mono-culture, but the emergency of new cultural forms. It does not mean the end of nations, or the imposition of a world government, but the emergence of trans-national institutions and ad-hoc organizations founded on relationships and reflexivity. It does to mean an end to localization, but the need to re-examine its underlying assumptions in light of the complexities, ambiguities and paradoxes that characterize the global citizen that leaves anywhere and everywhere at precisely the same time-now. And Globalism means one more thing. It means noticing.

# 9

# Building a Global Culture of Peace

Dozens of other individuals and organization in many cities have provided leadership and support, and I thank you all. I also want to recognize that a city in florida, Sanibel, as the first U.S. city to endorse the Earth Charter. Congratulations go to Majoy Nola Theiss for her leadership in this initiative, which led to endorsement by the Florida League of cities. As many of you know, last June, the majors of Burlington, Vermont, and Berkeley, California, led the U.S. Conference of Mayors to endorse the Earth Charter at their annual meeting in Detroit. The growing world wide support for the earth Charter among local governments as well as NGOs is very encouraging. We have come together for these Earth Charter community summits at a time of shock and grief in America and with a new awareness of the grave dangers that we face as a nation and a free society. This is a time that will test our courage and commitments as individuals and as a nation. In the midst of the suffering in New York, Washington, and Pennsylvania, there have been many examples of bravery and self-sacrifice among fire fighers, police, doctors, nurses, and many others. Inspired by these men and women, we must rededicate ourselves to the highest ideals of our nation—to freedom, respect for diversity and the rights of the individual, solidarity in the midst of adversity, and the democrative way.

Terrorism is a form of criminal activity and barbarism that strikes at the very foundations of civilization. President Bush has wisely called on the nations of the world to unite together with the U.S. in the a campaign against terrorism. It appears likely that military action will be necessary to bring to justice those responsible for terrorist acts and to defend our nation against future attacks. However, as the Bush administrative has pointed out, it is also essential to use diplomatic, legal, financial, and economic tools in the effort to end terrorism, and thee means may prove to be the most effective. We should be supportive of the caution and restraint that our leaders are showing in the use of military force.

Moreover, we make a mistake if believe that terrorism by itself is the major global challenge e face today. Terrorism is a deadly threat, but it is only one part of a much larger complex of problems. This becomes clear if consider the global situation and take a long-term view. Looking at the bigger picture can put the struggle against terrorism in perspective, and it can help us an individuals, organisation, and local communities find intelligent and compassionate ways to respond to the crisis immediately at hand. I want to take this approach this morning, using the Earth Charter as a guide and a source of hope.

## A Global Culture of Peace

The only long-term answer to the problem of terrorism is to build a global culture of peace. Again, this requires a world wide partnership of all nations and all peoples. If this is our long-term objective, we must ensure that whatever military or other action we take to combat terrorism will prove in the long run to be a means to the end of creating a planetary culture of peace. The ends—no matter how noble—do not justify any means, in part because the means we use determine the nature of the ends we will actually achieve. Just as one cannot preserve and build a free and democratic society by using authoritarian and undemocratic means, so one cannot build peace if your primary means is war and violence. Military action may be necessary in certain situations to defend against the aggression of another state or to stop terrorism and genocide, but other creative means are required to build peace.

Herelies the relevance of the Earth Charter to the events of September 11 and the challenges of the 21st century. The Earth Charter culminates with a vision of peace, and the principles in the Earth Charter identity the essential elements of a culture of tolerance, nonviolence, and peace. The earth charter, for example, recognizes that there will be no peace without social and economic justice. This includes the urgent need to eradicate the poverty in which 1.3 billion people live hopeless and desperate lives. A war on terrorism must include a war on global poverty if it is to have any chance of lasting success.

We must also recognize that 85% of the world's resources are in the hands of 20% of the world's people, and the gap between the rich and the poor continues to widen. Such conditions generate resentment and anger that me young people easy targets for religious fanatics, revolutionaries, and terrorists.

Another condition of enduring peace is democracy. Democracy gives a voice to the people an opens the door to participatory decision making. It involves creating the kind of vibrant civil society that finds expression in gatherings such as these Earth Charter community summits. It provides a social and political environment in which women and men can secure their human rights and fundamental freedoms.

The spread of democracy and its triumph over fascism and communist totalitarianism throughout much of the world may well be the most significant human achievement of the 20$^{th}$ century. Building a global culture of peace means renewing our own democratic institutions at home an supporting other peoples in their efforts to create democratic institutions appropriate to their distinct cultures. It means making more democratic the international institutions that govern world trade and international relations.

In addition, the only firm foundation for justice, economic well-being, democracy, and peace is ecological security. Earth's ecological systems provide us with clean air, fresh water, the food we eat, other essential natural resources, and the natural beauty that gives us artistic and spiritual inspiration. In the most comprehensive study to date of the health of the biosphere, an international team of scientists sponsored by the United Nations, the World Resources Institute, and The World Bank reports that human beings are degrading all of Earths basic ecological systems at an accelerating rate. If this trend is not soon reversed, it will have a devastating impact on the human community, the larger living world, and future generations.

Much has been done over the past thirty years to address our environmental problems. Here in Florida exemplary work is being done in restoring the Everglades ecosystem. However, in general our response has been at beast half-hearted and woefully inadequate. The warning signs are everywhere. A massive extinction of species is underway. Global warming is occurring. Ocean levels are rising, threatening low lying cities and villages. The water table in many regions of the world is drop in rapidly. Tropical and temperate rain forests that produce goods and services essential to the well-being of life on Earth are being burned and cut down. Major ocean fisheries have collapsed. Half of the world's coral reefs are dying. The scarcity of essential resources like water is increasingly a cause of conflict and violence. What kind of world do we want to leave for our grandchildren?

In our interdependent world, then, as we mount a campaign against terrorism, we must remember that the long-range goal is a world woe partnership for peace. Enduring peace means promoting environmental protection, the eradication of poverty, democracy, human rights, gender equality, respect for cultural and religious diversity, and nonviolent conflict resolution. This is the message of the Earth Charter.

The meaning and importance of this message will become clearer if we consider more closely some of the major ideas that have shaped the document.

**Interdependence**

One way of understanding the Earth Charter is to think of it as a declaration of global interdependence and universal responsibility. When this nation was founded, we issued a Declaration of Independence. Over 200 years later, we confront a very different world, and we urgently need a national and international declaration of interdependence. World wide interdependence is to a large degree the result of American technology, industrialization, and trade. Our nation has been the leader in the process of globalisation, and yet, have not fully understood the ethical implications and practical consequences of living in the world we ourselves are actively creating.

The reality is that we have entered a planetary phase in the development of civilization—what the historians call an era of global history. Diverse communities, nations, and cultures have their own stories, but more and more all o our lives are also part of one story. We are a proud and free people and a mighty nation, but we must also recognize today that we are an interdependent member of the larger human family and the greater community of life. With this interdependence goes a vulnerability we cannot escape. As the Earth Chapter puts it: In the midst of our cultural diversity, we are "one human family and one Earth community with a common destiny."

Our global interdependence is ecological, economic, political, cultural, and spiritual. There is not one major problem that we face—whether it be environmental protection, economic prosperity, the control of infectious disease, crime and drugs, or terrorism—that a community or nation can manage alone. Global cooperation is absolutely essential. Furthermore, if we want other nations to help the US address problems like terrorism about which we are especially concerned, then we must be willing to work more collaboratively with them on other critical global problems like poverty, economic opportunity for all, global warm in, and arms control. Isolationism and unilateralism in our international policy is short-sighted and self-defeat in. It is in our national interest to be critical global citizens, who work cooperatively with others for the common good.

In addition, we must recognize that none of the fundamental problems that face our communities, our nation, and the world can be effectively addressed in isolation. This, too, is part of the meaning of interdependence. Our environmental, economic, social, cultural, and spiritual challenges are interconnected. Poverty, for example, is both a case and a consequence of environmental degradation. Our economy is a subsystem of the planet's ecological system, and environmental degradation and the depletion of resources will eventually undermine our best efforts to build healthy economies. When our ethical and spiritual life is weak and confused, it leaves our economic and social life without meaning and purpose. In the light of these considerations, holistic thinking, interdisciplinary collaboration, and integrated problem solving are essential.

**Global Ethics**

In an interdependent world where cooperative problem solving is a prerequisite for progress, agreement on common goals and shared values is necessary. Effective international and cross-cultural collaboration requires a new global ethics. We urgently need a shared vision of basic values that will provide a basis for world wide partnership and an ethical foundation for the emerging world community.

The mission of the Earth Charter initiative is to help establish such a foundation. The Earth Charter endeavours to make clear that in the final analysis the problems the world faces are ethical ones. If we are to create a secure world and better future for all, we must revise our idea of the good life and our understanding of right conduct, and we must do this together as global citizens. The objective is not to impose the values of one culture or tradition on everyone else or to create some new monoculture. The goal is to learn from one another and to find common ground through dialogue in the midst of our rich cultural diversity.

The Earth Charter is a demonstration that e can meet this complex challenge. It is a product of a decade-long, world wide, cross-cultural, interfaith dialogue on shared values. This dialogue went on in face-to-face encounters in local, national, and international meetings in a series of internet conferences, and by e-mail and fax. Hundreds of organisations and thousands of individuals were involved. The Earth Charter sets forth a consensus on ethical values that is taking form in the emerging global civil society. In the course of the global dialogue that generated the Earth Charter, there were often significant differences, but what impressed me most was the good will of all the participants and their determination to find common ground in the midst of difference.

### Sustainability

The ethical principles of the Earth Charter are described as "interdependent principles for a sustainable way of life" that provide a common standard for individuals, organizations, communities, and governments. The concept of a sustainable way of life and of sustainable development has become a new, powerful organizing idea like freedom or democracy. The concept of sustainability ha a narrower and a broader meaning. An activity is sustainable if it can be continued indefinitely. Patterns of production and consumption are considered to be ecologically sustainable if they respect and safeguard the regenerative capacities of our oceans, rivers, forests, arm lands, and grasslands. However, using the term in the broader sense, one can talk about building a sustainable global society. In this connection, sustainability includes all the interrelated activities that promote the long-term flourishing of Earth's human and ecological communities. The principles of the Earth Charter provide an inclusive definition of sustainability this broader sense.

Finding our way to a truly sustainable way of living together is our hope for the future. It is the path to building a culture of nonviolence and peace.

### An Ethic of Respect and Care

At the heart of the Earth Charter vision is an ethic of respect and care for all life forms and the greater community of life, of which humanity is an interdependent part. This ethic of respect and care is articulated in the first two principles of the Charter, and all the other principles follow from and elaborate the meaning of these first two.

The sense of ethical responsibility begins with an attitude of respect. Respect involves recognition and appreciation. What is worthy of respect also warrants moral consideration. The Earth Charter challenges us to expand our moral awareness and to respect and value all life forms and Earth, our planetary home that has made the development of life possible. Before the awesome mystery of life, respect can deepen into a reverence for life.

The ethical life begins with an attitude or respect of or life, but it only takes form when respect develops into a deep sense of caring. Respect and care together create an ethically responsible human being. The attitudes and values associated with caring are a foundation upon which to build our public as well as private lives Caring involves feeling as well as thinking and acting—our whole being. "To care for" means to respect and value. It means to prevent harm and to proote healing and well-being. Our caring is most profound and effective when it is inspired and guided by the integration of the head and the heart knowledge and compassion, science and love. Communities that have lost their capacity for care show the environmental and social effects of in difference, narrow self-interest, short-term thinking, neglect, and abuse.

At this juncture in human evolution, extending our sense of respect and care to embrance the whole human family in all its diversity, the greater community of life, and future generations has become an ecological and social necessity. In the vision of the Earth Charter, caring for people and caring for Earth are two interrelated aspects of one great task. Only such an expansion of our moral consciousness will transform industrial-technological civilization and lead toward a genuinely sustainable way of life and peace on Earth.

We all have a role to play in implementing the ethic of care, in achieving just and sustainable communities, and in building a global culture of peace. This is the meaning of universal responsibility in an interdependent world. Looking forward form September 11 in the spirit of the Earth Charter, what can you and I do?

In times like these, we need the wisdom that flows from a clear mind and a pure heart. Taking time to centre ourselves through prayer, meditation, and being with family, friends, and members of one's faith community can be a great help. Remember that the goal is to decrease hatred and violence and to build peace. This can to be achieved with hatred and violence but only through a life-affirming ethic of care. As we struggle to protect ourselves from terrorism, we must also seek to understand and address the conditions and causes that produce hatred and violence at home and abroad, if we want long-term solutions.

There is an urgent need for a new and deeper dialogue between Western culture and the Middle Eastern Islamic world. This is a good time for interfaith dialogue involving Christians Jews and Muslims and members of other religious traditions as well. The Earth Charter can be used as a catalyst for exploring common ethical values in these exchanges. We can also demand that throughout the world our religious leaders take strong measures to prevent religion from becoming an instrument of hate.

We must let our government leaders know that we support a spirit of collaborative engagement in world affairs—not just regard, we must give the United Nations strong and consistent support, financially, diplomatically, and morally. The UN was founded first and foremost to prevent war and to promote peace, and it is absolutely essential at this stage in human history. A year from now, the United Nations will convene the World Summit on Sustainable Development, and our government representatives should now the we want the Unties States to play a creative leadership role at this critical world meeting.

All of us can work to alter our lifestyles and to implement those Earth Charter principles that are relevant to our organisations, businesses and local communities.

Share the Earth Charter with teachers in your local schools and with government officials and business leaders. Use it to generate discussion and debate on the major challenges and choices we face. Urge your local governments to use the Charter as a guide to sustainable development and a tool to assess progress toward that goal.

Thousands of local, national, regional, and international organisations have now endorsed the Earth Charter. The mot recent endorsement has come from the Parliament of the World's Religions. Invite your organisation to consider endorsing the Earth Charter, if you have not already done so. The more support we have from civil society and local government, the greater the chance of endorsement by the United Nations General Assembly in 2002.

The emerging global civil society, of which all of us here are a part, has become a third force shaping world affairs alongwith government and business Through the ballot box and our purchasing power in the marketplace, we have the collective ability to influence profoundly influence government and business. There are many encouraging examples of the of such activism.

In my home sate of Vermont, the Earth Charter is being transported across the state from town to town in a beautiful, handcrafted Ark of Hope by people walking in a spirit of peace. In addition to the Earth charter, the Ark of Hope contains the prayers and poems of many Vermonters. The global challenges before us are great, but if we unite behind the kind of vision affirmed in the earth Charter, there are grounds for hope. Humanity has the knowledge, technology, and financial resources required to protect Earth's ecological systems and to make progress in creating a just and peaceful world.

# 10

# Socialism in Undeveloped Countries

What do we mean by "socialism"? The word is often used very vaguely, but it is not difficult to give it a precise meaning. The definition of socialism consists of two parts, one economic and one political, one concerned with the production and distribution of goods, the other with the distribution of power. As regard production, all land and capital must be the property of the State—though perhaps the state might sometimes delegate possession to some large body of producers or consumers, such as a trade union or a co-operative society. As regards distribution, what I paid for each kid of work must be fixed by a public authority, with a minimum of what is required for bare necessaries, and a maximum of what will give the greatest incentive to efficient work. There is no need of equality of income for all as part of the definition of socialism; the fact that Chaliapin is paid more than a scene-shifter does not suffice to prove that Russia is still bourgeois. What is essential is that a man should not be able to extort profit by his possession of means of production, whether land or capital.

But socialism certainly has as its ideal equality of income, subject only to such modification as may be imposed by the special needs of various classes of workers. On the political side, socialism is not compatible with autocracy or oligarchy, but demands tat all sane adults should have an equal share of ultimate political power. Even the Bolsheviks, who oppose democracy during the time of transition, regard it as part of their ideal, and admit that socialism will not be fully realized until it is possible to restore liberal democratic institutions, such as universal suffrage, free speech and free press. (This appears in their writings, and was confirmed by Kamnev in a conversation I had with him while in Russia.) The different forms of socialism—State socialism, guild socialism, etc.—do not differ on this point, but only on the extent to which proximate political power is concentrated in the democratic State or diffused through various federated bodies. For reasons which we have already considered it seems impossible that industrialism should continue efficient much longer unless it becomes socialistic.

This is partly because the system of private profit rouses the discontent of the workers and gives them a sense of injustice, partly because the private ownership of land and capital confers upon the owners a degree of control both over private citizens and over the State which is dangerous, since it is used to increase private power and profit and not for the benefit of the community. But the transition from the present system to socialism is full of difficulty, and it is doubtful whether the attempt will succeed or will result in a return to barbarism. Marx, whose prophetic insight was remarkable but not impeccable, conceived the transition with a schematic simplicity which does not appear at all likely to be realized. He thought—as was natural from the experience of England in the first half of the nineteenth century—that the line between capitalist and proletarian would always remain quite sharp so long as capitalism survived, and that the proletarian could never obtain more than starvation wages, i.e., just enough to keep himself and his family alive. Gradually the capitalists would grow fewer through the concentration of capital, and the proletariat would grow more discontented and more organised through experience of their misfortunes and struggles against them. Their struggles would be first local, then national, then international; when they became international they would be victorious, owing to the immense numerical preponderance of the proletariat. Then, suddenly, by a revolution, the whole economic system would be changed, and international socialism would be established. In all these respects Marx has proved to be partly mistaken. The line between capitalist and proletarian is not sharp: trade union leaders with comfortable incomes enjoy bourgeois comfort, associate with capitalist on equal terms, and often acquire much of the capitalist mentality. The iron law of wages, invented by orthodox economists to discourage trade unions and accepted by Marx to encourage revolution, was an economic fallacy: wages in America, and even in England, now afford far more thana bare subsistence to the majority of wage-earners. The concentration of capital in few large enterprises has not meant a diminution in the number of capitalists, owing to the growth of joint-stock companies. The proletariat have not grown more discontented; they were certainly more revolutionary in England a hundred years ago than they are now, It I true that they have grown more organized nationally, but the are showed the complete futility, up to the present, of international organisation. And if to-morrow a war were to break out between America and Japan, the proletariat of both countries would equal the capitalists in enthusiasm and surpass them in patriotism. Finally, the numerical preponderance of the proletariat has only been realized in a very few countries (of which Great Britain is one). Elsewhere they are outnumbered by the peasant proprietors, who as a rule side with the capitalists. In this last respect, however, time may yet justify Marx. Lenin's scheme of electrification is designed to industrialize agriculture, and thus give to the peasant the mentality of the proletarian. It is possible that technical improvement in agricultural methods may produce a similar change, less intentionally, in other countries. This is a very important consideration, and one which may decide the whole future of socialism, but unfortunately it s a matter as to which prophecy is exceedingly difficult. The establishment of a communist government in Russia brought to the fore a new set of considerations, which partly confirm and partly confute Marx. The Bolsheviks attempted to establish communism in a country almost untouched by capitalistic industrialism. This raises the question whether capitalism is, as Marx believed, a necessary stage on the road to socialism, or whether industry can be developed socialistically from the outset in a hitherto undeveloped country. For the future of Russia and Asia this question is of the most vital importance. The Bolsheviks came into power with the intention of establishing communism at the earliest possible moment, and this intention they no doubt still entertain. But apart from all external difficulties, the internal obstacles have proved greater than they expected. This led them to adopt what is called the "New Economic Policy," which is, at any rate for the moment, a practical abandonment of communism. The reasons for this step may be gathered from a very candid article on "The Meaning of the Agricultural Tax" by Lenin, published in English in the first number of the Labour Monthly (July 1921),[1] What he says of Russia would be equally applicable to a socialistic China, or to India if it threw off the British yoke and became Bolshevik. Lenin distinguishes, in present day Russia, elements at five different levels of economic development, namely:

1. Patriarchal, i.e., to a large degree primitive, peasant production.
2. Small commodity production. (This includes the majority f peasants who sell corn.)

3. Private Captalism.
4. State Capitalism.
5. Socialism.

The term "State Capitalism" occurs frequently in this article, as well as in others of his writings. It seems to mean the running of enterprises by the State for profit, i.e. in the same any as they would be run by private capitalists. It appears in the course of the article that it includes the running of railways by the State, whether in Soviet Russia or in pre-war Germany The term is not defined in the article, and I do not profess to know its exact meaning. But the essence of the matter seems to be tat under State Capitalism the state sells the goods or services concerned, instead of supplying them gratis to those who have a claim to them.

Lenin regards the later stages as higher in the economic scale then the earlier ones, and considers any development from one of them to the next as and development from one of them to the next as an advance. He also seems to hold—though this is scarcely reconcilable with Bolshevik policy—that no stage can be skipped, but all must be passed through in their proper order. He argues that small commodity production must be encouraged because it is an advance on patriarchal peasant production; that larges-scale private capitalism is better than small production (though he hardly ventures to say his government should encourage it); that State capitalism should not be opposed by socialists, because it is so much better than private capitalism; and that socialism cannot be brought about quickly even by a government which bends its whole energies to this task. He quotes the following passage from a pamphlet of his written in 1918. . . . State Capitalism would be a step in advance in the present state of affairs of our Soviet Republic. If, for example, State Capitalism could establish itself here during the next six months, it would be an excellent thing and a sure guarantee that within a year Socialism will have established itself and become convincible.

Later on in the article he says: In the above-quoted arguments of 1918, there are a number of error in connection with periods. Periods prove to be much longer than was then assumed. But the question of speed need not concern us at present; it is the nature and direction of the movement towards socialism in undeveloped countries that I wish to investigate. If one examines Lenin's argument closely, one finds (if I am not mistaken) that its upshot is this; A government of convinced communists can limit the phase of private capitalism to rather small businesses, replacing large-scale private capitalism by State capitalism; also they can, by propaganda and by initiating industrial advances, enormously accelerate the movement from anyone phase to the next; but they can not enable a community to skip any of the phases altogether, or overcome the laws of economic evolution.

A few further quotations will help to elucidate the position taken up in this very important pronouncement.

State Capitalism is incomparably higher economically than our present economic system (i.e. that of Russia in 1921). Socialism is impossible without large capitalist in technique. Socialism is impossible without the domination of the proletariat in the State.

I will first of all, quote a concrete example of State Capitalism. Everybody will know this example: Germany.

A victorious proletarian revolution in Germany would immediately and with tremendous ease smash the whole shell of imperialism...and would for certain bring about the victory of world Socialism.

If the revolution in Germany is delayed our task

becomes clear, to learn State Capitalism from the Germans, and to exert all our efforts to acquire it. We must not spare any dictatorial methods in hastening the Westernization of barbarous Russia, and stick at no barborous methods to combat barbarism.

The problem of power is the root problem of all revolutions. Our poverty and ruin is such that we cannot immediately establish large State Socialist Factory Production.

It is necessary to a certain extent to assist the re-establishment of small industry, which does not require machinery.

What is the result of all this? Fundamentally, we get a certain amount (if only local) of Free Trade, a revival o the petty bourgeoisie and Capitalism. This is undoubted, and to close one's eyes to it would be ridiculous.

After explaining the folly of attempting to prevent all private trading, with a half-confession of the fact that this policy has been vigorously pursued hitherto he explains the new policy which he now advocates:

Or (and this is the only possible and sensible policy) we can refrain from prohibiting and preventing the development of capitalism and strive to direct it in the path of State Capitalism. This is economically possible, for State Capitalism exits in one or another form and to one or another extent everywhere where there are elements of Free Trade and Capitalism in general.

He proceeds to mention concessions and co-operative societies as examples of this policy.

On the subject of fitting the peasantry into a socialist system, he says:

Is it possible to realize the direct transition of this state of pre-capitalist relations prevailing in Russia to Socialism?

Yes, it is possible to a certain degree, but only on one condition, which we know, thanks to the completion of a tremendous scientific labour. That condition is: electrification. But we know very well that this "one" condition demands at least ten years of work, and we can only reduce this period by a victory of the proletarian revolution in such countries as England, Germany and America.

Capitalism is an evil in comparison with Socialism, but Capitalism is a blessing in comparison with medievalism.

It must be the aim of all true workers to get local industry thoroughly going in the country districts, hamlets and villages, no matter on how small a scale. The economic policy of the state must concentrate on this. Any development in local industry is a firm foundation, and a sure step, in the building up of large-scale industry.

I have thought it necessary to make these numerous quotations, because they contain admissions, based on experience, of many things which socialistic critics have vainly urged upon the Bolsheviks both in Europe and Asia. The problem of what can and what cannot be done towards the hastening of the advent of Socialism in undeveloped or partially-developed countries, is made much clearer by Lenin's exposition of his difficulties. The great importance of the problem lies in the fact that, while technical and economic conditions are more favourable to socialism in advanced countries, the political conditions are more favourable in backward countries, for reasons which I shall discuss presently. If, therefore, the technical difficulties could be overcome by the Bolsheviks, they would have immensely facilitated the introduction of world-Socialism. But the Bolshevik method has not only the difficulties recognized by Lenin. It has also others at least as formidable, as I shall now try to show. The result seems to be that, in spite of the political difficulties, there is more hope of the inauguration of successful socialism in the advanced countries than in those which have hither to escaped any large development of capitalistic industrialism.

Industrialism in an undeveloped country (as we saw in an earlier chapter) must be aristocratic, and must at firs entail great poverty for the bulk of the population unless it is inaugurated by foreign capital. The Bolsheviks are obliged to manage industry as autocratically as any Trust magnate, and are enable to afford more than a bare subsistence to their employees. Moreover, the attempt to dispense with the assistance of foreign capitalists has had to be abandoned since the resumption of trade and the adoption of the policy of concessions. The policy of developing industrialism without outside help entails such terrible hardships, over and above those that are in any case inevitable, that no nation, not even Soviet Russia, can face them. It is true that in England industrialism was built up without foreign capital, but the circumstances were very special, and not such as can be repeated. Coal and iron were plentiful and in close proximity to each other; new inventions, all English and confined to England by the Napoleonic wars, were cheapening production enormously; and above all, there were no other industrial nation to compete. In spite of all these advantages, the poverty and overwork of the operatives were appalling, and such as can only be imposed upon a nation subject to an aristocratic tyranny. We cannot hope, therefore, that a modern undeveloped nation, without special advantages, can become industrial without the help of foreign capital.

Under thee circumstances, is it possible for a country like Russia or China to pass straight to what Lenin calls State Capitalism, without passing through the stage of large-scale private capitalism? To make the matter concrete, is it possible to have railways, docs, etc., built and owned by the State, and mines worked by the State, by means, partly, of borrowed capital, but without allowing the lenders any voice in the management. A strong State can do analogous things for ordinary purposes; for example, the holders of war loan were not allowed a representative at G.H.Q. to see that the war yielded good dividends. Nor did the French investors who lent to the Tsarist government demand a voice in the management of the secret police, although they knew that revolution might mean repudiation. In such matters, it is assumed that the interests of governments and their creditors are identical, and that therefore governments need not be interfered with by private capitalists. But the development of new industrial resources a different point of views I customary, and a government can seldom effect a loan without selling some part of the national independence. In china, for example, foreign investors expect the concession of monopoly rights—customs, railways, mines, etc.—before they will end to a government. This makes State capitalism impossible in so far as the rights granted to foreigners are concerned. The money that they end to the government is spent in bribery, paying troops, etc, not in productive enterprises; the productive enterprises remain in the hands of foreign capitalists.

In Russia, the Bolsheviks hope to restrain this policy of concessions within narrow limits, and to retain the bulk of the nation's resources in the hands of the state if they could succeed decisively, the Russian State, or perhaps the communist party, might in the end replace the foreign capitalist as the exploiter of China, and might acquire a hold there which foreign nations would find very hard to loosen. The success or failure of Russia will probably decide whether it is possible to pass to Socialism through State Capitalism rather than through large-scale private capitalism. If the Bolsheviks succeed, Asia may escape the advanced forms of private capitalism; if they fail, the whole world will probably have to arrive at the stage at which the advanced industrial countries are now.

The success or failure of the Bolsheviks turns on three kinds of factors, military, economic, and moral.

It is, of course, obvious that success is impossible without an army sufficiently strong to repel all attacks that can be easily provoked. Any trade agreements the Bolsheviks conclude are the fruit of their success in defeating Koltchak and Denikin and holding the Poles at bay. If at any moment a combination of (say) Japanese, Poles and Rumanians had a good chance of defeating them, such a combination would, of course, at once declare a holy was against them. The only thing that may in time alter this state of feeling will be the investment of large amounts of new foreign capital in the form of concessions which a White government might repudiate. It is chiefly the military strength of Russia that gives it pre-eminence above other undeveloped countries

The economic factors introduce more difficult considerations. It is necessary for the Bolsheviks first to import from abroad the minimum of machinery, rolling-stock, etc., required for reviving agriculture and restoring industry to its pre-war level. When this has been done, and it has become possible to purchase food from the peasants by supplying them with goods instead of paper, it will become possible to revive and increase the pre-war export of food and raw materials, and at the same time to develop Russian industry enormously. It is the early steps n this process that are the most difficult and dangerous. Imports are needed first of all, and although a few of the most indispensable can be paid for in gold, the bulk will have to be paid for in concessions, since exports are impossible in these days of famine and collapse of transport. Russia's need being desperate, the concession-hunters will exact very severe terms. Each concession will become a centre of private trading, and will make it more difficult to keep the bulk of foreign commerce in the hands of the State. There will be loopholes for corruption, and it may well be doubted how much of the later phases in the economic recovery will take place on the lines of State capitalism. All thee difficulties are in no way peculiar to Russia, but are bound to occur in any undeveloped country which attempts a method of developed country which attempts a method of development disliked by foreign capitalists. But though the difficulties are great, they are not economically insuperable; by sufficient honesty, determination, and energy on the part of the rulers they could probably all be overcome in time.

This brings us to the moral factors of success. It is here that the difficulties of the Bolshevik programme are greatest. Few governments in history have had more honesty, determination, and energy than the Soviet government; yet it may well be doubted whether even they, in the end, will be found to have enough for the carrying out of their original intentions. If the periods of time involved had been, as Lenin believed in 1918, six months or a year, or even a few years, the men who initiated the movement could have themselves carried it to a triumphant conclusion without any great chance meanwhile in their own outlook and disposition. But it is now six years since the October revolution, and by Lenin's confession the work is scarcely begun. When the Bolsheviks speak of the period during which the dictatorship will have to continue, they seem to contemplate at least a generation. Meanwhile many of the original leaders will have died, while those who remain and those who replace them will have acquired the habit of arbitrary power. The practice of negotiating with capitalists and their governments will tend to produce an acceptance of their assumptions, as it often does in trade union leaders. Capitalists will endeavour to extent their concessions, and will offer corrupt bargains to induce such extensions. It is hardly to be assumed that all officials will be always incorruptible.

It is, of course, possible, for a time, to secure a very high moral level through enthusiasm and hope. Revolutionary ardour will do wonders while it lasts, but it does not last for ever. The road form pre-industrial production to well-developed State Capitalism (to say nothing of Communism) is so long that it cannot be traversed during an outbreak of revolutionary ardour; and after such an outbreak there is usually a period during which demoralization and corruption are even more rampant than in normal times. An attempt to establish socialism in an undeveloped country, while the developed countries remain capitalistic, must pass through two phases, the first purely militant, in which the forces of internal and external capitalism are resisted, the second constructive, when the work of industrial development is undertaken under State management, and the population (probably with foreign help) is taught the more difficult parts of industrial processes. Russia is perhaps at the and of the militant phase, and has been successful so far as fighting is concerned; but the constructive haseis a more difficult test. During the militant period, men's combative instincts as well as their nationalism assist the enthusiasm for a new economic order. But when peace is restored it becomes natural to want an easier life and to grow tired of everything strenuous and tense. At this moment the foreign capitalists, in their concessions, begin to offer all kinds of advantages, from well paid work for the ordinary wage-earner up to a fortune for the technical expert. To resist tem by means of mere laws will be very difficult, as difficult as it have been found to prevent small private trading—an attempt which Lenin frankly declares to have been a mistake. There is, it would seem, only one force which could keep communism up to the necessary pitch of enthusiasm, and that is nationalism, developing into imperialism as foreign aggressions are defeated. Otherwise the period during which revolutionary ardour can be kept alive will not be so long as the period required for the militant and constructive stages together. And if imperialism once gets the upper hand, it is of course vain to hope that any genuine communism can result. Marxians, who believe that economies causes along operate in politics, ignore such difficulties as well have been considering, because they are psychological, not economic. But the difficulties are none the less real on that account. Nor is it safe fro rulers to treat themselves, in the Bolshevik manner, as exempt form human weaknesses, t subject to psychological laws, and certain to retain their original purposes unchanged throughout any number of years of difficult power.

In spite of all these obstacles the Bolsheviks may succeed; and if they do they may quite possibly become a model for China and India. There is one very important think that they have make clear, and that is, that Socialism in undeveloped countries must be aristocratic, an affair of a few energetic intellectuals leading that small percentage of the population which consists of "class-conscious proletarians." It is impossible for progress in these countries to come as it has come in the West, because the men who are capable of leading revolutions have absorbed the latest eastern thought, and will not be content with anything acknowledged to be out of date in England or France. Miliukov might have been content with a revolution like Cromwell's, Kerensky with one like Danton's; but the Bolsheviks, who alone had the energy required for success, wanted Marx's revolution, which Western revolutionaries still believed in because it had not yet happened. In the west, however, as in Marx's thought, his revolution had always been conceived as democratic. In Russia, where democracy is as yet impossible, some form of oligarchy had to be found until education could become more widespread, and this form of oligarchy was found in the dictatorship of the communist party. For the same reasons, namely, that democracy is not yet possible in Russia, it was in the name of democracy that capitalism criticized and attacked the Bolsheviks. Thus both sides lost sight of an important part of the truth: the Bolsheviks, practically if not theoretically, of the fact that democracy s part of the aim of socialism; their opponents, of the fact that democracy cannot be achieved all at once in an uneducated nation.

The Bolsheviks have, however, made a very important contribution to the solution of Eastern political problems by discovering an oligarchy which is neighter that of birth nor that of wealth, but that of believers in a certain economic and political creed. When this creed is progressive and constructive, like that of the communists, it is likely to produce a better oligarchy than any other that is politically feasible, except for the one reason that it rouses the hostility of the outside world. This is, however, such a very large disadvantage that t is scarcely possible to strike the balance. If the governments of the Western Powers were socialistic, or even more or less neutral, there would be no such disadvantage. But while the wage-earners of England and America continue to elect as their chosen representatives men whose delight it is to oppress, starve and imprison all who advocate the interests of the wage-earners, less developed nations must reckon with our hostility, or with our insincere and corrupting friendship, as the price they have to pay for attempting any-short cut to Socialism. It remains to be seen whether they can afford to pay the price.

We are thus brought back to international questions as dominating the problems of socialism in undeveloped countries. If (what is unlikely but not impossible) China also comes in time to be dominated by communists, ten—assuming Lenin's new methods successful in keeping the peasants contented—it is quite possible that Asia and Russia may be strong enough to succeed in a line of development displeasing to Europe and America, and ending in the establishment of their economic independence on a basis of socialism. But there are so many ifs in this argument that probability is against it. It is more probable that china will remain and Russia will relapse, under the economic dominion of the Western Powers, until such time as their industry shall have been developed by capitalistic methods. In that case, the ultimate victory of Socialism, if it comes, will have to come from the advanced countries, as was universally assumed before the Russian Revolution.

# 11

# Class and Culture in Global Systems

The work of Immanuel Wallerstein has been criticized bycertain anthropologistsfor not having takenculture into proper account. He has beenaccused of the sinof political economy, a not uncommon accusation, a reflex of the 80's anthropological jargon that might finally today be exhausted. Years earlier a number of social scientists were engaged in a critical assessment of the social sciences from a distinctively global perspective. Wallerstein, Frank and others were at the forefront of this critique which had a powerful impact on anthropology. The global perspective was not a mere addition to anthropological knowledge, not a mere of extension of the use of the culture concept i.e. Before it was local and now it is global, before culture stood still, but now in the global age, it flows around the world. It was a more fundamental critique, or at least it implied a more fundamental critique. This critique could only be attained from a perspective in which they very concept of society was re-conceived as something very different, as a locus constructed within a historical fore field which was very much broader than any particular politically defined unit.

The world system perspective grew from several different

sources. Wallerstein and others argued that no understanding of the history of the West could be attained without understanding the relation between regions. This was a crucial rewriting of the history of the last 500 years. It was more, however, since it said something crucial about capitalism that was often forgotten by ideologists of various persuasions. The control over the way in which wealth circulated, the way it was accumulated, the destiny of any particular area or country, was not simply a reflex of local production and consumption. On the contrary, any particular locale was dependent upon the way it related to the larger arena of the total economic process.

Now there are surely differences in the particular interpretations of history involved here. There are those who would see the world systemic or global as something essentially modern, there are those who would push it back to the Medieval world with its Middle Eastern, Indian and Chinese centers, and there are those who would push it back to the Ancient world, even 5000years. The questions are we still talking about capitalism in all of this? Is there not a fundamental difference between mercantile systems of the past and the modern world system? Are there parallels, at least between such systems if their dynamics are not identical? These are all unsolved questions under debate, questions that may lead to important progress in understanding the history of the world.

With all these differences, however, there is something common in this perspective. The commonality is, in fact, twofold. First it is a realization that the conceptual structure of social sciences needs to be revised in order to account for the global nature of social reproduction. The second is the imperative need to deal with the radical issue of people's control over their conditions of existence which is so critically recast in the world system perspective From 'socialism in one country" to survival in any country is the issue that bears down on those who urgently sense that something has got to be done.

The globalisation framework has a very different origin. It is best described as a self-reflective awareness that something new has happened. In all of its various forms it tends to insist on the specificity of the present, often in unabashedly evolutionist terms. Before we were local but now we are global. The global is seen as a new level of social, economic, political integration that has now, finally, been attained. There are various prototypes, from business economics (Ohmae 1990) to cultural studies, especially of the post-colonial variety. The movement from local to global, from national to transnational is an additive process that acts upon former structures, disintegrating or otherwise transforming them. They lost their power and significance as organizers of social existence, of if they don't they should and shall. The TNC's take economies out of the hands of the state, just as the global media, and transnational populations take social organisation out of the hands of the nation. Below I hall discuss this as an ideological transformation rather than a scientific discovery. The reason for this is that the discourse of globalisation appears as the immediate product of a growing awareness by intellectual and other elites that something has happened and not the result of serious research. This does not detract from the value of this awareness, but it requires that we situate the awareness socially and attempt to account for its appearance as well as seriously considering those aspects of reality which it claims to represent.

The fundamental difference between global systems and globalization approaches is that the former represents a theoretical framework within which the institutional structures of the world are themselves generated and reproduced in global processes which are not something a that is a result of the pas few decades of "evolution" but which are structural aspects of all social dynamics, while the latter is a historical or development list image of a contemporary change. For example, to claim that culture today flows across the world, filtered through states, markets, movements and everyday life (Hannerz 1992), is to assume these structures are the units between which flows occur and are not themselves structured and transformed by global relations. If the latter were the case then the global flow model could not be expressed in such terms.

## Out of Anthropology: Ethnography and Global Systems

From an anthropological perspective, the discovery of the global dimension was quite revolutionary. After all, the ethnographic enterprise was predictated on the self-efficiency of the local in explanatory terms. Several generations of anthropologists were imbued with the notion that the field of fieldwork was all that was necessary to accede to an adequate understanding of the other. When we embarked upon the critique of the local in global terms, it was precisely because we had come to an understanding that the very constitution of local situations in the guise of communities and societies was only adequately accounted for in terms of a larger set of relations. If the very constitution of the social—not merely certain institutions, but the very forms of sociality in asocial field—is dependent upon larger processes of the global system, then the notion that society is the sufficient explanatory whole must be seriously questioned. This is not to say that the rear no structural logics of local listence, nor that societies are in fact constituted and practiced as closed entities. On the contrary, and this is perhaps the major difference between a global systemic versus a globalisation perspective, it is one thing to acknowledge the existence of such relatively closed logics and another to assume that their constitution is autonomous with respect to broader processes. This is a difference of crucial proportions. It is difference of levels of levels of analysis. Global systemic relations are not visible as such. They are not behavioral connections between individuals. They refer to the analytical or theoretical properties of processes that are posited by the researcher, that is hypotheses concerning the way in which social formations are constituted and transformed over time.

In such terms global system theory s epistemologically equivalent to Levi-Strauss definition of structuralism as opposed to structural functionalism. The latter is a form of abstract description. Levi-Strauss epitomized it with the express: "the function of the stomach is to digest food." A mere abstract reiteration of the observed processes that are summed up in the world digestion. Radicliffe-Brown proposed the study of kinship as networks of relations of descent that were directly observable and could be classified into distinct types. Levi-Strauss proposed that the constitution of descent groups was an aspect of a larger structure of alliance and reproduction (1949). He proposed that kinship could be understood as a dynamic of exchange in which what appeared as separate classes of system could be shown to be logical transforms of one another and which could be reduced to a few basic underlying structures. The logic of reciprocity was not an observable but a theoretical model exiting in the head of the anthropologist, in the same way that gravity was a model of the relation between bodies in the universe. In both cases, the model was not a description of observed reality but a hypothetical construction that could product reality effects, i.e., falling bodies, changing tides, and eight section marriage systems. The models were not, of course, assumed to be mere constructs but to model the real properties of reality, but properties of reality are not directly observable since they do not correspond to concrete objects and events.

Globalisation studies have a very different frame of

reference. They are based on a direct experience or a realization of something that has changed, most often in the experience of the observer. Globalisation is about something that has happened, not about the basic nature of social realities. It does not propose a novel approach to the social, but instead proposes that the world has changed. This is apparent in so many of the texts whose underlying discourse is predicated on a transition from the local to the global, from the national to the transnational. This perspective is not focused on underlying structures, but on directly observable or experienced realities. It is about transnational phenomena as such, behavioural "transnational connections" of various kinds, about the movement of goods, people and information, not about the nature of such movement. This is why such discourse so often concludes with the simple statement of the existence of global realities and wit its moral implications. Globalizers often seem, for clearly ideological reasons, to by very much taken by the novelty and liberation involved in the mere existence of globality. After all it would appear to the liberating for those who write about it in a such terms. In a more general sense, how even globalization can, as a I suggested above, be understood as the analogue of structural functionalism to global system theory's structuralism. This is because of its pre-occupation with events and happenings and behavioural relations. But the analogy stops thee since it is not terribly interested in discovering abstract principles of the observed realities.

Here another approach seems to have colored globalizing anthropology, one dependent upon Geertz's textualization of the culture concept (1973). The latter assumes the objectivity of the "other as text, which can be read by the anthropologist without the benefit of the "others" intervention. Culture is read over other people's shoulders. The eye of the observer becomes supreme in this kind of anthropology. It is the other for-us, the other as part of our experience which becomes the core object of analysis. This is how such poisted realities as hybridity, creoloization, and the like can emerge. These are the ethnographic "realities" that form the culture mainstay of globalization. If the city landscapes in Stockholm now combine ethnically and linguistically mixed populations and store signs in American English, if We observe (at the airport) the Nigerian, Congolese or Papua New Guinean sporting a can of coke and a hamburger...is this to be interpreted as creolizaiton in the sense of cultural mixture? Is it to be interpreted as hybridity in the sense of the liminal sphere between the modern Western and the pre-modern, non-Western, assuming that the other is associated with a whole array of pre-modern behaviours and representations of reality (Canclini 1995)? What is really going on in such referred to realities? Does anyone have to ask or is the observation enough. What about other peoples' experiences, internationalities and lives? Are not such hybrids defied as such because they seem to be betwixt and between our own "modern western" categories, i.e. Hhybrids for us? This of course, is not merely a question for global anthropologies, but is a more serious issue of method. The tendency to substitute one's own experience for those who we are supposed to be studying has not been discussed with respect to the anthropology of globalization. With all the discussion of ethnographic authority, with multi-vocalization. With all the discussion of ethnographic authority, with multivocality and multi-siting, there is a certain disinterest in what kind of knowledge we are aiming for. This can be concretized in terms of the different kinds of questions that can be asked of informants or of the field within which informants may make their lives. Questions of the type: how do you do that? Whom do you marry, why do you adopt you own grandchildren? Etc. Such questions elicita certain frame of reference in the responses, one that takes the form of abstract formulations with generalized we's and I's. Very different kinds of responses are elicited by longer term and more intimate contacts, what, in clearer fashion, is present in some of the more phenomenological anthropological work and even sociological work of the past and present (Mannheim 1982, Kapferer 1998, Csordas 1994). The difference between these two kinds of anthropology is not a trivial matter. It is the difference between an anthropology that strives to grasp the living experience of others and one that is content with our objectified aspects of those other lives. The presence of other people's voices is of course an important aspect of the necessary breakdown of an ethnographic authority that was itself a structure of global hegemony. But the other voice must include more than simply objectified knowledge if we are to grasp what other lives, or any lives, are about.

## Globalization and Ethnography

There is an important connection between current versions of globalised anthropology, the way in which communication is carried out and the kinds of knowledge that are ultimately produced. The current interest in globalized objects and the identification of other people's identities as Creole and/or hybrid exemplifies this linkage between superficiality and globality. When I have questioned whether or not the subjects described as Creole or hybrid actually experience themselves in such terms, or in terms that are easily interpreted as such, I am usually told that this is a question of objective culture and not of experience. That is, global cultural products are like texts that already contain their meaning before the reader engages them. I find this a quite disconcerting understanding of cultural process. This is a notion in which meaning is actually objective, and can therefore be read by the anthropologist without reference to the subjects whose worlds we are describing. Can this actually be the case? To some extent it is implied in a strongly textual notion of culture and is an extraordinary demonstration of ethnographic authority.

This authority is explicit, it assumes that culture can be read, and reading is indeed the metaphor of the authoritarian observer. No need to ask, to engage the other, certainly not to participate, as in participant observation. One need only participate to the degree that it avails one of a good spectator seat, i.e. good place from which to observe, for reading is a kind of observation. It assumes that meaning is thoroughly pubic and objective and thus requires no intention on the part of the "native". The understanding of culture as public text was first emphasized by Greez, but has become an implicit assumption for many. And while Geertz himself has been concerned with the understanding of other people's construction of selfhood and inspired many an anthropologist to embark on such understanding, it is difficult to understand how his insights into the Balinese person as mask which nothing behind it could have been attained. Thick description, of course, implies that meanings are subtle, but it is not clear how one can arrive at such understanding by means of mere observation, or at least it would be interesting to now what ought to be observed to arrive at deeper conclusions concerning other people's experience of the world. The recent critique by Unni Wikan (1995) demonstrates that a deeper understanding can be arrived at by engaging with other people in a more intensive way. Whether one agrees or not with her interpretation is beside the point. What it crucial is that she argues directly from the combination of social practices and social discourses and representations. From here it is possible to maintain a dialectical and detective like procedure in trying to grasp other strategies and constructions of life worlds.

In the aftermath of Geerth and quite to his own apparent consternation (1988), there has been a postmodern (or at least post-Geertzian) questioning of the entire ethnographic project focused very much on the issue of ethnographic authority. This has led to an important critique of many of the assumptions of classical ethnography, not least its localist bia. But this bias is more complete than at first meets the eye, and it is here that things may have gone wrong. While one may have indeed rightly criticized the authority of the ethnographer, one did not get into the details of what this authority of the ethnographer, one did not get into the details of what this authority comprised. It is significant that the question was first raised by James Clifford, a non-anthropologist. The latter did indeed realize that the problems raised by "being there" were left in a state of tension and insecurity by Conrad, while institutionalized away by Malinowskian authority, but he does not explore this important insight further. It is here—precisely here—that the major issues can be raised. What does it mean to understand another world and what can be said about such understanding in methodological or even theoretical terms? This is a question that can be said to lead in two related directions: towards a phenomenology of social existence and towards a structuralism of the properties of social life. This first concerns the nature of experienced social life, the socially shared aspects of lived reality on the one hand, and those aspects of reality that are not present to consciousness but present in the unconscious and in the non-conscious. This is that unconscious aspect of human reality that can be known and elicited at least in principle. The non-conscious refers to the properties of reality that are not available to consciousness without a process of learning. The former refer to the repressed, the forgotten or that which is in one way or another absent from awareness yet necessarily present in practice. The latter refers to those properties of reality that are simply not present in awareness because they never were part of consciousness. This category depends upon processes of knowledge and awareness production within a social field itself. Thus properties of global or world system cycles or business cycles, or even the structures of kinship-based alliance systems, are not conscious unless made so by a learning process. This does not mean that their properties do not exist, but that they exist in consciousness only via their effects, and where such is the case the conscious elaboration of such effects results in partial or mythical representations. If we accept this understanding of ethnographic reality, a number of results follow: First, the understanding of another world—based on the assumption that other worlds may indeed be different from our own—can only be approached via the experiences that other people have within that world. Second, there are aspects of other worlds that can only be accessed via rather complex methods of elicitation and analysis since they are not part f immediate awareness. Third, there are aspects of other words, those which ay also be part of our own (global systemic) reality, that can only be accessed by means of a series of analytical and hypothetical propositions since they are not available to consciousness except via their effects on people's lives.

This kind of discussion has not been taken up recently within anthropology. Rather the issues have remained focused on the question of authority itself, on the questions of voice ad location. They have been very much assimilated by the experiences of anthropologists themselves, experiences that dovetail more generally with those of many intellectuals and academics (not necessarily the same thing) as well. This has led to the conflation, delineated above, between the experience of the observer and that of the observed. And it is this which has become the mainstay of much of the globalization literature. The latter consists primarily in statements based on external interpretation, not least of the meaning of events and objects. This is the basis of the discourse on hybridity with a few exceptions. It is significant that much of this discussion is itself focused on objects, not unoften objects at an exhibition. Clifford's analysis of anthropologist M. O'Hnlon's paradise: Portraying the New Gunea highlands, the catalogue of which s published by the British Museum, deals with the way in which local traditional objects are mixed up the western consumer goods (Clifford 1997). Foster (1999) has also discussed this in a recent article, namely the way n which a traditional shield in the exhibit can be decorated with the logo of South Pacific Lager. It turns out that thee was specific motivation for this hybrid product; hat the designer "had been asked by senior men to incorporated a representation of a beer bottle on the shield, to make the point that 'it was beer alone which had precipitated this fighting,' and the question that springs to mind is what was this all about" (1997:68). Drunkenness was directly involved in the conflict that inspired this shield. One might well have made a more intensive study of the way in which shields are decorated in order to rasp the way in which motifs are incorporated, i.e., the way in which the "modern" might well have bee a totally irrelevant property of beer in the process of creating the shield. Is this a question of hybridity in the sense of fusion and mixture, or of a very specific and motivated articulation, one that does not leave the experiential world of the creator but seems matter out of place to an anthropologist dependent on an idea of culture as text, i.e., as objectified meaning? Foster suggests, following Marcus (1995), that to arrive at such understanding we need to "get up and move out of intensively investigated single sites" (Foster 1999:144). But it is precisely the de-intensification of ethnographic praxis that enables us to substitute our own experience of the object for that of those whom we are purportedly trying to understand.

## The Anthropology of Experience and Cultural Production

A solution to this problem can only be worked out at the theoretical level. We must propose the kinds of relations we should expect to find linking global processes and the production of cultural form. This requires, in its turn, that we examine more closely the nature of cultural production itself rather than simply assuming that culture is a substance or thing in itself that can, as a result, move in global flows. Culture is attributed meaning and must be actively maintained as meaning in order to continue to exist. This aspect of meaning is not often taken seriously, since meaning is often stabilized in institutional forms related to the stabilization of communication itself. Any archeologist knows that meanings cannot be read from remains without making all kinds of assumptions of equivalence to some given scheme of established interpretations. What is it that makes such attributed meaning shared meaning is a complex issue, related to the way in which social worlds are organized and enforced for larger groups of people. Power is converted into authority and the latter into forms of socializations; the formation of subjects and of subjective experience. Such processes are incomplete since the activities involved do not occur in a vacuum devoid of other intentionalities. However, such processes do create a field in which shared experiences and shared modes of meaning attribution are effected. Such fields might be sad to be fields of resonance in which what Mannheim referred to as conjunctive communication can occur. Such fields are hierarchical. They are also the fields within which shared cultural forms are created.

This might appear to be an argument for the local basis of cultural production, and this does not seem to square with globalization. After all most of the phenomena of world culture, from pop music to clothing styles, to green movements and popular cults, are not apparently based on the kind of shared experience that is forms in delimited fields of social interaction. This is an important issue and a two tiered analysis: First, one must ascertain to what degree the same meanings are being attributed to the same phenomena and/or projects in the global arena.

Second, one must ascertain the ways in which there might be said to be overlapping resonances or analogous experiences being produced that allows a broader possibility for identification of the same things in the same way. There are serious sociological issues here: for example might it be argued that similar kinds of youth cultures are produced in the Caribbean and in the Anglo-American dominated areas of the Pacific that make reggae a formidably powerful attractor and that these are related to the forms of social transformation that have occurred in both places? While the two worlds that became articulated to capital it modern it to the forms of social transformation that have occurred in both places? While the two worlds that became articulated to capitalist modernity might be very different, and this accounts for difference in the original musical forms in the two areas, it could be that more general properties of those words, such as egalitarian village structure lacking autonomous political structures, with strong forms of pooling rather than exchange, with a certain similar form of oppress on by white colonial society all might have come together to produce a "structure feeling" which enables such transoceanic musical resonance. This kind of approach, in any case, would seem to be more interesting than simply saying that the cultural item, reggae had become global by moving around the world on the sound waves. There are certainly more important questions to be understood here.

The argument for the centrality of socially shared experience and its constitution is not an argument against globalization, of course, but an argument for a more systemic understanding of the latter as a cultural process. By not assuming that cultural meaning is a substance (a curious essentialist tendency among globalization "theorists") by deconstructing it, it should be possible to then reconstruct the way in which it is constituted by others in the global contexts of their particular existences.

## Cultural Transnationalism as Ideology

One of the reasons that the cultural is taken for granted among cultural globalizers, is that it is an instrumental part of the very identity of those who hold this approach. This identity is not an artificial construction as such. It can in itself only be understood. If we take a broader view of the transformation of the world system today. While ll academic discourses are situated and can be subjected to ideological analysis. In the case of the globalization literature this is much more obvious simply because there is a surprising lack of empirical research involved. The discourse is best characterized, instead, as authoritarian and often implicitly—and even explicitly—normative (Appadurai 1996). This is a style that is fully consistent with a self-relegated authority in which description and interpretation are merged. Never is a hypothesis suggested! Rather, reality is simply defined in a certain way dependent upon the author's experience of everyday life (rarely) or films and other media (more generally). This is fully consistent with the tetualist bias in both cultural studies and anthropology. The research of others may well be used to make an argument but it is often purely illustrative rather than openly interpretive. Appadurai's recent discussion of violence in relation to globalization is a case in point (1998). Using selected examples it is proposed that violence is a means of eliminating ambiguity," Matter out of place." foreigners who look like nationals, the liminal products of migratory hybridization. Now while there are significant case of military questioning of busloads of short tutsi or tall Huru as well as their murder, it is not at all clear that this is about the fear of mixture in itself. On the contrary there is evidence that it is the ear/hate of the other as such and that the ambivalence is a mere problem of identification. After all most of the people killed in ethnic warfare are quite clearly identifiable. Appadurai's cavalier use of the material to which the himself refers is evidence of the conflation of interpretation and description.

The argument that seems to organize the discussion is that globalization is producing a world of hybridity which is causing reactionary violence on the part of those who would continue to maintain a belief in ethnic purity or ethnic absolutism as it is fashionably called today. An author like Hannerz (1992), more aware, perhaps, of the problem of the empirical material, avoids this problem by qualifying practically all his statements to the point of extinction. Thus, in an article on the withering away of the nation, we are informed after many meanindering words that the nation may not be disappearing, but it is in any case changing. Such breathtaking risks can only e understood as a kind of fear of theoretical flying. Appadurai is quite the opposite, predicting the evolution form a national to a postnational world, an evolution that is bound to be bloody but which in the end shall free us all from that old fashioned institution, replaced at last by the cultural freedom afforded by disasporas! While this is not presented as a hypothesis and with little argument to back it up, it does have the quality of being fallsiable on several counts, not least the assumption that alls well that end's well, as if we were fast approaching the end of history, the multicultural diasporic and hybrid world of globalized capitalism. Why were should feel safe in our disasporas is difficult to understand, and why majority, non-diasporic, populations, should be defeated by these new transnationals, and why all this appears as brad new s also quite strange given the evidence that some aspects of globalization, the most powerful economic aspects have been coming and gong petriodically for a very long time. There is, in fact some evidence that we may well be in the midst of a period of contraction.

The core of transnationalism appears to be a will and desire to transcend boundaries and everything that they represent in the form of closure, locality, confinement, terms that are associated with backwardness, provincialism and curiously a lack of culture, supposedly in the sense of cultivation. This mode is one that polarizes the cosmopolitan with respect to the local and defines the former as progressive, as the future of the world, as the civilized while relegating the latter the barbaric, the red-necked, the reactionary and racist. This polarity is not a recent invention, but is very much part of the cosmological structure of the global system. Its historical appearance might be said to be salient in periods when real polarization occurs, when global elites exist in theory and practice from the local and national fields in which they were previously embedded.

## Globalization, Class and Culture

A global systemic anthropology should aim at understanding both the world and the cultural identities and derivative discourses that are generated by the structures of that world. In several recent publications 1999a, 1999b) I have suggested that there is a dual process involved in the current process of globalization. The first of these is a decline in centrality or hegemony in the world system, a decline expressed in the weakening of the nation states of the former centre of the world system, i.e., in the West. This has been accompanied by the disintegration of the Soviet Empire as a hegemonic structure and of some of the weakest links in the world system, especially Africa. Thee is a great deal of variation involved, this process has involved massive decentralisation and the emergence of new or renewed politized identities, It has also involved massive disorder and dislocation of populations, and a resultant mass migration to traditional centres that are now facing their own internal crises. The most general property of this new disorder is expressed in a wave of ethnification resulting in a cultural and political fragmentation of formerly larger units. The ethnification consists in a strong re-identification that is clearly advantageous for those who so identify but also increases the conflict potential in the larger world. The rise of indigenous movements, regional movements, immigrant minority politics and increasing nationalism are all in such terms expressions of the same transformation-fragmentation process of identification in the world arena. While this was occurring in the relatively declining" areas, the rising areas of the world system in East and Southeast Asia demonstrated an opposite rise of national and regional identities, a new modernism and a decline, often forced, of minority politics. This is not to say that minorities disappeared, but that their political demands were either accommodated by successful integrative politics or simply ignored or even suppressed. That this process has been reversed in the current Asian crisis is well exemplified by the rapid increase of ethnic conflict in Indonesia after many years of relative peace and by the apparent liberation of East Timor after years of attempted integration.

The hypothesis involved here is simply that areas rising in the system tend to become increasingly centralized within delimited zones (national states, territorial states) wit an accompanying decline in sub-state identification, and that the reverse occurs in periods of loss of global position. This hypothesis refers to specific tendencies in a complex reality in which there are other forces that might offset such tendencies. For example there is presently a regionalization in the world that is part of the process of economic globalization that may be crucial in understanding the tendency to a three way division of the world among the EU, NAFTA and APEC as competing potential hegemonic zones. This must be seen, of course, against the background of the dual division of the world that arose out of the Second Word War and of the virtual monopoly of the United States as western hegemon until the 60's. The change involves a combined fragmentation in former centres and weak links and a consolidation in new rising zones.

## Cultural Production in the Global System

This discussion is meant to provide a way of modelling cultural production in the global system. The model is based on an understanding of shared social experience, experience that has existential meaning for those who partake in it. This raises questions of the intentionality involved in cultural elaboration and transformation, and in the resonance which makes cultural form work as a social phenomenon. Such social experiences are formed within a hierarchy of constants and dynamic processes that link global process with the local structuring of social lives. It treats globalisation particular phase process in the larger system, one that is linked with declining hegemony i older centres, with decentralization of capital accumulation—in other words, globalization of capital—and a double tendency toward globalization of eilities and localization of middle and lower classes. The current politization of elites and locals of the upqardly and downwardly mobile is combined with a cultural fragmentation that strikes the dehegemonizing zones of the world arena, leading to a complex combination of ethnification and class polarization. The latter give rise to various cultural transformations and an intensive creativity, one that is not a celebration of cultural liberation but of deep contradiction in the real lives of the people that social scientists should be trying to understand. This understanding has been the programme of World-Systems, Analysis and a larger family of global analyses. It is one that is founded in a critical perspective and distance itself from pervasive ideologies, including those concerned with globalization itself. Wallerstein has dedicated his research to the understanding of the systematic nature of the historical processes of the world areena. The attack on this attempt by postimpressionist, postcolonialists and others who identify increasingly with the freedom that seems to be offered to them via the advantageous financing of cultural elites must become part of the analysis rather than a merely an opposed intellectual position.

# Bibliography


Ashford, Douglas E., *Ideology and Participation, Library of Social Research,* Vol. 3, (Beverly Hills, Sage, 1972).

Bailey, F.G., *Strategems and Spoils: A Social Anthropology of Politics* (Oxford, Balckwell, 1969).

Beteille, A., *Castes: Old and New: Essays in Social Structure and Social Stratification* (Bombay, Asia, 1969).

Bryant, C., *Managing Rural Development: Peasant Participation in Rural Development, Development Monographs No. 1,* (West Hartford, Kumarian Press, 1980).

Chambers, R., *Rural Development: Putting the Last First* (Longman, 1983).

Chaturvedi, H.R., *Bureaucracy and Local Community: Dynamics of Rural Development* (New Delhi, Allied, 1977).

Chaturvedi, H.R. and Mitra, S.K., *Citizen Participation in Rural Development* (New Delhi, Oxford Publishing Co., 1982).

Clegg, S., *The Theory of Power and Organisation* (Routledge and Kegan Paul, 1970).

Commission on Church's Participation in Development, *People's Particiaption and People's Movements* (Geneva, World Council Churches, 1981).

Curtis, D., *et al., Popular Participation in Decision Making and the Basic Needs Approach to Development*: *Methods, Issues and Experiences* (Geneva, International Labour Organisation, 1978).

Dak,T.M., *Social Inequalities and Rural Development* (New Delhi, National, 1982).

Deshpande, V.D., 'Code of Conduct for Rural Voluntary Agencies', *Economic and Political Weekly*, XXI (30), 1304-1306 (1986).

Esman, M.J. and Upholff, N.T., *Local Organisations: Intermediaries in Rural Development* (Ithaca, Cornell University Press, 1984).

Esman, M.J., *Local Organisations and Rural Development: The State of the Art* (Ithaca, Cornell University, 1982).

Fernades, W., 'The National NGO Convention: Voluntarism, the State and the Struggle for Change', *Social Action*, 36 (October-December 1986, 431-441).

Franda, M., *Voluntary Associations and Local Development in India: The Janata Phase* (New Delhi, Young India, 1983).

Freedman, D.H., 'Popular Participation and Administrative Decentralisation' in *F. Lisk* (Ed.), 1985, pp. 127-147.

Frankel, F.R., *Indian Political Economy 1947-77: The Gradual Revolution* (New Jersey, Princeton University Press, 1978).

Freeman, J.M., *Untouchable: An Indian Life History* (George Allen Unwin, 1979).

Fuchs, S. *At the Bottom of the Indian Society* (New Delhi, Munshiram Manoharlal Publishers, 1981).

Gandhi, I., *Community Development and Panchayati Raj in India 1952-72* (New Delhi, Ministry of Agriculture, Department of Community Development, Government of India, 1973).

Ghai, D.P. *et al., The Basic Needs Approach to Development: Some Issues Regarding Concepts and Methodology* (Geneva, International Labour Organisation, 1977).

Goulet, D., *On the Ethics of Development Planning* (Los Angles, University of Galifornia, 1975).

Harari, D. and Jorge G.B., *Social Conflict and Development* (Paris, OECD Development Centre, 1983).

Heredero, J.M. *Rural Development and Social Change: An Experiment in Non-Formal Education* (New Delhi, Indian Social Institute, 1977).

Hirschman, A., *Shifting Involvements* (Oxford, Martin Robertson, 1982).

Huque, W., *et. al.*, "Towards a Theory of Rural Development", *Development Dialogue*, 2, 7-137 (1977).

Ishwaran, K., *Politics and Social Change*, 1966.

Jain, L.C., *Grass Without Roots: Rural Development with Government Auspices* (New Delhi, Sage, 1985).

Killian, L.M., 'Social Movements', In Robert E.L. Faris (ed.) *Handbook of Modern Sociology* (Chicago, 1964), p. 433.

Klass, M., *Case: The Emergence of the South Asian Social System* (Institute for the Study of Human Issues, 1980).

Laski, H., *A Grammar of Politics* (George Allen and Unwin, 1939).

Lindenberg. M. and Crossby, B., *Managing Development: The Political Dimension* (West Hartford, Kumarian Press, 1981).

Lisser, J., *The Politics of Altruism* (Geneva, Lutheran World Federation, 1977).

Lutheran World Federation, *Workshop on Community Development in Latin America: A Report* (Geneva, LWF, 1977).

Overseas Development Institute, *Proceedings of the Conference on NGOs in Development*, (ODA 1987).

Oyugi, W.O., 'Popular Participation and Access to Basic Needs in Kenya' in *F. Lisk* (ed.)., 1985, pp. 148-185.

Pan American Institute for Development, *Papers of Seminar on Effective Participation in Integrated Rural Development with Emphaiss on Grassroots* (Nigeria, 11-21 September, 1978).

Patel,, A.R., 'Rural Development: A Challenging Task for Voluntary Agencies,' *Kurukshetra*, XXXIV (11), 24-28 (1985).

Pearse, A. and Stiefel, M., Debarter Comments on "Inquirty into Participation: A Reseach Approach" (Geneva, United Nations Research Institute for Social Development (1981).

Rahema, M., "The Growing Role of NGOs: Autonomous Actors of Part of the Delivery System?" *Society for International Development*, 18th. World Conference Paper C.1., Rome (1985).

Ramamurthy, S.R., 'Government Functionaries Must Wholeheartedly Accept voluntary Agencies,' *Kurukshetra*, XXXIV (1), 10-13, 1985.

Rao, M.S.A. (ed.), *Social Movements in India: Peasant and Backward Class Movements*, Vol. I (New Delhi, Manohar Publishers, 1978a).

Richardson, A., *Participation* (Rouledge and Kegan Paul, 1983).

Robertson, A.F., *People and the State: An Anthropology of Planned Development* (Cambridge, Cambridge University Press, 1984).

Roy, R. and Srivastava, R.K., *Development Dialogues in Development: The Individual, Society and Political Order* (New Delhi, Sage 1986).

Sen, Jai, 1986, *On Anti-Voluntarism. Lokayan Bulletin*, 4 (3/4), 9-37.

Sen Gupta, B., 'Self-sufficiency of Community Health Programmes: Rhetoric or Reality?' *Link, 3*, 7-12 (1983).

Sethi, Harsh, 'Rural Development: Alternate Strategies', *Economic and Political Weekly*, Special Number, (1978).

Sethi, Harsh, 'Redefining Politics, Power, and Development: Some Reflections on Voluntary Agencies and Social Change,' *Bulletin, XII* (12), S.176-S.185, 1982.

Sharma, M.L. and Dak, T.M., *Caste and Class in Agrarian Society* (Delhi, Ajanta Publications, 1985).

Sheth, D.L., and Dak, T.M., *Caste and Class in Agrarian Society* (Delhi, Ajanta Publications, 1985).

Sidel, V.W. and Sidel, R., 'The Health Care Delivery Systems of the People's Republic of China' in *K. Newell* (ed.), 1975, pp. 1-12.

Srinivas, M.N., *The Dominant Caste and Other Essays* (New Delhi, Oxford Publishing House, 1987).

Staudt, K.A., *Women and Participation* (New York, USAID, 1978).

Todaro, M.P., *Economic Development in the Third World* (Longman, 1977).

United Nations, *Popular Participation in Decision Making for Development* (New York, United Nations, 1975).

United Nations, *Popular Participation in Selected Upgrading Programmes in Urban Areas* (New York, United Nations, 1986).

United Nations, *Department of International Economics and Social Affairs, Popular Participation Politics as Methods Advancing Social Integration* (New York, Untied Nations, 1987).

Uphoff, N.T. *et al.*, *Fessibility and Application of Rural Development Participation: A State of the Art Paper* (Ithaca, Cornell University, Rural Development Committee, 1979).

Wesergaard, K., *People's Participation, Local Government and Rural Development: The Case of West Bengal* (Copenhagen, Centre for Development Research, 1986).

White A.T., 'Why Community Participation?', *Assignment Children*, 59/60, 17-34 (1982).

White, M. B. and White, H.D., *The Power of the People: Community Action in Kerala* (Singapore, East Asia Christian Conference,).

Wolfe, M., *Participation: the View from Above, Dialogue About Participation, 3,* (Geneva, United Nations Research Institute for Social Development, 1983).

*Yojana, Special Issues on Voluntary Agencies*, 28, 20 and 21, November 1984.

# Index

***